ReFocus: The Films of Sohrab Shahid Saless

ReFocus: The International Directors Series

Series Editors: Robert Singer, Stefanie Van de Peer and Gary D. Rhodes

Editorial Board: Lizelle Bisschoff, Stephanie Hemelryck Donald, Anna Misiak and Des O'Rawe

ReFocus is a series of contemporary methodological and theoretical approaches to the interdisciplinary analyses and interpretations of international film directors, from the celebrated to the ignored, in direct relationship to their respective culture – its myths, values and historical precepts – and the broader parameters of international film history and theory. The series provides a forum for introducing a broad spectrum of directors, working in and establishing movements, trends, cycles and genres including those historical, currently popular, or emergent, and in need of critical assessment or reassessment. It ignores no director who created a historical space – either in or outside of the studio system – beginning with the origins of cinema and up to the present. *ReFocus* brings these film directors to a new audience of scholars and general readers of Film Studies.

Titles in the series include:

ReFocus: The Films of Susanne Bier
Edited by Missy Molloy, Mimi Nielsen and Meryl Shriver-Rice

ReFocus: The Films of Francis Veber
Keith Corson

ReFocus: The Films of Jia Zhangke
Maureen Turim and Ying Xiao

ReFocus: The Films of Xavier Dolan
Edited by Andrée Lafontaine

ReFocus: The Films of Pedro Costa: Producing and Consuming Contemporary Art Cinema
Nuno Barradas Jorge

ReFocus: The Films of Sohrab Shahid Saless: Exile, Displacement and the Stateless Moving Image
Edited by Azadeh Fatehrad

edinburghuniversitypress.com/series/refocint

ReFocus:
The Films of Sohrab Shahid Saless

Exile, Displacement and the Stateless Moving Image

Edited by Azadeh Fatehrad

University Press

This book is dedicated to Deep, for his true love

Edinburgh University Press is one of the leading university presses in the UK. We publish academic books and journals in our selected subject areas across the humanities and social sciences, combining cutting-edge scholarship with high editorial and production values to produce academic works of lasting importance. For more information visit our website: edinburghuniversitypress.com

© editorial matter and organisation Azadeh Fatehrad, 2020, 2022
© the chapters their several authors, 2020, 2022

Edinburgh University Press Ltd
The Tun – Holyrood Road
12 (2f) Jackson's Entry
Edinburgh EH8 8PJ

First published in hardback by Edinburgh University Press 2020

Typeset in 11/13 Ehrhardt MT by
IDSUK (DataConnection) Ltd

A CIP record for this book is available from the British Library

ISBN 978 1 4744 5639 5 (hardback)
ISBN 978 1 4744 5640 1 (paperback)
ISBN 978 1 4744 5641 8 (webready PDF)
ISBN 978 1 4744 5642 5 (epub)

The right of the contributors to be identified as authors of this work has been asserted in accordance with the Copyright, Designs and Patents Act 1988 and the Copyright and Related Rights Regulations 2003 (SI No. 2498).

Contents

List of Figures	vii
Acknowledgements	ix
Notes on Contributors	x
Foreword by Vahid Alaghband	xiii

    Introduction   1
    Azadeh Fatehrad

Part I The Life and Work of Sohrab Shahid Saless

1. Slow, Closed, Recessive, Formalist and Dark: The Cinema of Sohrab Shahid Saless   7
Hamid Naficy
2. Point of View, Symbolism and Music in Sohrab Shahid Saless's *Utopia*   28
Christopher Gow
3. The Blind Owls of Modernity: Of Protocols, Mirrors and Grimaces in Sohrab Shahid Saless's Films   43
Matthias Wittmann
4. *A Simple Event* from a Historical Perspective: What Do We Talk About When We Talk About Realism?   64
Majid Eslami

Part II Creative Exiles

5. Sohrab Shahid Saless and the Political Economy of the New German Cinema   79
Michelle Langford
6. The Aesthetic of Diaspora in Moving Image Practice   101
Azadeh Fatehrad

Part III The Stateless Moving Image

7 Curating the Nomadic: Film and Video at Ambika P3   123
   Michael Mazière
8 A Certain Tenderness   131
   Gareth Evans
9 Statelessness as Practice: Sohrab Shahid Saless and the Work of Exile   141
   Pierre d'Alancaisez
10 Screening Sohrab Shahid Saless's Work: Contemporary Perspectives   151
   Dario Marchiori

Interview by Behrang Samsami (Journalist) with Bert Schmidt (Shahid Saless's Cinematographer)   159
Sohrab Shahid Saless's Filmography   166
A Film about Shahid Saless   170

Index   177

Figures

2.1	Heinz's abusive behaviour (*Utopia*)	29
2.2	Heinz's rehearsal (*Utopia*)	32
3.1	Michael looking out of the window (*Time of Maturity*)	45
3.2	The railway guard's wife looking out of the window (*Still Life*)	46
3.3	Rosie, Helga and Monika looking out of the window (*Utopia*)	46
3.4	The railway guard and his family having dinner (*Still Life*)	47
3.5	The cooking pot (*Still Life*)	48
3.6	The railway guard's glasses (*Still Life*)	48
3.7	The railway guard leaving his home (*Still Life*)	52
4.1	Mohammad in the classroom (*A Simple Event*)	68
4.2	View from outside the building (*Taste of Cherry*)	71
4.3	Mohammad outside the doctor's house (*A Simple Event*)	72
4.4	Mohammad's mother in the school principal's office (*A Simple Event*)	73
4.5	In the school principal's office (*The Traveller*)	73
6.1	Michael hiding outside the neighbour's apartment (*Time of Maturity*)	106
6.2	Michael arrives home (*Time of Maturity*)	107
6.3	Michael sitting alone at the foot of the staircase (*Time of Maturity*)	108
6.4	Domestic setting (*Jeanne Dielman, 23 quai du Commerce, 1080 Bruxelles*)	110
6.5	The lonely woman and her room (*I, You, He, She*)	111
6.6	Conversation in the kitchen (*No Home Movie*)	113
6.7	The couple on the sofa (*Nightsongs/Die Nacht singt ihre Lieder*)	117
6.8	The lonely man on the sofa (*Nightsongs/Die Nacht singt ihre Lieder*)	117

7.1	Seven-channel HD Video installation of *Chantal Akerman, Now*	125
7.2	Seven-channel HD Video installation of *Chantal Akerman, Now*	125
7.3	David Hall's *1,001 TV Sets (End Piece)*	127
8.1	*Gastarbeiter*	133
8.2	*Gastarbeiter*	133
9.1	Rabih Mroué and Catherine Deneuve in *Je veux voir*	146
9.2	*Your Country Doesn't Exist (Do it Yourself)*	147
In.1	A break in filming: actor Josef Stehlik and director Saless. Saless is partially covering the written slogan on the Slovakian production company's car	160
In.2	The exterior shots for *The Willow Tree* on a tributary of the Danube on the Slovakian–Hungarian border	161
In.3	Behind the scene of *Hans – A Young Man in Germany*	162
In.4	On the set of the film: Sohrab Shahid Saless and Bert Schmidt, his assistant director	163
OA.1	Sohrab Shahid Saless in his studio	171
OA.2	Sohrab Shahid Saless in Germany	172
OA.3	Sohrab Shahid Saless in Bandar Torkaman, Iran	173
OA.4	Sohrab Shahid Saless: portrait	173
OA.5	Bandar Torkaman site visit	174
OA.6	Bandar Torkaman site visit	174
OA.7	Bandar Torkaman site visit	175
OA.8	Poster for the film	175

Acknowledgements

ReFocus: The Films of Sohrab Shadid Saless has been developed as part of my ongoing practice-based research on the representation of diaspora and double agency within the medium of the moving image. The initial starting point was a personal fascination with the work of this remarkable filmmaker, which led to the development of the first UK retrospective on his work (co-curated with Nikolaus Perneczky, October 2017 to January 2018), alongside the first English-language book on the director. During the retrospective, eleven films were screened at three sites – Close-Up Cinema (East London), Institute of Contemporary Art (Central London) and Goethe-Institut London (West London) - to reach as wide an audience as possible and share our admiration for Shahid Saless's outstanding practice. We are pleased to report that the project was a great success.

Through *ReFocus: The Films of Sohrab Shadid Saless*, its selected chapters and contributions from remarkable scholars, you will notice the unique condition of Shahid Saless's films as a stateless archive and will be provided with a deeper insight into the filmmaker's practice, as well as the notion of curating stateless moving images.

This project has been made possible through the generous support of many individuals and institutes. I would like to thank Professor Fran Lloyd, Professor Stephen Barber, Gillian Leslie, Gary D. Rhodes, Robert Singer, Aras Khatami, Vahid Alaghband, Ezzidin Alwan, Helen Glenn, Jane Pavitt and Jo Reeves, as well as Kingston University's Visual and Material Culture Research Centre, Iran Heritage Foundation, Art Council England, Edinburgh University Press and Kingston School of Art, for their invaluable help and advice throughout its genesis.

Notes on Contributors

Omid Abdollahi is a filmmaker and member of Iranian Short Film Association (ISFA) and Iranian Documentary Filmmakers Association (IDFA). With his short and documentary films he has participated in numerous festivals and has won various awards, such as the Bronze Medal at the Festival of Nations, Ebensee, Austria; the IDFA Bertha Fund award; the Jury Prize from the Ismailia International Film Festival; and the Jury Mention Special Prize from Clermont Ferrand International Short Film Festival. http://omidabdollahi.com

Pierre d'Alancaisez is a curator and is founding director of *waterside contemporary* in London. Alongside curating some forty exhibitions at *waterside* and offsite, d'Alancaisez has presented numerous public performance works, talks and screenings, and was publisher of a gallery magazine and a series of exhibition catalogues. http://waterside-contemporary.com/

Majid Eslami is an Iranian journalist and a film and literary critic. Eslami has been Chief Editor of chahaar.com (an art and literature website) since 2017 and a journalist for *24 Film Magazine* since 2011. He has also translated several publications such as, among others, *Films of Akira Kurosawa* by Donald Richie in collaboration with Hamid Montazeri; *In the Labyrinth: A Novel* by Alain Robbe-Grillet; *A Sketch of the Past* by Virginia Woolf (autobiography); *The Third Man* by Graham Greene (screenplay); and *Lost Highway* by David Lynch (screenplay).

Gareth Evans is a London-based writer, editor, film and event producer, and Whitechapel Gallery's Adjunct Moving Image Curator. He produced the essay film *Patience (After Sebald)* by Grant Gee and has executive-produced the feature-length artists' works *Erase and Forget* (Andrea Luka Zimmerman, Berlinale Panorama, 2017), among others. He is co-director of production agency Artevents and has curated numerous film and event seasons across the UK, including 'John Berger: Here Is Where We Meet' and 'All Power to the Imagination! 1968 and its Legacies'. He edits *Artesian* and co-edits for Go Together Press and House Sparrow Press, whose recent publications include original titles by John Berger and Anne Michaels.

Azadeh Fatehrad is an academic, artist and curator based in London. Her practice ranges from still and moving images to fictional stories, short films and art books that have been exhibited internationally at the Royal Academy of Art (London) and Index: The Swedish Contemporary Art Foundation (Stockholm), among others. She has curated many public programmes such as 'Sohrab Shahid Saless: Exiles' at the Close-Up Film Centre, Goethe-Institut and Institute of Contemporary Arts (ICA), London (2017–18), and 'The Feminist Historiography' at IASPIS, Stockholm (2016). Fatehrad is on the editorial board of the peer-reviewed *Journal for Artistic Research* (JAR) and is St John's College Artist in Residence 2018 at the University of Oxford.

Christopher Gow conducted his postgraduate research into Iranian cinema at both the University of London (School of Oriental and African Studies) and the University of Warwick, exploring the relationship between the New Iranian Cinema and émigré Iranian filmmaking. He currently resides in Scotland and has taught courses on Iranian cinema at the University of Glasgow. *From Iran to Hollywood and Some Places In-Between* (2011), based on his doctoral thesis, was his first major publication. He has presented papers on Iranian cinema at a variety of international conferences and has published articles on various aspects of Iranian cinema, including *Moviement*, *Asian Cinema* and *Directory of World Cinema: Iran 2*.

Michelle Langford is Senior Lecturer in Film Studies in the School of the Arts and Media at the University of New South Wales, Sydney, Australia. Her research spans the cinemas of Iran and Germany. She is author of *Allegorical Images: Tableau, Time and Gesture in the Cinema of Werner Schroeter* (2006) and editor of *The Directory of World Cinema: Germany* (2012, 2013). Her work on Iranian cinema has appeared in leading film studies journals, including *Camera Obscura* and *Screen*, and she has published on Sohrab Shahid Saless in *Screening the Past*. She is currently completing a book entitled *Allegory in Iranian Cinema: The Aesthetics of Poetry and Resistance*.

Dario Marchiori is a curator and director of the Department of Performing Arts, Image and Screen at Université Lyon 2, France. https://passagesxx-xxi.univ-lyon2.fr/marchiori-dario-601067.kjsp

Michael Mazière is an artist, curator and currently Reader in Film and Video at the University of Westminster. He is the co-founder and curator of Ambika P3, an experimental research space for international contemporary art, and an active member of the Centre for Research and Education in Arts and Media (CREAM);

recent exhibitions include Victor Burgin (2013), Chantal Akerman (2015) and Lindsay Seers (2017), among others. Mazière is co-editor of the *Moving Image Review & Art Journal* (MIRAJ), an international peer-reviewed scholarly publication devoted to artists' film and video and its contexts.

Hamid Naficy is Professor of Radio-Television-Film and Hamad Bin Khalifa Al-Thani Professor in Communication at Northwestern University, where he is also an affiliate faculty member in the Department of Art History and a core faculty member on the Middle East and North African Studies Programme. Naficy is a leading authority on cultural studies of diaspora, exile, post-colonial cinemas and media, and Iranian and Middle Eastern cinema. He has published extensively in English and Persian, including the award-winning four-volume *Social History of Iranian Cinema*, published in 2011–12, and a two-volume book on documentary cinema theory and history, *Film-e Mostanad*.

Behrang Samsami is a Research Assistant at the German Bundestag and works as a freelance journalist, publishing numerous pieces on the life and work of Sohrab Shahid Saless. He is author of *The Disenchantment of the East: The Orient in the Travel Literature of Hermann Hesse, Armin T. Wegner and Annemarie Schwarzenbach* (2011; in German), and co-editor of *The Risky Project: Modernity and its Mastering* (2011, 2015; two vols in German) and of *Nicholas II: Splendour and Fall of the Last Tsar* by Essad Bey (originally published 1935, reissued 2011; in German). www.behrangsamsami.com

Bert Schmidt was assistant director to Rosa von Praunheim and Sohrab Shahid Saless. Following this, he pursued his own film projects: *Selection: Books* (Berlin Film Festival 1987, in competition), *The Suitcase* (German National Film Award 1992) *Dance of Sisyphus* (a feature documentary on a dynasty of jugglers, 2004). and *Motorbike* (Royal Anthropological Institute Film Festival, 2012). www.strandfilm.com

Matthias Wittmann is a film and media scholar, film critic, film curator, and research assistant at the Seminar for Media Studies (University of Basel), focusing on Iranian cinema, which he is currently exploring in the framework of an ongoing project supported by the Swiss National Science Foundation on 'Afterimages of Revolution and War: Trauma- and Memoryscapes in Post-revolutionary Iranian Cinema'. He is author of *MnemoCine: Die Konstruktion des Gedächtnisses in der Erfahrung des Films* (2016). His upcoming publications include 'Im Warteraum der Filmgeschichte: Nachbilder der Revolution in Mohsen Makhmalbafs Nāṣer al-Dīn Shāh Āktor-e Sīnemā (Iran, 1992) and Salām Sīnemā (Iran, 1995)' in Agnes Hoffmann and Annette Kappeler (eds), *Theatrale Revolten* (2017).

Foreword

Sohrab Shahid Saless was a proponent of Iranian New Wave Cinema. He made his mark on the international film festival circuit with the enormous success of his two Iranian-made feature films: *A Simple Event* (*Yek Ettefaq-e Sadeh*, 1974) and *Still Life* (*Tabiate Bijan*, 1974), the latter winning the Silver Bear at the Berlinale in 1974. After his move to Germany in 1975, from 1975 he went on to direct a considerable body of feature-length projects, including long works for television, and culminating in the drama *Roses for Africa* (*Rosen für Afrika*, 1992), for which he was awarded the German Television Prize. While his Iranian films were concerned with the marginal lives of the downtrodden and disenfranchised, in Germany, this 'guest-worker' (as he would call himself) looked to the agony of homelessness and displacement, and the cruelty of the bureaucratic system: a reflection of his own life in Germany, without permanent residency status and fighting continuously for film funding.

Despite his long career in the German film industry and the acclaim that has greeted his films, Shahid Saless is rarely mentioned in scholarly literature and, except for a few short articles, there is a total lack of scholarship in English on the life and work of this visionary and transnational artist. The present book, which follows in the footsteps of the first UK retrospective of his work in 2018, promises to fill the lacunae. Iran Heritage Foundation is proud to have supported the UK retrospective and the publication of this book.

Vahid Alaghband
Trustee, Iran Heritage Foundation

Sohrab Shahid Saless in his studio. (Source: Unknown photographer, Tehran, 1958.)

Introduction

Azadeh Fatehrad

You feel less *here*, and more *there*. Where 'here'? Where 'there'? In dozens of 'heres,' in dozens of 'theres,' that you didn't know, that you don't recognize. Dark zones that used to be bright. Light zones that used to be heavy. You no longer end up in yourself, and reality, even objects, lose their mass and stiffness and no longer put up any serious resistance to the everpresent transforming mobility.[1]

This volume is the first English-language book on this remarkable but neglected Iranian–German filmmaker (1944–98). Shahid Saless's work belongs to no single place or canon; it is a continent of its own – a central massif of cinema, as one critic notes. The director's slow-paced films tell simple stories almost without words, in meditative but searing images that register the smallest of details. His close attention to the routines and repetitions of everyday life is mirrored in the rhythmic flow of his films and in the clockwork-precision play of sound and silence. In addition to cinema, he engaged in other mediums such as television and literature. Moving across cultures, from pre-revolutionary Iran to post-war West Germany and the former Czechoslovakia, he observes the world with an unflinching eye, alert to cruelty and injustice, but never judging.

Shahid Saless led a fascinating, if at times sad and lonely, life. Fleeing from his native Iran in 1974 and making Germany his new home, he did enjoy some success there but eventually had to leave in 1992, due to the difficulty of securing funds for his projects and finding it hard to support himself generally. He died just a few years later, alone in a rental flat in Chicago. This book provides an overview and analysis of Shahid Saless's lifetime work, produced in Iran,

Germany and the USA, through a set of comprehensive contributions from leading scholars in the field.

The book is divided into three major parts. The first covers Shahid Saless's time in Iran, including the inspiration he took from the great Chekhov, and his minimalist mise-en-scène and use of non-professional actors in *A Simple Event* (1974) and *Still Life* (1974). It continues by reflecting on Shahid Saless's work in West Germany; this includes *Utopia* (1982), which offers a form of social critique of the life of women in Berlin during the 1970s. This is followed by theoretical reflections on categorising Shahid Saless's work as an Iranian filmmaker abroad – from exilic to diasporic, émigré, ethnic, cosmopolitan and beyond. Here, the ironic language of Shahid Saless's filmmaking, as witnessed in *Time of Maturity* (1976) and *Far from Home* (1975), is seen as offering a 'counter-protocol' to the norms prevailing in society at that time.

In the second part, the book refers to the notion of 'cinema of exile', using Shahid Saless as a case study to reflect on certain aesthetic, stylistic, financial and socio-political regularities in the lives of those creatives who have chosen to make a new place their home. The book also discusses Shahid Saless's situation in the political economy of New German Cinema and considers how the emergence of a 'cultural mode of production' in Germany, which relied heavily on state subsidies and television co-productions, helped him not only to re-establish his career in exile but actually to emerge as an important proponent of what the Germans called the *Autorenfilm*. Engaging with various socio-cultural factors, this part also reflects on the notion of individual struggle to navigate a path through complex social relations and the diverse negotiations of agency within artistic practice. *Time of Maturity* is reflected upon to explore the notion of 'in-betweenness' in the Iranian–German filmmaker's work, and his aesthetic and stylistic approach that masterfully leads the viewer from one uncomfortable scene to the next.

The major theme of *ReFocus: The Films of Sohrab Shadid Saless* is related to exiled and displaced moving image practitioners: their ethics, aesthetics and modes of production, as well as their precarious lives and often uncertain legacy. Therefore, a parallel is drawn with Belgian film director Chantal Akerman's work, as well as that of Romuald Karmakar. In particular, selected scenes from Akerman's *Jeanne Dielman, 23 quai du Commerce, 1080 Bruxelles* (1975) and Karmakar's *Nightsongs (Die Nacht singt ihre Lieder*, 2004) are analysed to provide a wider context for the 'cinema of exile'.

Considering that Shahid Saless's body of work consists of a stateless archive of footage held in various locations such as Film Museum München (in Germany) and the Centre for the Intellectual Development of Children and Young Adults (Kanoon) (in Iran), with the copyright being held by various individuals and institutions around the world, it becomes almost imperative to allocate a section of this book to the matter of 'accessibility':

the way in which researchers and curators can access stateless archival films such as Shahid Saless's, and how the public can also see these invaluable creative productions. Therefore, in the third part of this book we explore the notion of the 'stateless' moving image and the processes and challenges for researchers and museums and galleries involved in working with such materials, all of which is designed to provide a deeper insight into working with the uncertain legacy of creative exiles like Shahid Saless.

The text also looks at some developments in distribution channels, such as galleries and digital platforms that were not available to Shahid Saless during his time. Film curators and academics at both private and publicly funded institutes have provided their insight into the persistent problems concerning the archiving and transmission of transnational or 'stateless' film – Shahid Saless's work being a case in point in comparison to his that of his contemporary counterparts.

The final three additional sections are dedicated to Shahid Saless's filmography, including full details of cast and crew, along with production information. We have also provided images from production shoots, screen grabs and more. There follows an interview between journalist Behrang Samsami and Bert Schmidt (Shahid Saless's cinematographer), to give an even deeper insight into the filmmaker's work. The final section discusses a film that has been made about Shahid Saless, written and produced by Omid Abdolahi.

In *ReFocus: The Films of Sohrab Shadid Saless* my aim has been to create an opportunity for artists, scholars and the engaged public to reflect on the director's work and on its implications for creativity in diasporic conditions of urban displacement. I have personally found Shahid Saless's work a great inspiration in terms of the context we share in common as creative foreigners struggling in a new land to obtain a residency permit and to integrate. His slow-paced, minimalist evocations of the everyday have inspired the work of Chantal Akerman (mentioned above) and the legendary Abbas Kiarostami. Today, moving image artists such as Romuald Karmakar are also claiming a kinship with Shahid Saless, whose films speak forcefully to the traumas of displacement and migration.

NOTE

1. G. Didi-Huberman (2018) *The Eye of History: When Images Take Positions*. Boston: MIT Press, p. 11.

PART I

The Life and Work of Sohrab Shahid Saless

In 1974, facing increasing government pressure and censorship, Shahid Saless left his native Iran – where he had realised two incisive feature films and co-founded the New Film Group – for West Germany. Without permanent residency status and locked into a continual struggle to secure funding, this self-described 'guest-worker' of German cinema was to create a unique but critically neglected body of films that speak forcefully to the traumas of displacement and migration.

CHAPTER 1

Slow, Closed, Recessive, Formalist and Dark: The Cinema of Sohrab Shahid Saless

Hamid Naficy

Iranian filmmakers in the diaspora form one of the most active transnational filmmaking groups in the world. However, they do not constitute a unified bloc. Their identities are varied and evolving – from exilic to diasporic, émigré, ethnic, cosmopolitan and beyond – and they work in many countries, using different modes of production and making a variety of types of film in multiple languages. This chapter discusses these issues by placing Sohrab Shahid Saless's life and films in the context of the Iranian diaspora since the 1960s and the 'accented cinema' that they produced.[1]

If Masud Kimiai's movies *Dash Akol* (1971) and *Qaisar* (1969) consolidated the conventions of the popular Tough Guy movie subgenres of *dash mashti* and *jaheli*, respectively, Dariush Mehrjui's *The Cow* (*Gav*, 1969) combined some of the textual features that became characteristic of New Wave art-house movies, particularly those of Sohrab Shahid Saless, the most loyal dramatist of naturalism and realism in Iranian cinema. Reality – faithfulness to the external world – and realism – faithfulness to the conventions of classic realist cinema – were two intertwined features that set the New Wave films apart from the fantasy-driven and narratively chaotic commercial *Filmfarsi* works (in the Farsi language), such as the Tough Guy movies. These were foundational features of this counter-cinema, which set the reality of ordinary peoples' lives, treated with empathy and respect, against the fiction of the official culture of spectacle perpetrated by the Pahlavi government and commercial cinema. These features gave the New Wave films their 'luminous truth', a phrase used by Giuseppe Ferrara to describe the Italian neorealist films (Liehm 1984, 132). The audiences for the popular *Filmfarsi* genre movies were ordinary people, while those for the art-house movies were predominantly more educated.

EARLY CAREER AND FILMS IN IRAN BEFORE EXILE

Sohrab Shahid Saless was born in Qazvin in 1944. He received his film production training in Austria and France, and began making films in Iran in the late 1960s as a contract employee of the Ministry of Culture and Art, earning 9,000 tomans a month. He made twenty-two documentaries and short films for the ministry, several of them about the performing arts and dance, designed for foreign distribution through Iranian embassies and consulates. Among these were *Bojnurd Folkdances* (*Raqs ha-ye Mahhali-ye Bojnurdi*, 1970), *Torbat-e Jam Folkdances* (*Raqs ha-ye Mahhali-ye Torbat-e Jam*, 1970) and *Turkman Folkdances* (*Raqs ha-ye Mahhali-ye Turkaman*, 1970).

He directed his first feature, *A Simple Event* (*Yek Ettefaq-e Sadeh*, 1974), under the guise of working on a twenty-minute short. Many key features of his style emerged in this first fiction film, and were reconfigured in the second and last feature that he made inside Iran, *Still Life* (*Tabi'at-e Bijan*, 1974). Unlike his contemporary New Wave director Parviz Kimiavi, who had a generally optimistic and expansive view of the world and whose films were playful and open, Shahid Saless was pessimistic and his work adopted a recessive and closed style. The action in these two films is staged with meticulous Chekhovian naturalism, and they are filmed in a signature minimalist and formalist style involving a slow pace, and a static and observational camera prone to long takes, long shots and slow pans. In fact, Shahid Saless might be considered as one of the progenitors of what nowadays is called 'slow cinema' in film studies circles.

Additionally, Shahid Saless's films are concerned with the life of ordinary people and their daily routines, rendered with an ironic and objective distance. Space is closed and pre-ordained; time is still or passes slowly. Unlike some New Wave filmmakers, Shahid Saless generally shunned symbolism. With time, his films became darker, yet luminous in their darkness.

As the result of his troubled exile, his lengthy, dystopic and dysphoric films, and his difficult personality and style of work, as well as the Eurocentrism predominant in much of film studies world in the 1980s and 1990s, he did not gain the respect and recognition that he deserved, either in Germany where he made all his post-Iran films, as a contributor to the vibrant New German Cinema, or in international circles, as the great auteur director that he was. Likewise, it is not surprising that he would not currently be recognised as one of the fathers of slow cinema. Those who are usually cited as pioneers of this film style include Andrei Tarkovsky, Ingmar Bergman, Michelangelo Antonioni, Aleksander Sokurov, Béla Tarr, Chantal Akerman and Theo Angelopoulos. I would nevertheless add his name to this list of great cinematic slowcoaches!

The first two feature films that he made inside Iran not only showcased his luminous style but also garnered widespread praise among Iranian critics and at international film festivals. *A Simple Event* concerns the daily routines of a student, who lives in Bandar Shah, at the end of the south–north rail line, with his alcoholic fisherman father and his sick mother; the latter soon dies. *Still Life* deals with the everyday life of a railway guard at some far-off junction in the northern part of the country, who is about to lose his job. The joyless existence and drudgery lived through by these characters stood in high contrast to the era during which the films were made, particularly *A Simple Event*, which was filmed during the lavish 2,500th anniversary celebration of the Iranian monarchy. The characters are played by non-actors, but the films treat these ordinary people with dignity: a dignity that the state had withdrawn from its citizens. Critics praised *A Simple Event* and it influenced rising filmmakers, such as Abbas Kiarostami. Critic Jamal Omid called it a 'sincere, noble, and truthful' work; Feraidun Moezimoqaddam characterised it as a 'long poem'; and Jamsheed Akrami, playing on its title, called it 'a significant event' (Omid 1995, 659–62). Shahid Saless himself called it 'the noblest film I ever made in my life' (Sar Reshtehdari 1998, 45). With this seminal work he made a name for himself nationally by winning the top directorial award at the Second Tehran International Film Festival.

Both *A Simple Event* and *Still Life* were entered in the Berlin International Film Festival, where they both won awards, the latter the Silver Bear (for best film). Such prizes brought Iranians a sense of pride. Ironically, Iranians (mis)recognised themselves in the dark mirror that Shahid Saless held up to them. That his films had become a source of pride was evident from the critic Feraidun Moezimoqaddam's review in *Sinema 53* magazine:

> I feel proud and honoured. My international friends all congratulate me, and the Iranian residents and students in Germany (even those with criticism) are delighted and proud . . . I think the highest reward that Shahid Saless received was the compassionate looks of Iranians who had made their way to Berlin from all around Germany and witnessed that he was not returning home with empty hands, thanks to his films. (Omid 1995, 691)

In Iran, only *Still Life* received a public screening, and that just in one Tehran movie house, Capri Cinema. It did unexpectedly well, however. Despite, or perhaps because of, its success, the government did not give the director a production permit for his next film, *Quarantine* (*Qarantineh*), causing Shahid Saless to choose voluntary exile in Germany, where he made fifteen lengthy and searing films in twenty-three years. Exile internationalised Iranian filmmakers in a more fundamental way than either their training abroad or their participation in film festivals. Of Shahid Saless's movies made in exile, the only one shown in Iran before the revolution, to a packed auditorium in the

Iran–Germany Cultural Society, a venue for the Tehran International Film Festival, was his *Far From Home* (*In der Fremde/Dar Ghorbat*, 1975), about a Turkish guest-worker in Germany. Like his other exilic films, this one steered clear of Iranian matters – stories, characters, locations – but it did deal with a personal issue: life as an immigrant in an inhospitable foreign land. With this film, the director's closed-form aesthetics became more prominent and his dark tonality thickened.

Far From Home deals with Turkish industrial guest-workers in Germany, who formed a large labour force essential to Germany's post-World War Two economic recovery but who never received the recognition they deserved. An alienated worker named Hussein (Parviz Sayyad) maintains a crushingly routinized job as a beaten-down but earnest operator of a factory's monstrously noisy machines. While work gives him an income and a much-desired structure, it is a prison. His austere life outside the factory is laden with fear and loneliness; his attempts to enter German society fail. Even though he shares an overcrowded communal apartment with other guest-workers, he feels isolated. Hussein's only contact is a younger man named Kalim (Muhammet Temizkan), who claims to have a German girlfriend. He borrows money from Hussein to sustain this relationship – money that he gambles away and never returns. In the end, the girlfriend turns out to have been imaginary, a figure of desire which both men used in an attempt to emplace themselves in the midst of their total displacement. An urgent letter forces Kalim to return to Turkey – a return that is dreaded, foreclosing his dream of freedom and connection to Germany, even though his actual experience there is far removed from that idyllic German dream of an elsewhere (*Fernweh*). In this dystopic figuration of the exilic return, *Far From Home* ran counter to the accented films that celebrate actual or imaginary homeward returns. Shahid Saless himself neither harboured the fantasy of a glorious return to his original homeland nor attempted such a return.

Though unique in his artistry, Shahid Saless was nevertheless part of the large Iranian diaspora, begun in the 1960s, and the cinematic productions that stemmed from it; this deserves exploration. Since Mehrjui's *The Cow* in the early 1970s, Iranian art-house films have been making major headlines in the international press and at film festivals, winning top awards. This trend intensified many-fold with the emergence of the new post-revolution art-house films, which, in addition to receiving a laudatory press and myriad top awards at international film festivals, were given commercial exhibition in movie houses and on TV, college campuses and streaming sites. As early as the start of the 1990s, the Toronto International Film Festival and New York Film Festival began calling Iranian cinema 'one of the pre-eminent national cinemas' and one of the 'most exciting' cinemas in the world, respectively. Abbas Kiarostami, Amir Naderi, Dariush Mehrjui, Bahram Baizai, the Makhmalbaf family, Rakhshan Banietemad, Tahmineh Milani, Bahman Ghobadi, Majid Majidi, Jafar Panahi and Mohammad Rassoulof have all become practically household names among the cinephiles of the world. What has not received sufficient attention is the significant work that Iranians have been producing outside Iran, in their wide diaspora.

A survey of some sixty-one countries in 2009 by the International Monetary Fund concluded that Iran has the highest rate of 'brain drain' in the world and that 'every year more than 150,000 educated Iranians leave their home country in the hope of finding a better life abroad'. This number, which has now reached around 180,000, is a massive and alarming development, with far-reaching consequences for the future of Iran, Iranians in diaspora and the receiving nations.

What is remarkable is that, simultaneously, post-revolution Iran also topped the list of the world's largest refugee havens, with the number of displaced Iraqis reaching 700,000 after the Halabja chemical bombings in 1988, and the displaced Afghan population reaching three million at its peak in 1991 (Hakimzadeh 2006, 8–9). Both of these movements of displaced populations – emigration and immigration – have had profound repercussions for Iranian cinema and Iranian filmmakers, particularly in broadening and deepening their horizons, and diversifying and globalizing their output.

Most Iranians emigrated to Europe and North America, with those in the USA forming the largest population outside Iran. Although highly concentrated in Southern California, the group is dispersed widely across the country, with heavy concentrations in New York, Texas, Virginia, Maryland, Florida and Illinois. This population is also widely heterogeneous in terms of social and class affiliation, profession, politics, ethnicity, religion, gender and generation. As a result, it is misleading to speak of an Iranian community outside Iran as if it were singular and homogeneous. The same is true of the Iranian mediamakers.

I conducted three research projects on these mediamakers, each leading to a book. One dealt with Iranian popular culture and television programmes in Los Angeles, a second with displaced Middle Eastern and North African filmmakers, including Iranians, and a third with displaced Iranian filmmakers only; these provide a context for Shahid Saless's works.

IRANIAN POP CULTURE AND TELEVISION IN LOS ANGELES

The first study, undertaken in the 1980s and the early 1990s, established the vitality and extensive cross-fertilisation of Iranian exilic popular culture and television, produced in Los Angeles and disseminated throughout the diaspora.

It showed that, in their first decade of emigration, from 1980 to 1991, Iranians in the USA produced and transmitted sixty-two regularly scheduled television programmes, totalling over seventeen hours of programming per week. For their TV broadcasts, they used the new 'lease access' provision of the cable television law that required cable companies to air community-produced shows. In addition, Iranians produced twenty-seven feature films, primarily in the USA, many of them by veteran, Pahlavi-era filmmakers. Finally, Iranians in Los Angeles – the capital of Iranian pop culture, also called 'Persian Motown' in those days – produced eighteen regularly scheduled radio programmes in this period, eigthy-six Persian-language printed periodicals, and numerous music albums and music videos, and formed numerous cultural and political associations, university student societies and nightclubs (Naficy 2002, 249–67).

Iranian ethno-religious minorities proportionately outnumbered their Muslim compatriots among television producers in California: of 46 producers, 28 were Muslim, 12 Christian (6 Armenians, 5 Assyrians, 1 Protestant), 2 Jewish and 4 Baha'is (Naficy 1993, 82). Interethnicity – the presence of subgroups within an immigrant group – also figured large in the Los Angeles pop music industry, resulting in fascinating cross-fertilisation. For example, in the 1980s, Jewish businesspeople were generally the producers and distributors of the music that Muslim singers sang and Armenian musicians performed. In addition, Jews were apparently the most active music-buying, concert-going and party-giving group among Iranians, perhaps partly due to their financial success as a result of their very high self-employment rate in Los Angeles.

Over the years, Iranian exilic television underwent a radical transformation. While the early exilic TV productions consisted of single shows, produced by an individual producer and aired in the 1980s and 1990s by broadcasters, cablecasters or public access outlets for Iranian exiles primarily in Los Angeles, the twenty-four-hour satellite channels that emerged from the 2000s on were diasporic, in that they addressed not only Iranian exiles in Los Angeles, but also those elsewhere in the diaspora and inside Iran. These channels thus became important players in the new, mutually antagonistic public diplomacy – soft power relations – particularly between the Islamic Republic of Iran, Iranians in the diaspora, and the United States. The satellite era began with National Iranian TV, operated by former pop singer Zia Atabay, and quickly grew to include over two dozen Persian-language channels as other governments and entities entered this controversial but lucrative intersectional media public diplomacy.

IRANIAN-ACCENTED CINEMA IN DIASPORA

My second study, conducted in the late 1990s, argued that a new global cinema had emerged, created by the displaced filmmakers of the world since the 1960s. I called this an 'accented cinema' because – in its non-linear, fragmented style, its multilingualism, its concern with themes of home and elsewhere, and its marginal and displaced characters – it offered an alternative to mainstream cinemas, which were presumably without accent. My study showed that Middle Eastern and North African filmmakers in their diaspora formed a surprisingly large and diverse group of accented directors, numbering 321 from 16 sending countries, who made a minimum of 920 films in 27 receiving countries, mostly in Europe and North America (Naficy 2001, 18). The study showed that, in the 1990s and early 2000s, the output of Iranians topped the list of Middle Eastern and North African diasporic filmmakers: Iranians produced 307 films, followed by Armenians (235), Algerians (107), Lebanese (46), Palestinians (35), Turks (25), Moroccans (25), Tunisians (23) and Israeli/Jewish (24).

My third, extensive study, of Iranian filmmakers working abroad only, conducted for my four-volume book, *A Social History of Iranian Cinema*, not only revised their total output considerably upward from the previous two studies but also provided a fascinating socio-cultural and cinematic profile of that output. The geographical locations in which Iranians made films give us a good idea of the dispersal and concentration of the diaspora communities, and the number of films they created indicates the relative size and cultural capital of the Iranian population in each location. Iranians made films in twenty-one countries, with the United States ranking first (505 films), followed by France (138), Canada (107), Germany (90), Sweden (77), Austria (68), Great Britain (67), the Netherlands (42), Australia (19), Norway (18), New Zealand (11) and Denmark (10). The dominance of those in the USA is not surprising, for America houses both the largest population of Iranians outside Iran – as well as numbers of Iranian entertainers and mediamakers – and the most powerful film industry in the world (Naficy 2012, 376).

There are some exceptions, however, as Iranians in France made more films than those in Sweden and Germany, even though at the time both of the latter had a larger Iranian population; and while Iranians in France, which has a smaller population of Iranians, produced a larger number of films than other European countries, those in Israel, which has a higher ratio of Iranians, apparently did not produce any. The disproportionate number of films to population in certain countries is partly due to the over-productivity of a few individuals in those places: for example, Ghazel Radpay in France, Sohrab Shahid Saless in Germany and Houchang Allahyari in Austria. Such areas need more work and more accurate data.

IRANIAN IMMIGRATION WAVES AND THEIR FILMIC OUTPUT

The influx of Iranians into the USA occurred in three broad waves: from 1950 to 1977, from 1979 to 1986, and from 1987 to 2012. The first was motivated by the rapid, top-down Westernisation spearheaded by the Shah, the second by the bottom-up popular social revolution, eventually led by Ayatollah Khomeini, and the third by economic misery, the eight-year war with Iraq, and political repression; this produced three different types of population. While the first wave was comprised chiefly of permanent economic immigrants or of temporary immigrants, such as a large number of students, much of the second wave was made up of political refugees and exiles with high class-capital (Bozorgmehr 1997, 443–4). The third wave consisted of highly qualified professionals, on one hand, and of working-class economic refugees, on the other, who emigrated after the ceasefire with Iraq in search of better opportunities; these are the émigrés (Hakimzadeh 2006, 3).

Even though a small sojourner population, the first immigrant and student wave produced many films – 78 in North America and Europe. The second, larger wave of exiles and refugees was even more productive, with 135 films. In the ensuing years, between 1987 and 2012, as exile evolved for many into diaspora, ethnicity and permanent immigration and these people were joined by a new third wave of working-class émigrés; their output grew steadily, reaching an all-time high of 896 films (Naficy 2012, 381).

Just as the Iranian populations in the diaspora are not homogeneous, the films that they make are also not homogeneous. They could be discussed in various ways, under aesthetic, stylistic and formal rubrics or under the types of film made. Here I will discuss them based on the social placement of their authors. As such, this is primarily an authorship approach to the diaspora cinema to the films of Shahid Saless.

MODALITIES OF IRANIAN-ACCENTED FILMS

The films that Iranians made abroad are part of the new global cinema of displacement – accented cinema – created by differently situated displaced filmmakers who, despite their many fundamental differences, share certain features in their films, which constitute the latter's accent (Naficy 2001). If the dominant cinema in each country were considered universal and without accent, the films that displaced subjects make there would be accented. Likewise, if the dominant world cinema, that of Hollywood, were considered universal and without accent, the films that displaced global filmmakers make would be accented. However, this accent emanates not so much from the accented speech of the diegetic characters as from the displacement of the filmmakers themselves, in their alternative artisanal production mode, and in the style, aesthetics, narratives and politics of their films.

I divide Iranian filmmakers working abroad into at least five recognisable but overlapping types: exilic, diasporic, émigré, ethnic and cosmopolitan. This classification is based on the filmmakers' different types of displacement and subsequent placement within the immigration waves to which they belong, and the manner in which displacement shapes their films. Iranian filmmakers, like many other Middle Eastern filmmakers, moved through several countries and across several identities. Some claimed multiple identities – both simultaneous and sequential – while others denied any form of particularistic identity. Some never returned home, while others periodically visited their homelands, where they made films. Some moved among too many worlds, often leaving behind inadequately documented histories. A few deliberately obfuscated their history in order to conceal their tracks. Such fluidity and camouflaging, characteristic of displaced positionality, makes it difficult to pin down with certainty some filmmakers' country of origin or residence, let alone their other markers of identity, such as ethno-religious affiliations. As a result, it is important to note that some filmmakers fall into more than one category. What is more, many started in one category of identity but evolved and made films in other categories, in tandem with their own personal and professional journeys and evolution of identities. In addition, not all Iranians abroad made accented films. Some worked in the dominant film and television industries and engaged in popular cinematic practices, making mainstream movies. I briefly discuss prominent filmmakers in each category, including Shahid Saless as a transnational cosmopolitan accented filmmaker.

EXILED FILMMAKERS

The term 'exile' refers principally to external exiles: Iranians who voluntarily or involuntarily left their country but who maintained both an ambivalent and a highly cathected relationship with their original and adopted homes. Although these exiles did not return to Iran – and many could not, they maintained an intense desire to do so, a desire that was projected in potent return narratives in their work. The exiled filmmakers, like exiled writers, who were generally older, suffered from the discrepancy between their higher-status identity prior to exile and their generally lower-status identity in foreign lands. In addition, being deprived of their original language, culture and audience robbed them of their natural bedrock and tools of expression (Naficy 1993, 1–31). If, at home, they were regarded as stricken by the West (*gharbzadeh*), in exile they became deeply stricken by home (*ghorbatzadeh*). Finally, filmmakers who were forcibly driven away tended to define, at least during the initial period of their exile, all things in their lives not only in relationship to the homeland but also in strictly political terms. Their connection was one of inheritance and descent.

Among such exiled filmmakers are Parviz Sayyad in the USA, with his feature fiction movies, *Checkpoint* (*Sarhad*, 1987) and *Mission* (*Ma'muriat*, 1983), and Reza Allamehzadeh in the Netherlands, with his feature fiction *The Guests* of *Hotel Astoria* (*Mehmanan-e Hotel-e Astoria*, 1989) and documentaries critical of the Islamic Republic's conduct, including *Iranian Taboo* (2011), which details the persecution of the Baha'is in Iran.

There is, of course, another modality of internal exile. If this modality were to be defined as '[i]solation, alienation, deprivation of means of production and communication, [and] exclusion from public life' (Row and Whitfield 1987, 233), then many Iranian intellectuals, artists and filmmakers, particularly arthouse cinema directors, could be considered to be working in internal exile within their own country. Jafar Panahi, Mohammad Rassoulof and Mojtaba Mirtahmasb, working in Iran, are among these internal exiles, who, despite various impediments, including official and unofficial bans, engage in a kind of guerrilla-style filmmaking.

DIASPORIC FILMMAKERS

Diaspora, like exile, often begins with trauma, rupture and coercion, and involves the scattering of populations to places outside the original homeland. Sometimes, however, the scattering is caused by a desire for increased trade, work and financial, artistic, professional and other opportunities. Like the Iranians in exile, those in diaspora have a prior identity in Iran, and their diasporic identity is constructed in resonance with that earlier descent identity. However, unlike exile, which may be individualistic or collective, diaspora is necessarily collective, in both its origination and its destination. As a result, the nurturing of a collective memory, often of an idealised homeland, is constitutive of the diasporic identity. In addition, the exiles' identity involves a near-exclusive, vertical descent relationship with the Iranian homeland; the diasporic consciousness is multisited, involving horizontal relationships with Iranians at home and with Iranian compatriot communities elsewhere across the globe. As a result, plurality, multiplicity and hybridity are structured in dominance among the diaspora filmmakers, while among the political exiles binarism and duality reign.

Among the Iranian diasporic filmmakers is Babak Shokrian, who made feature films dealing with Jewish subjects, the Jewish diaspora and Jewish Iranians: *Peaceful Sabbath* (1993), *America So Beautiful* (2001) and *Shah Bob* (2015). Because of their subject matter and Shokrian's Iranian–Jewish background, these could also be classified as ethnic films. Persheng Sadegh-Vaziri, a Kurdish–Iranian American, made many documentaries about Iranian national and ethnic belonging: *Journal from Tehran* (1986), *Far from Iran* (1991), *A Place Called Home* (1998) and *Women Like Us* (2000–2). Some of these focused more on Kurdish ethnic identity, including her own, some on Iranian diasporic identity, and others on gender identity. Shokrian and Sadegh-Vaziri live and work in the USA. Working primarily out of Great Britain and the USA, Tina Gharavi made experimental documentaries about gender and sexual identity, some involving herself, such as *Mother/Country* (2002), as well as others, such as *I Am Nasrin* (2013), that focus on Iranian teenage refugees in north-east London.

These diasporic filmmakers are also émigré filmmakers, in whose works their own personal, sexual, ethnic and national identities are explored.

ÉMIGRÉ FILMMAKERS

The émigré filmmakers are defined as those who, like exilic and diasporic subjects, left Iran and immigrated to other countries, where, after a period of resistance and adaptation, they consented to becoming permanent residents and citizens while maintaining a variety of attachments to their original home country. Though present in some form, the trauma of displacement, the cathected direct relationship to a lost homeland, and the burning desire for a grand homecoming are not constitutive of immigrants' lives, as the forces of consent relations with the adopted country attenuate those that favour descent relations with the homeland.

Émigré European filmmakers were the engines of the American studio system in the 1920s to 1950s. The first heads of the five major US studios in the 1920s were all Jewish émigrés from the Soviet Union and Eastern Europe, while many major studio directors of the 1930s and 1940s were émigré filmmakers escaping the Nazis. In subsequent decades, other émigré filmmakers from other lands joined in, consolidating the classical realist film style and enriching the American cinema – indeed, world cinema – and culture.

The doyen of Iranian émigré filmmakers was veteran television director Reza Badiyi, born in 1930 in Arak, Iran, and trained by the United States Information Agency unit in Iran to make documentaries about development issues. After moving to the USA in 1955 and earning a degree from Syracuse University, he made a prodigious number of mainstream US television series and films in the period between the 1960s and the 2010s. Among these were the following popular TV series: *Get Smart* (1965), *Mission Impossible* (1969), *Mannix* (1972), *The Six Million Dollar Man* (1974), *Baretta* (1978), *Hawaii Five-O* (1979), *Knots Landing* (1979), *Fame* (1982), *T. J. Hooker* (1986), *Falcon Crest* (1990), *In the Heat of the Night* (1994), *Star Trek* (1994–6), *Cagney & Lacey* (1995), *Baywatch* (1997), *Buffy the Vampire Slayer* (1997), *La Femme Nikita* (1997) and *Mortal Combat* (1999). He was so prolific that he was called the 'Godfather of American television', logging in 'more hours as a director than anyone in history': about 423 in all (Naficy 2012, 396). He died in 2011.

Another type of émigré filmmaker turned to the art world to create installations and art-house films. Working out of New York, Shirin Neshat made several dual-projection films for museums and galleries, becoming a renowned international artist. In 2009, she moved into feature filmmaking with her powerful adaption of Shahrnoush Parsipour's story, *Women Without Men*. All her video works and her first feature deal with Iran or Iranian subjects. However, her latest film, *Looking for Um Kulthum* (2017), extends her reach, dealing with the life and time of the great Egyptian singing star.

ETHNIC FILMMAKERS

Ethnic filmmakers are born to exilic diasporic, and émigré populations in the adopted countries, whose own relationship to their ancestral homeland is often indirect, second-hand, abstract, and sometimes mediated solely through memory, fantasy and mediawork. Iranian émigrés and ethnics in the USA, like other similar groups before them, are hyphenated, bicultural and multicultural subjects, who assiduously play the politics of the hyphen to construct new identities out of their descent relations with their parental homes and consent relations with their own current homes.

The adoption of the hyphen by Iranians in the USA and by accented filmmakers and writers has both positive and negative implications. It could be viewed positively as an indicator of becoming fully American, like other multicultural citizens, or, alternatively, it could be seen as a resistance to the homogenising power of American melting-pot ideology. In this case, both assimilation and resistance would be regarded positively. On the other hand, the hyphen could imply a lack, or an idea that hyphenated Iranians are somehow subordinate to unhyphenated people and that they would never be totally accepted or trusted as full citizens. Many Iranians in the USA at first resisted the hyphen on a class basis, as it implied admitting that they were not fully American and white, like many other lower-class, poor and disenfranchised people of colour in America. They also resisted it because retaining the hyphen could suggest a divided allegiance, even disloyalty, which was particularly dangerous during the periodic waves of anti-Iranian and anti-Muslim sentiments in the USA.

Interpretation of the politics of the hyphen is quite complex. In a nativist and chauvinist reading, generally favoured by exilic and diasporic populations, the hyphen provides a vertical link to an authentic essence that lies outside ideology and pre-dates, or stands apart from, the new adopted nation. The hyphen is a link that emphasises descent relations to Iran and to roots, depth, inheritance, continuity, homogeneity and stability. The filmmakers' task in this modality, in Stuart Hall's word, is only 'to discover, excavate, bring to light and express through cinematic representation' that inherited collective cultural identity, that 'one true self' (Hall 1994, 393). However, in its contestatory adoption, primarily by émigrés and ethnics, the hyphen can operate both vertically and horizontally, playing descent relations against consent relations. In this modality, filmmakers do not strive to recover an existing, authentic past or to impose an imaginary and often fetishised coherence on their fragmented experiences and histories. Instead, by emphasising discontinuity, heterogeneity and specificity, they demonstrate that they are in the process of becoming, that they are 'subject to the continuous "play" of history, culture and power' (394). Read as a sign of hybridised, multiple or constructed identity, the hyphen can become liberating because it can be performed and signified upon. In reality, each hyphen is a nested hyphen, consisting of several intersecting and overlapping hyphens that provide inter- and intra-ethnic, racial, religious, temporal and national linkages. This intersectionality works against essentialism, nationalism and binarism, characteristic both of modernity and of exile.

In the past four decades in which Iranians have settled in large numbers in the USA, they have played a fascinating and evolving game of identity, sometimes with, and sometimes without, the hyphen. During the hostage crisis, and its virulent backlash against Iranian residents in the USA in the 1980s, some denied being Iranian, identifying themselves, instead, as 'Latino', 'Mexican' or 'Greek'. In due course, with Iranian success in business, science, the arts and academic fields, some openly adopted the hyphenated 'Iranian–American' moniker, joining the roster of other successful hyphenated ethnic Americans. Others, harking back to the roots of ancient Iran to modulate, soften or avoid entirely any negative associations with the current Islamic Iran, adopted 'Persian' or 'Persian–American' as their preferred identity. This identity invoked an ancient, almost mythical and tolerant empire that pre-dates both the religion of Islam and the current intolerant Islamic Republic's regime, an identity that has been romanticised in Hollywood movies and popular literature.

The latest and most public use of this latter Persian strategy is in Bravo TV's reality series *Shahs of Sunset*. Begun in 2012, the series was very successful, going into its seventh season in August 2018. Relevant to the topic under discussion here, Bravo TV's website described the participants as six 'Persian–American' friends in Los Angeles, 'who try to juggle their active social lives and careers while also balancing the demands of their families and traditions'. In the series, the players proudly declare themselves to be 'Persian' and engage in all the usual youthful American lifestyles and past times featured in other reality shows – living, loving, dating (both homo- and heterosexual partners), partying, fighting, marrying and working.

Among ethnic filmmakers is Caveh Zahedi, born in Washington, D.C., in 1960, who made fascinating and challenging autobiographical and avant-garde documentary features such as *A Little Stiff* (1991), *I Don't Hate Las Vegas*

Anymore (1994), *I Was Possessed by God* (2000), *In the Bathtub of the World* (2001), *I Am a Sex Addict* (2005) and *The Sheik and I* (2012). In all of these, the director is also the principal subject and actor, his own biography, persona, family relations and politics of the hyphen shaping the films' humorous, contentious, entertaining and experimental narratives.

TRANSNATIONAL COSMOPOLITAN FILMMAKERS

Transnational cosmopolitan filmmakers are mobile both in their places of residence and in the places in which, and about which, they make their films, regardless of their own places of birth and residence; their films are about a variety of topics, often multicultural, transnational and intersectional. Cosmopolitan filmmakers resist any attachment to place, nation and roots; instead, they emphasise routes, individualised identities and auteurist authority. They reject the politics of the ethnic hyphen and generally do not make films about Iran or Iranians. If they do, they do not tell their own personal stories.

Abbas Kiarostami was one exemplar of the cosmopolitan filmmaker, who continued to live inside Iran but who made most of his later films outside the country – in Africa, France and Japan, among other places. Funded by transnational sources, these works involved non-Iranian stories and actors, were filmed in foreign locations and in foreign languages, and were screened not in Iran primarily but at international film festivals, where they received acclaim, and were distributed on international art-house and academic circuits.

Amir Naderi is another cosmopolitan filmmaker living primarily in the USA. His US-made features, *Manhattan by Numbers* (1993), *Avenue A, B, C . . . Manhattan* (1997), *Marathon* (2002) and *Sound Barrier* (2005), are all about homelessness and [un]belonging of one sort or another, and are mostly centred on Manhattan, where he lived. He has also made films in Japan – *Cut* (2011) – and Italy – *Mountain* (2016). In all of these, his characters are on the move, on the run, in perpetual motion and on a search of one kind or another. These active, mobile characters pursue their goals obsessively, in the way that Captain Ahab chases the white whale Moby Dick: forcefully, indefatigably and relentlessly, signalling larger epistemological, psychological and philosophical issues. None of these films deals with Iran or Iranians. Like Shahid Saless, Naderi does not want to be considered as a member of a group – a filmmaker in exile, an Iranian filmmaker or even an Iranian–American filmmaker; instead, as he told me forcefully in an interview, he prefers recognition as a universal film auteur.

> I want to make a complete break, destroy all the bridges. I want to have nothing to do with Iran, my family, Iranian cinema, or being an Iranian exile filmmaker. I want to be a great filmmaker, period. [pause]

I have undergone a blood transfusion [no longer carrying Iranian blood]. I don't care about family, country, language, and the great poets like Ferdowsi, Hafez, or Sa'di. I have broken away from all that. I am here and now, and I want to make my mark on history not as an Iranian or an Iranian–American filmmaker but as a filmmaker, pure and simple. (Naficy 2012, 508)

SOHRAB SHAHID SALESS, A COSMOPOLITAN FILMMAKER IN EXILE

Shahid Saless can best be described as a cosmopolitan subject and filmmaker, even though there are strong strands of exilism in his life and works. After the two fiction films he made inside Iran before the revolution, he made fifteen intense and lengthy features in Germany about alienation and anomie, such as *Utopia* (1982), which one critic called 'dark as tar'. With each film, this darkness intensified, but this was no ordinary darkness; it was intense, luminous and illuminating. As part of his politics of identity and hyphen, none of his films deals with Iran or with Iranian subjects, hyphenated or not. Instead, they focus on homelessness, homeseeking, and the burning desire for an elsewhere and for another time, not for a previous home or for a return to an originary home. Like Naderi, Shahid Saless disavowed any particularistic subnational, ethnic, national or hyphenated affiliation or identity – particularly Iranian – in the interest of being recognised as a stateless, universal and transcendent auteur director. However, under such emphatic disavowals lurk complex crosscurrents of identity politics and psychology.

After the national and international successes of his New Wave films, *A Simple Event* and *Still Life*, Shahid Saless left Iran in 1974 semi-clandestinely, for what became a permanent exile. The reason for the stealth was that he did not have the exit permit then required of all passengers, so pretended to be an important director on his way to Germany for a major film co-production deal (Sar Reshtehdari 1998, 56–7). The primary impetus for his departure was the stifling conditions governing society and the film industry under the Shah, which had put a stop to his production of *Quarantine*, a film he never completed.

Because he left voluntarily, as he told me, he did not consider himself an exile, and he did not pine for return, another characteristic of those in exile. Instead, following the German–Jewish film scholar Lotte H. Eisner, about whom he made the affectionate documentary *The Long Vacation of Lotte H. Eisner* (1979), he preferred to speak of his lengthy sojourn abroad as a kind of 'long vacation'. It is this conceptualisation that allowed him to express neither remorse nor nostalgia, which are constitutive of exilic structures of feeling. In a series of lengthy interviews with me in Los Angeles, conducted over a three-day period a year before his untimely death, he shared his candid thoughts about his life and films:

> I do not belong to the Iranian diaspora cinema. I left the country in 1974 because of certain difficulties that had been placed in my filmmaking path and because I was very interested in filmmaking, like any young person. I left the country voluntarily and worked for twenty-three years in Germany without returning home, despite encouragement by the regimes of both the Shah and Khomeini to do so. I must admit with extreme sadness that I have no nostalgic longing for Iran. When each morning I set foot outside my house, whether it was in Germany, France, Venice, or the Soviet Union – the places where I have lived and made films – I would feel at home, because I had no difficulties. I am essentially not a patriot . . . I think one's homeland is not one's place of birth, but the country that gives one a place to stay, to work, and to make a living . . . Germany was my home for a long time. (Naficy 2012, 501)

Despite this exilic denial, Shahid Saless's darkly luminous, dystopic and dysphoric films point to a deep undercurrent of exilism and criticism of the societies in which he lived. He was at home neither in Iran nor in Germany; he was alienated from both. Most of his over a dozen difficult films for cinema and television, some of them three hours long, examine the psychology of social displacements, disillusionments, anomie and alienation in German society. The inhabitants – including immigrants – seem to be suffering from some sort of internal exile, a claustrophobic, contentious, ennui-ridden existence.

In displacement, the author and the work map on to one another more tightly. Home is transformed from a physical place to one's art, one's films, to cinema. Like many accented filmmakers, Shahid Saless makes films that resonate autobiographically, their despondency reflecting his own exilic-feeling structures. If there is nostalgia in them, it is not for a lost homeland but for a lost mother, while father figures are rare. These figurations have deep personal sources: Shahid Saless lost his mother when she abandoned the family before he was two years old, and he was not particularly close to his father. As he told me: 'I saw my mother only once, in Austria, when I was eighteen years old, and we ended up having a fight' (Naficy 2012, 501). Shahid Saless had a daughter with a German woman to whom he was not married, a daughter whom he did not see after she reached her fifth month. These fractured relations and profound loneliness haunt his movies. His most autobiographical film in Iran is his first feature, *Still Life*, while his most autobiographical exilic film is his last feature, *Roses for Africa* (1992). Of the latter, he said:

[It] is all about myself, even though it is an adaptation of a novel. I have changed the story a lot and, at any rate, Paul's attitude and behaviour is exactly like mine. Whatever he does, I do. I wanted to see myself on the screen as I am. (Naficy 2012, 502)

What is this most autobiographical film about? It is not about escaping the trap of here and now by *returning* to an earlier home, as those in exile would want to do; rather, it is about the unfulfilled wish of people pinned in their own stifling societies to *escape* the trap of here and now for an idealised elsewhere, named 'Africa'. As such, the film is about the protagonist's home-founding journey – one that fails terribly due to suicide, like Shahid Saless's own tragic journey, or long vacation, which ended in a bloody death in Evanston, Illinois. Despite their manifest differences, all of his films ruminate on the common dilemma of pervasive homelessness. Collectively, they constitute one of the most sustained and searing critiques by an émigré filmmaker of his adopted homeland, Germany. In *Far From Home*, he offers an undesired return home; in *Utopia*, a form of internal exile; in *Order* (*Ordung*, 1980), amnesia; and in *Roses for Africa*, suicide in a phone booth, while the image of the plane taking off for Africa is reflected in the protagonist's irises, poignantly signalling his failure to achieve his life's wish to go to a desired elsewhere.

Despite his hard work and accomplishments, Shahid Saless remained an outsider to the New German Cinema. Chief among the reasons for this was his uncompromising attitude. He removed his name from *Hans – A Young Man in Germany* (*Hans – Ein Junge in Deutschland*, 1985) because the producers demanded that he shorten his three-and-a-half-hour film. He refused, causing the film to be broadcast without his name, until four years later, when he finally shortened it to his liking and allowed his name to be used. There was also his difficult personality and demanding work habits, which, since *Utopia*, required the intermediary of a lawyer, as well as his minimalist filming style, critical dystopia, and bitter and dark-feeling structures, which made watching his films a challenging experience for ordinary spectators. Although there are numerous reviews of his films in various languages, Eurocentric film scholars in Europe and North America paid little attention to him, treating him as more of a guest than a contender (his films are difficult to find, as well). Given the dystopic trajectory of his films, it is no surprise that, in a short and sardonic piece, he would call cinema a 'whore's milieu', one that does not do 'much for one's potency' (Shahid Saless 1988, 56). The designation of filmmakers as impotent whores working in capitalist societies to which they do not fully belong and from which they cannot truly escape (like the prostitutes in *Utopia*) is a pessimistic but realistic assessment of accented filmmakers' interstitial conditions.

This metaphor became a reality for Shahid Saless in the mid-1990s. Up to then, state-subsidised funding in West Germany had helped to shield alternative filmmakers (including accented filmmakers) from the vagaries of the market. Like the New Wave filmmakers under the Pahlavi regime and early art-house directors under the Islamic Republic, economic dependence on the state meant that these West German filmmakers did not gain a mass following because 'government subsidy ensured that they never needed to gain one' (Kaes 1989, 21). However, after Germany's unification and the triumph of capitalism, involving media privatisation, which profoundly transformed both the country and its film industry, Shahid Saless could no longer continue to make his type of slow, dark and lengthy art-house films. The transformation worsened the whorish competitiveness he had critiqued. Unwilling to compromise, he was now not only an outsider but also a true stranger in a strange land, because of which he became more despondent and darker in outlook. Interstitial authorship by diasporic, exilic, émigré, ethnic and cosmopolitan filmmakers takes a high toll:

> After *Roses for Africa*, for six years I could not make a single film. I had three great screenplays, which people in the know thought could be made into successful films. Unfortunately, one by one they were rejected by the producers who wanted films with happy endings – the type of films I'd never made before. When all three screenplays were rejected, I began drinking all alone from the crack of dawn until five in the afternoon. At five o'clock I would fix myself a meal, eat it, and then make numerous phone calls to friends in different parts of the world. All of them would admonish me for drinking. After hanging up the phone, I would fall into a state of stupor until the next morning. I did this for three years. Without any films to make, I was totally undermined and vanquished; while when I was making films, nothing in the world mattered to me. (Naficy 2012, 503)

His refusal to play along meant that there was no place for him in Germany, even in its interstices. *Roses for Africa* seems to have acted as a prophetic, proto-exilic film, foreshadowing Shahid Saless's second exile and death. Unlike Paul, his alter ego in the film, who, unhappy with life in Germany and unable to go to his idealised African elsewhere, commits suicide with a gun in a telephone booth, Shahid Saless succeeded in leaving for another elsewhere: the USA, where he settled in 1995 in the hope of making his first US feature. If, for two decades, he had felt at home – albeit marginalised – in Germany, he was downright uncomfortable in the USA, largely because of its history of interventionist foreign policy in Iran and elsewhere: 'I do not feel at home here for I have an open account with America that cannot be closed,' he said (Naficy 2012, 503). As in *Utopia*, the place of comfort was inside, in a nondescript apartment complex in the San Fernando Valley suburbs of Los Angeles, where he lived with his stepmother, Farrokh Kamravani Shahid Saless (where our interviews took place). Alas, he was unable to finance any film projects in Los Angeles, forcing him to move to a Chicago suburb, where he had to battle with a series of long-standing illnesses, including tuberculosis, cancer, pneumonia, alcoholism and an ulcer, to which he finally succumbed at the age of fifty-four; it was a sad, lonely and bloody death in a small apartment in Evanston, like Paul's in the telephone booth in his final film, *Roses for Africa*.

Chicago-based filmmaker Mehrnaz Saeed-Vafa, perhaps the last person to interview him on camera for a film, described his last days to me. Shahid Saless had promised his friends to go cold turkey and stop drinking alcohol. After several days of not hearing from him, a friend, Mohammad Pakshir, decided to check up on him. When he knocked on the door to the director's apartment but received no response, he called the police, who, upon breaking the door down, discovered a grisly scene: Shahid Saless lying supine on the floor behind the door, dead, naked and covered in his own blood. He had had another bout of severe bleeding, years earlier in Philadelphia, when his stepmother and brother had been around to help rescue him. Not this time. The doctors estimated that he had died within the previous 48 hours, declaring 1 July 1998 as his date of death; however, Saeed-Vafa thinks he may have died on his birthday (28 June), a bitter irony that would fit his films. The path from the bathroom to the door and the back of the door were bloodied, indicating that he had struggled to crawl to the door and to open it. His telephone, his lifeline to the outside world, had been cut off ten days earlier because of his failure to pay his bills, a perennial problem. His brother had his body cremated without an autopsy and had the ashes posted to him, so that he could divide them up with his stepmother. That way each would have something 'to spread on water'. No memorials were held (Naficy 2012, 504).

Shahid Saless's profound homelessness in exile – despite his denial – come through in his elegiacally dystopic films, in the snippets of my interviews with him quoted here, in the way he lived and died, and in the final short film (fifteen minutes long) that Saeed-Vafa made about him, *Sohrab Shahid Saless Far From Home* (1998). What, more than anything else, turned him into an exilic figure, causing his departures from his previous homelands, was not national belonging, but rather obstacles in his filmmaking path. Cinema was his true home, not Iran, his country of birth, nor Germany, where he made all of his post-Iran films, nor the USA, where he failed to make any films at all. As he said to me, as we returned to his apartment from a visit to the local liquor store with a bottle of whisky:

> From the time that I went after film and became a filmmaker until today, I have not felt for a moment that I am Iranian. But that which gave me everything and was my home, my wife, my father, my mother, my

children, my life was filmmaking. If one day they tack a red ribbon on my lapel, that says 'Filmmaking Forbidden,' I won't commit suicide because I hate people who do so, but I think I will die within two years' time. (Naficy 2012, 504)

Although he was not forbidden to make films in the USA, he was unable to raise funds for them there, which was tantamount to receiving a 'filmmaking forbidden' ribbon on his lapel. In truth, it was more than that. It was tantamount to a death sentence. And that is where he died.

While such an obsessive passion for cinema is peculiar to only a few exilic filmmakers, such as Sohrab Shahid Saless, Amir Naderi and Luis Buñuel, the empowering function of filmmaking, which helps exiles cope with deterritorialisation by creating new narrative homes, motivates all accented filmmakers.

NOTE

1. This is a considerably modified version of two sections on Shahid Saless's films taken from my four-volume book (Naficy 2011, 393–8 and Naficy 2012, 500–4), as well as from my other writings referenced throughout.

BIBLIOGRAPHY

Bozorgmehr, Mehdi (1997), 'Iranians', in David Levinson (ed.), *Encyclopaedia of American Immigration Cultures*. New York: Macmillan.
Hakimzadeh, Shirin (2006), 'Iran: A Vast Diaspora Abroad and Millions of Refugees at Home', Migration Policy Institute: Migration Information Source, September, <http://www.migrationinformation.org/feature/print.cfm?ID=424> (last accessed 1 June 2018).
Hall, Stuart (1994), 'Cultural Identity and Diaspora', in Patrick Williams and Laura Chrisman (eds), *Colonial Discourse and Post-Colonial Theory: A Reader*. New York: Columbia University Press.
Kaes, Anton (1989), *From Hitler to Heimat: The Return of History as Film*. Cambridge, MA: Harvard University Press.
Liehm, Mira (1984), *Passion and Defiance: Film in Italy from 1942 to the Present*. Berkeley: University of California Press.
Naficy, Hamid (2012), *A Social History of Iranian Cinema, Vol. 4: The Globalizing Era, 1984–2010*. Durham, NC: Duke University Press.
— (2011), *A Social History of Iranian Cinema, Vol. 2: The Industrializing Years, 1941–1978*. Durham, NC: Duke University Press.
— (2002), 'Identity Politics and Iranian Exile Music Videos', in Richard Young (ed.), *Music, Popular Culture, Identities*. Amsterdam and New York: Rodopi.
— (2001), *An Accented Cinema: Exilic and Diasporic Filmmaking*. Princeton: Princeton University Press.
— (1997), Author's interview with filmmaker Sohrab Shahid Saless, Los Angeles, CA, USA (10, 11 and 12 April).

— (1993), *The Making of Exile Cultures: Iranian Television in Los Angeles*. Minneapolis: University of Minnesota Press.

Omid, Jamal (1995/1374), *Tarikh-e Sinema-ye Iran, 1279–1375*. Tehran: Entesharat-e Rowzaneh.

Row, William, and Teresa Whitfield (1987), 'Thresholds of Identity: Literature and Exile in Latin America', *Third World Quarterly*, 9, 1: 229–45.

Sar Reshtehdari, Mehdi (1998), *Bar Lowh-e Ruzegar: Goftogu ba Sohrab Shahid Saless*. Los Angeles: Qaf.

Shahid Saless, Sohrab (1988), 'Culture as Hard Currency or: Hollywood in Germany (1983)', in Eric Rentschler (ed.), *West German Filmmakers on Film: Visions and Voices*. New York: Holmes and Meir.

CHAPTER 2

Point of View, Symbolism and Music in Sohrab Shahid Saless's *Utopia*

Christopher Gow

Sohrab Shahid Saless's three-hour opus about the relationship between an abusive pimp and five female sex workers operating out of a brothel in 1970s West Berlin, *Utopia* (1982), was the director's sixth feature film made in West Germany, not counting his earlier documentaries about Lotte H. Eisner and Anton Chekhov (the latter being made in the Soviet Union). It was his eighth feature film in total, taking into account his first two award-winning Iranian films, *A Simple Event* (1974) and *Still Life* (1974), both of which established his reputation in West Germany and further afield. By the time *Utopia* was released, Shahid Saless had been living and working in West Germany for nearly decade, after leaving his home country of Iran in the mid-1970s, when he was prevented from working on what would have been his third feature film, *Quarantine* (Naficy 2001, 200–3). During that time he continued to practise and hone the techniques that would become characteristic of his filmmaking style. With specific reference to *Utopia*, Hamid Naficy has described these techniques as consisting of 'a slow pace, slow acting style, and slow line delivery; a rather static and observational camera that is prone to long takes, long shots and slow pans; and a concern for the life of ordinary people and the routine practices of their everyday existence, rendered with an ironic distance' (Naficy 2001, 200).

Narratively, *Utopia* also revisits the subjects to which Shahid Saless would return obsessively over and over again during his career: his concern with and empathy for society's outsiders, reflective of his own 'outsider' status in German society (and, to a lesser extent, even within Iran); the theme of isolation, and the alienation of his characters from their surroundings and from other people, including their own family members, as well as society at large; and the effects of trauma and its various causes, such as the death of one's mother, the loss of one's job and, particularly in *Utopia*, the use of violence to terrorise and control. For example, there is a scene in *Utopia* in which the pimp Heinz (Manfred Zapatka) punches the youngest of the sex workers, the rebellious student Susie (Gabriele Fischer), directly in the face. It is not the first time that we have seen Heinz use physical violence against the women who work in his brothel. Indeed, as early as the film's opening pre-credits sequence, we witness Heinz drag his long-suffering partner Renate (Imke Barnstedt) into his car by her hair, whereupon he drives her to a specific location and forces her out on to the street to work at night, as he looks on impassively from behind the wheel of his car, parked nearby, smoking a cigarette. In another scene, he repeatedly slams Renate's face into the counter of the bar in the brothel, where they serve their clients alcohol. We have even seen him assault Susie already once, in an earlier scene, slapping her when she threatens to leave the brothel and berating her co-workers for putting up with Heinz's abusive behaviour. The threat of physical violence, as a means of intimidation and control over Renate and Susie, as well as the other women – Rosie (Gundula Petrovka), Helga (Johanna Sophia) and Monika (Birgit Anders) – permeates the entire film and informs every interaction Heinz has with them (Fig. 2.1).

Yet the moment when Heinz strikes Susie remains shocking, not least because of the suddenness with which Heinz lashes out, with little to no emotion or concern for the consequences, as if it were a reflex action. Misogyny and violence are evidently so ingrained in the character of Heinz, that his actions seem almost instinctual, as if he were lashing out like a wild animal. Moments like these run throughout Shahid Saless's films: not moments of violence necessarily, but rather moments that jolt us out of the sense of familiarity into which we are frequently lulled, even if that sense of familiarity is not always comforting or reassuring. Instances that spring to mind include the startling conclusion to *A Time of Maturity* (1976), when the film's young

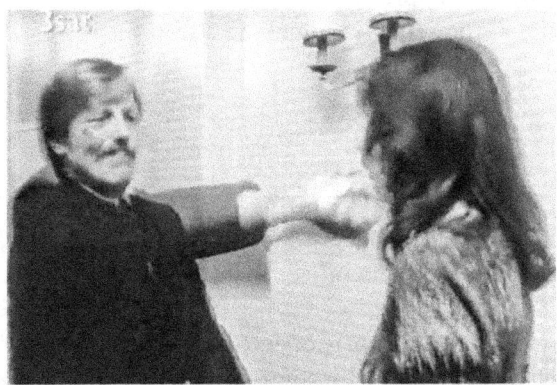

Figure 2.1 Heinz's abusive behaviour. (Source: screen grab from *Utopia* 1982.)

child protagonist Michael returns home early to his mother's flat from school one day, and stumbles upon his mother – once again, a sex worker – performing fellatio on one of her clients. Or the closing moments of *Diary of a Lover* (1977), when the police discover the dead body of Michael's 'lover', Monika, hidden underneath his bed. Or the murder scene that occurs early on in *The Willow Tree* (1984) – adapted from the short story of the same name by Chekhov – the close-up of the mace connecting with the victim's head, accompanied by a sickening dull thud, and shattering the image of the seemingly idyllic, pastoral world that has been constructed in the opening moments of the film, the murder taking on an almost biblical resonance, as if we are watching Cain slay his brother Abel.[1]

As typical as *Utopia* undoubtedly is of Shahid Saless's broader style, it is nevertheless one of his most atypical films in a number of ways. While most of his stories are presented from the point of view of one main character, *Utopia* is very much an ensemble piece, where the story is told from multiple perspectives. Moreover, whereas Shahid Saless's protagonists are predominantly male and can be viewed as ciphers for Shahid Saless himself – he was particularly honest about the extent to which the character of Paul in *Roses for Africa* (1992) was a self-portrait (Naficy 2001, 201–2) – five of the six central characters in *Utopia* are female. Regardless, Shahid Saless manages to continue the autobiographical streak running throughout his films, by way of his use of symbolism, reflecting his own sense of displacement in West Germany. Indeed, Shahid Saless's use of symbolism in *Utopia*, especially his use of music, feels more explicit – though no less powerful – than in any of his other films. It is worth while taking the time to examine these differences more closely, not only because they will help us to understand and appreciate *Utopia* better, as well as Shahid Saless's other works (*Utopia*'s sheer length and relentless bleakness make it one of his most challenging films, despite the beauty of its design and structure), but also because it sheds light on the director's versatility as a filmmaker, and his ability to approach different content and marry it to the appropriate form, while at the same time making a film that can still be understood as very personal.

THE GAZE AND POINT OF VIEW

As noted, *Utopia* is one of Shahid Saless's most uncharacteristic films, not least because, unlike nearly all of his other films, which usually focus on one lone protagonist, in *Utopia* our point of view is dispersed across the film's six central characters, with no single perspective displacing or being given significant prominence over the other. Furthermore, that point of view is almost exclusively female rather than male. The narrative is framed entirely from the point of view of Renate, Rosie, Susie, Helga and Monika, with the exception of some scenes in which, uncomfortably, our point of view is aligned with that of Heinz, and some others in which we are left alone in the company of Heinz, usually in his own room-cum-office, which is also located within the brothel. However, even these latter scenes raise more questions than they provide answers about Heinz's character. For example, in one scene Heinz experiences what looks to be a very painful migraine, clutching his head and moaning as he kneels down on the floor in agony. The reason for these migraines is never explained, nor do we see Heinz seeking any medical treatment for them. Likewise, in another scene we see him looking at what appear to be family photos, including one of himself when he was younger, but apart from some background information from Renate as to how she and Heinz first met and her first (positive) impressions of him, we learn nothing about his family history. One might construe that Heinz's hatred of women is linked to some traumatic event in his past, a troubled relationship with his mother perhaps, and that the migraines are some kind of physical symptom of the malignant hatred that will eventually destroy him, but Shahid Saless never makes this explicit. Heinz remains very much a mystery to us, an object of fear and cruelty, as well as a sadist.

This is not to suggest that there are not many powerful moments in Shahid Saless's œuvre that are presented primarily from a female perspective. His extended documentary interview with Lotte H. Eisner would be an obvious case in point. In terms of his feature films, the close-up of the disdainful expression on the face of the railway worker's wife in *Still Life*, as she looks at the young man who will eventually take over her husband's position disrespectfully guzzling down the meal she has prepared for him; and the heart-breaking scene in *A Time of Maturity*, when Michael's mother, staring at her reflection in a mirror, breaks down in tears upon returning home late one night, are two other moments that spring vividly to mind. But they are just moments. Even in said scene from *A Time of Maturity*, our viewpoint is, to an extent, filtered through the eyes of Michael, who lies in bed awake, unbeknownst to his mother, listening to her silently as she cries.

Utopia is markedly different in so far as Renate, Rosie, Susie, Helga and Monika are all fully-rounded characters in their own right, despite the way in which all of its characters are subject to the observational gaze of Shahid Saless's camera. Their conflicting outlooks on the world and their different approaches to Heinz emerge strongly during the course of the film. Renate has long since resigned herself to a life of victimhood, whereas Susie is more defiant and openly challenges Heinz on numerous occasions (and suffers the brutal consequences for doing so). Monika is new to her role as a sex worker and clearly insecure, whereas Rosie is far more experienced and sexually confident. Helga, meanwhile, attempts in one scene to seduce Heinz, declaring her love for him. The different tactics that the women employ, the distinctive attitudes that they have towards their work and their clients, and the way in which they negotiate their individual relationships with Heinz, before joining forces to kill him at the end of the film, are central to the drama of *Utopia*.

Nevertheless, despite their strong personalities, the fact that the lives of the women rotate so closely around the figure of Heinz, and that their behaviours are so heavily motivated by their fear of how Heinz will react, is reflective of the unequal power dynamics that exist within the brothel. Such an interpretation is supported by the importance that is ascribed to the act of watching throughout *Utopia*. Indeed, watching is an important act in many of Shahid Saless's films. In *Hans – A Young Man in Germany* (1985), set in Berlin during and in the immediate aftermath of World War Two, the titular half-Jewish protagonist gleans information from his surroundings by quietly observing the world around him, including its inhabitants. We spend a great deal of time watching Hans as he, in turn, silently watches events unfold before him and observes how human nature manifests itself, sometimes kindly but mostly cruelly. This is also true of Zamini, the schoolboy from *A Simple Event*, as well as Michael in *A Time of Maturity*. In fact, all of Shahid Saless's child characters watch and interpret the world around them, in order to understand their surroundings and survive. By stark contrast, the way in which the elderly railway worker from *Still Life* silently watches the world go by adds to the sense that he and wife are being left behind, as life and so-called 'progress' march on.

In even starker contrast, in *Utopia*, for Heinz the act of watching (like physical violence) is a means of control. This is displayed from the very beginning of the film, during the opening credits, as Heinz watches Renate from his car as she waits on the pavement for a potential client to accost her. At one point Shahid Saless cuts to an interior shot from the inside of the car, as if he were positioning the viewer in the back seat and placing them uncomfortably alongside Heinz, as he watches Renate through the windshield. These images are

Figure 2.2 Heinz's rehearsal. (Source: screen grab from *Utopia* 1982.)

counter-balanced to an extent by frontal shots of Heinz from outside the car, looking at him through the windshield as he calmly sits in the driver's seat and puffs away at his cigarette. The idea that watching serves as a means of control is reinforced in the scene where all of the women 'audition' for Heinz before the brothel's official opening, introducing themselves to him as they would to one of the brothel's clients (Fig. 2.2). In this scene Heinz inspects the women with clinical detachment and brutally critiques their 'performances'. He derides Monika's stiltedness and anxiety, while praising Rosie's flirtatiousness. (As noted, with the possible exception of Renate, the film establishes very early on that only Rosie has previous experience of working in a brothel, and is therefore more adept at pleasuring her clients and winning Heinz's praise.) The sense that the women cannot escape Heinz's watchful gaze, even when he is physically not in their presence, is emphasised throughout the film, perhaps most powerfully during one scene in which, in an act of defiance, Susie impulsively throws a bottle of alcohol at the bar and smashes a number of other bottles and glasses to pieces. Rosie quickly breaks down in terror at the thought of what Heinz will do when he returns to the flat and sees what they have done. In another scene, when Heinz goes to pour himself a drink, he notices that the amount of alcohol in the bottle has gone down because some of the women have secretly been consuming small amounts, in defiance of the ground rules that Heinz laid down upon opening the brothel. In *Utopia* there is an overwhelming sense that nothing escapes Heinz's scrutiny. Then there are the clients themselves, one of which, a policeman no less, is notably not interested in any kind of physical contact, but is rather a voyeur who prefers to gaze upon Helga as he masturbates in front of her.

The women, meanwhile, are often denied access to a powerful gaze, or rather their gaze is characterised by inaction. For example, when Renate, Helga and Rosie discover Monika covered in blood and unconscious in the bathtub, having cut her wrists in a suicide attempt, they can apparently do nothing but look on in horror for what feels like an eternity, frozen in the bathroom doorway. Likewise, towards the end, the other women can do nothing but look on in horror as Heinz forces Susie to perform a sex act upon him, seemingly forcing her to lick his anus. Rather than show us the act, Shahid Saless cuts away to focus instead on the faces of the women, as they remain frozen in the doorway to Heinz's bedroom, aghast at what they are witnessing but incapable of helping Susie. There is a similar moment in *Hans – A Young Man in Germany*, when Hans discovers his mother being sexually assaulted by one of her co-workers and simply stares at the scene before him, even though his presence prompts the attacker to desist and leave.

What little agency some of the women might possess is glimpsed only briefly, during their respective encounters with the various clients that frequent the brothel. These scenes are also important because of what they reveal about the different character of each woman and how they cope (or fail to cope) in their new line of work. In the first such scene Rosie is clearly in command of the middle-aged, visibly nervous man who picks her over the other women, using her experience, at the instruction of Heinz, to convince the man to spend more of his money on drinks. Likewise, in a later scene, Susie easily extracts more and more cash from the elderly man who picks her, charging him extra for every additional service he desires while refusing to kiss him. But for every scene in which the women are shown to possess some degree of control, there is another in which their lack of real power is reinforced. In addition to Helga's encounter with the voyeuristic policeman, Monika is verbally abused by one of her clients, a vile misogynist who berates her for her lack of enthusiasm as they have sex. It is this traumatic encounter that appears to drive Monika to try to kill herself. Even those scenes with Rosie and Susie feature long close-ups of their faces, as they lay on their backs for their clients and look into space off screen with dead eyes, serving to illustrate how they are reduced to sex objects. It is also noteworthy that both Helga and Monika have a common bond, in that they have both ended up in their current predicament through the failure of the men in their respective personal lives. Early on in the film, when we are first introduced to all of the women in quick succession before they begin working in the brothel, we learn that Helga, who has ambitions to run her own business, has been left penniless by her ex-husband's failure to provide continued financial support, while Monika confides in an elderly lady in a train carriage that she is travelling to West Berlin to make a fresh start of sorts, after having an affair in her home town with a married man who failed to commit to her.

This is not say that *Utopia* is a misogynistic film, although it should be clear by now that many of Shahid Saless's female characters have a very tough time of it; rather, it is a film *about* misogyny. It is notable that there is really only one scene in the entire film, significantly set outside of the brothel, in which a strong sense of female solidarity and camaraderie emerges. That scene is located in the hospital, where Renate, Helga, Susie and Rosie go to visit Monika, after the latter's suicide attempt (though, again, they are driven to and from the hospital by Heinz, who does not permit them to travel by themselves). The women laugh and joke together for what seems like the first time and show genuine concern for Monika, in contrast to how they seem to turn on each other when they are working in the brothel. Aesthetically, even the colour palette of this scene stands out from the rest of the film, with the white hospital walls providing a refreshing contrast to the darker, lurid tones of the brothel. The structure of *Utopia*, therefore, with the majority of its action being set in the brothel and its emphasis on the act of watching, displays the lack of agency possessed by its female characters, as compared to the power of Heinz's controlling gaze. It is perhaps significant, after all, that Heinz's death is initiated by Renate, who stabs him repeatedly in the stomach with a pair of scissors when, after raping her, he finally lets his guard down and finally closes his eyes to go to sleep.

THE MURDER AND SYMBOLISM

The murder scene, or rather its notably brief aftermath, is also interesting for what it reveals about Shahid Saless's use of symbolism in his films. One could argue that the murder itself is not really that important, despite how protracted it is, with Heinz berating the women before they gang up on him and beat him to death, with any object that they can find to hand after Renate has stabbed him. What is important is what the murder might represent. This is often the case in films where the fate of certain characters and the consequences of their actions are left deliberately unresolved. In *Utopia* there is not – as one might expect at this point, though perhaps not so much from a director like Shahid Saless – any dramatic denouement detailing *how* exactly the women go about disposing of the body. Nor indeed, are we even given any explanation as to what happens to Heinz's body. It simply disappears, and the women carry on running the brothel by themselves, as if Heinz never existed. Shahid Saless therefore obviously considers the act of killing Heinz itself, and the practicalities of covering up the crime, as being not so significant. But these details are not omitted for narrative convenience. As mentioned, it is rather what the act represents that is important. But what does it represent? As with many of Shahid Saless's films, there is some room for interpretation. On the one hand, the bitter irony of the women proclaiming their freedom, and imagining all of the things that they can do, now that they are no longer subject to Heinz's tyranny, only then to return to their daily routine and to continue to live and work in the brothel, is undeniable. Although they may have found freedom in one sense, in another they are still trapped within the brothel, prisoners of their environment. On the other hand, the women need no longer fear the abuse they suffered at the hands of Heinz and, moreover, have now gone into business for themselves, with all of the profits going to them alone. They would appear to have liberated themselves from their physical and economic slavery. As Naficy has observed,

> Shahid Saless himself has pointed out that both the prostitutes and their master are symbols: the former, of the citizens who dream of liberty; the latter, of their exploitative rulers whom they wish to overthrow. In his pessimistic view of humanity, once they have overthrown their masters, subject people often turn on each other... *Utopia*, however, leaves open the possibility that the masterless prostitutes may work cooperatively as independent sex workers, much like the interstitial filmmakers working in the capitalist postindustrial cinema – a cinema Shahid Saless condemned as a 'whore's milieu'. (Naficy 2001, 201–2)

This kind of ambiguity and open-endedness is present in many of Shahid Saless's films. In *A Simple Event*, it is far from clear what will become of the relationship between Zamini and his father following the death of his mother. In *Still Life*, although the film has a clear 'ending', with the railway worker and his wife departing from their home, we are left to wonder what might become of them in their (forced) retirement. *Diary of a Lover* and *Order* (1980) end on strikingly similar notes, with the image of each film's protagonist, Michael and Herbert, respectively, locked away in a psychiatric hospital, their fates left hanging in the balance. In *A Time of Maturity*, the film ends almost immediately after the aforementioned scene in which Michael discovers his mother with one of her clients. As in *Utopia*, there is no dwelling upon the aftermath of this final traumatic event because the event itself, in this case Michael's discovery, is ultimately unimportant. What matters is the impact that it might have upon Michael. But Shahid Saless does not give us an answer. Instead of reacting to what he has seen, Michael quietly sneaks away and exits the flat again, leaving his mother and her client alone. The film ends with the image of Michael sitting by himself at the top of the staircase outside of his mother's flat, the viewer left to guess at what effect this traumatic event may have upon Michael.

By contrast, a film like *Roses for Africa* would be a notable exception to this rule, concluding as it does with resounding finality when the main character, Paul, kills himself, an act which gives the film an added sense of gravity when we consider, as noted above, that Shahid Saless considered Paul to be very much representative of his own personality. Indeed, the closest that Shahid Saless arguably ever came to giving the viewer a 'happy ending' would be the conclusion to *Hans – A Young Man in Germany*, where the film ends on what could be considered an uncharacteristically optimistic (albeit understated) note, with Hans sawing away at the bars covering his kitchen window, having survived the war and refusing to remain a prisoner in his own home: a simple act therefore, or perhaps rather a simple event, but one that is powerful all the same. Nevertheless, with many of Shahid Saless's films, as gruelling and (particularly in the case of *Utopia*) as physically long as they may be, there is often the sense that there is another film to be made, or another story to be told, after the end credits roll. The individual stories of Zamini, the railway worker and his wife, Herbert, Hans, the young Michael and the older Michael may have concluded, but the effects of what has happened to them will continue to live with them for a long time thereafter.

For all of the parallels that can be drawn between *Utopia* and Shahid Saless's other films, therefore, in the same way that it is unusual for its focus on a predominantly female cast, it is also atypical for how it is more open to symbolic readings. Again, this is not to suggest that Shahid Saless does not frequently employ overt symbolism in his films. For example, the image of the retired railway worker looking at his distorted reflection in a cracked mirror, at the end of *Still Life*, could be construed as representing not only his fractured sense of his own identity, which has been intertwined so closely with his profession, but also his redundancy and expendability to society as a whole. Indeed, mirrors and reflections are a recurring motif running throughout Shahid Saless's body of work, cropping up time and time again at moments of crisis. In *A Time of Maturity*, when Michael catches sight of his mother with one of her clients, it is of their reflection in a mirror, rather than a direct observation with his own eyes. In a perverse inversion of Lacan's 'mirror stage', Michael's encounter with a mirror threatens to disrupt his understanding of the world around him, rather than reinforcing his sense of selfhood. However, both *Still Life* and *A Time of Maturity*, in addition to most of Shahid Saless's other films, despite their claustrophobic settings, generally adhere to what could be described as a 'realist' aesthetic, with their characters' lives strongly situated within a broader social context. Conversely, *Utopia*'s intensely oppressive atmosphere, its precise focus on the power dynamics between a small group of characters and its deliberately repetitive narrative structure readily lend themselves to symbolic interpretations, the sense that the social order portrayed within the confines of the brothel serves as a metaphor for something bigger.

MUSIC, AUTOBIOGRAPHY AND IRONY

Nowhere is this symbolic slant more apparent than in Shahid Saless's use of music, both classical and popular. There are two pieces in particular that dominate the film and that crop up again and again at important moments. The first is the plaintive introduction to *In the Greenhouse*, from *Five Poems for a Female Voice* (1857–8), Richard Wagner's interpretation of the poetic works of Mathilde Wesendonck (Wagner 1904, 26–9). We see and hear this piece being performed in an opera house at both the beginning and the end of the film. The fact that this piece bookends the events of the film suggests that, despite everything that has happened, and all of the experiences that Shahid Saless's characters have gone through, we have simply returned to where we started, that nothing has really changed. Although Heinz is gone, the women are still confined to the brothel and are still trapped, physically as well as psychologically. It also suggests that the social status quo goes on uninterrupted, as it did before, with the well-to-do members of the audience sitting comfortably in their seats, enjoying their 'high art'. They are oblivious to what is going in the real world outside of the opera house. This also demonstrates Shahid Saless's concern with class and the gulf between rich and poor, but at the same time the thin line separating so-called 'respectable' society from the seedy world inhabited by his characters. In one early scene, for example, where Heinz and Renate are selecting a flat out of which they can operate the brothel, in response to Renate's concerns that they might disturb the neighbours Heinz replies that they have nothing to be worried about, because all of the other flats surrounding theirs are law offices.

This piece is played on the soundtrack at ten different points in the film:

1. at the very beginning of the film, when Heinz sits in his car watching Renate, whom he has just thrown out on to the street to work
2. when Renate is left alone in the corridor at the bottom of the staircase leading to the flat, after Heinz has yet again berated her (and it is clear from watching Shahid Saless's films that many scenes are set on or around staircases and in corridors, these 'in-between', interstitial spaces)
3. when Heinz is lying on his bed alone as the first clients visit the brothel, his forearm covering his eyes and rubbing his fingers together, almost as if he were imagining the money the brothel will rake in
4. when Rosie is having sex with her first client, a close-up of her face showing her staring blankly off screen as the client gets on top of her
5. when Renate hides the scissors that she will later use to kill Heinz under her mattress and stares at the floor, perhaps envisioning that fateful moment in her mind
6. when Heinz is driving all of the women back to the brothel from the nearby health clinic, where he has taken them for a check-up
7. when Monika is brushing her hair in the bathroom alone, repeating her name to herself over and over again, as if to remind herself of who she is, that she still really exists
8. when Susie is having sex with the elderly man mentioned above, once again, like Rosie, staring blankly off screen in close-up
9. when Susie is left alone outside of Heinz's bedroom, visibly traumatised after being forced to perform the above-mentioned sex act upon him
10. and finally, when Heinz is seated in his car again, outside of the hospital where he has taken the rest of the women to visit Monika.

Many of these moments tend to highlight the characters' loneliness, alienation and trauma. But why is this piece of music so ubiquitous? Why does Shahid Saless employ it so often, besides the fact that it obviously sounds sad and ominous? A quick look at some of the lyrics to the piece might give us an answer. As noted, the piece is called *In the Greenhouse*, in which the narrator speaks to and empathises with the plants that surround them. Along with another piece called *Dreams* from the same composition, it features music that Wagner would use again in his famous opera, *Tristan and Isolde* (1857–9). In the extract below, the narrator describes the hopeless desire of the exotic palm trees, as they appear to reach out with their leaves to embrace nothingness, and the sense of affinity that they feel with the palm trees, removed as they both seemingly have been from their homeland:

> Slow and still your arms are weaving
> Mystic figures in the air,
> And a perfume, anguish breathing,
> Sorrow sweet, arises there.
>
> How ye show desire and longing
> In your mighty arms embrace,
> Grasping, while vain hopes are thronging,
> Only air and empty space.
>
> I, too, know it, prison'd palm-trees!
> One, our lot, one pain we bear.
> Tho' we're bathed in radiant sunbeams,
> Yet our homeland is not here! (Naficy 2001, 200)

On one level, these lyrics can most obviously be interpreted as a commentary on the plight of the women in *Utopia*, all of whom are homeless in a sense. There is perhaps also a bitter irony in using a piece from a work called *Five Poems for a Female Voice* in a film about five women who, individually and collectively, are denied a powerful voice. However, on another level, the lyrics can also be interpreted autobiographically, as Shahid Saless obliquely referring to his own sense of displacement, as an Iranian émigré filmmaker in West Germany. This would appear to contradict Shahid Saless's previous assertions, in conversations with Naficy, that, effectively, he did not regard himself as an exile and considered Germany to be his home for a long time (Shahid Saless, Haghighat and Rahgozar 1999, 175–80). And while it is unlikely that the double meaning present in the lyrics of *In the Greenhouse* can be attributed wholly to chance, it would also not be entirely fair (and perhaps somewhat insulting) to think of Shahid Saless as someone who lived nearly half of his life in denial, though this may very well have been an element of his personality. On the contrary, it is perfectly understandable (and logical) that an émigré would have conflicting emotions about their adopted homeland, as well as about the contradictory position that they occupy within that adopted homeland. Such feelings are not incompatible with one another, nor are they mutually exclusive. In *Utopia*, therefore, Shahid Saless's use of Wagner's piece, as a kind mournful motif, can be understood not only as referring to the (internal) exile of the film's female characters, but also as alluding to his own status as an outsider in West German society.

The other piece of popular music that Shahid Saless employs, on three separate occasions, could hardly be more different: namely, Barbara Streisand

and Donna Summer's disco classic *No More Tears (Enough is Enough)* (1979). As with *In the Greenhouse*, the use of this song could be interpreted as bitterly ironic. This song is, after all, about female empowerment, in which the singer proclaims that she can no longer continue in a loveless relationship with the man who seemed to be 'the perfect lover', but who 'turned out to be like every other man'. The singer declares her intention to kick the man out of her home and her life, and tells other dissatisfied women to do the same. The fact that the women in *Utopia* do the exact opposite, and at points even appear to submit to Heinz's tyranny – for example, Susie leaves the brothel initially after Heinz abuses her the first time, only to return later in the film – would seem to make Shahid Saless's use of this song all the more caustic. This applies to none of the women more strongly than Renate, who, as the film establishes early on, has a pre-existing relationship with Heinz and assists him in opening the brothel. In one moving scene, Renate explains to the other women how Heinz tricked her into believing that he was a good man, when she was younger and more trusting, and that she has been trapped in a relationship with him ever since. Despite this, Renate seems to hope naïvely (and somewhat unbelievably) that one day Heinz will reciprocate the affection that she used to feel for him, attempting to comfort him in one scene where he experiences one of his head-splitting migraines, only for him to throw her to ground, where she lays strangely motionless. Although, in the end, the women eventually overthrow Heinz, it is not before they have suffered more terrible treatment than any decent and humane person would deem acceptable, by a lover from their partner, or an employee from their employer. The extent to which the conclusion of the film can be viewed as empowering or liberating for the women has been discussed above, but regardless of one's opinion, it is fair to say that the subdued ending of *Utopia* does not match the fiery and defiant spirit of Streisand and Summer's song.

Indeed, what is perhaps more striking than the irony of using this song in a film like *Utopia* is *how* and *when* Shahid Saless uses this song throughout the film, and in what way it might shape our understanding of its conclusion. We first hear the song about thirty minutes into the film when Susie, much to Heinz's annoyance, puts a record on as the women all sit about the brothel, bored, waiting for their first clients to show up. Importantly, Susie does not start the song from the beginning but towards the end, after the slow introduction has finished and the disco beat has already kicked in. Later on in the film, when Heinz is absent, Susie puts the record on again and turns the chorus up to full volume, whereupon all of women dance together and enjoy themselves for a brief moment. We then hear the song one final time, after the women have killed Heinz and are preparing to meet their first clients on their own, but this time from the very beginning, as Streisand sings the lyrics: 'It's raining, it's pouring, my love life is boring me to tears.' Aside from how these lyrics act as a kind of ironic commentary upon the women's lives, it is significant that, as the film has progressed from its beginning to its end, Shahid Saless uses snippets of this song in reverse order, with the beginning of the song not being played until the very end of the film, before we return to the opera house and the performance of *In the Greenhouse*. As with the return to the opera house itself, it reinforces the idea that the women, as well as the viewer, have simply returned to where they started, that they are trapped in a kind of vicious circle, despite having rid themselves of Heinz.

CONCLUSION

On the one hand, *Utopia* is a film that feels very different from Shahid Saless's other output, for the reasons outlined above. On the other hand, it is a film that feels totally consistent with Shahid Saless's filmmaking style and broader artistic vision. Its treatment of violence, both physical and psychological in nature; its use of point of view and the cinematic gaze; its emphasis on structure and repetition and the 'everyday'; its use of music, sparse but considered and rich with symbolic meaning; the open-endedness of its conclusion and the different interpretations that can be ascribed to it – all these qualities add up to make a film that is both very specific to its context and yet intensely personal. While *Utopia* is very much a film about misogyny, exploitation and the plight of its female characters, it can also clearly be understood as reflective of Shahid Saless's own sense of displacement as an émigré. As such, it is a film that is universal in its outlook, despite its extremely confined setting, and continues Shahid Saless's concern with society's outsiders and outcasts, with whom he no doubt felt an affinity. We all feel pain, or as Abbas Kiarostami might say, we all get toothache (Jaggi 2009); we all observe the world around us; we are all moved by music; and our own day-to-day lives often feel messy, complicated and incomplete. Shahid Saless's uncompromising style can feel too alienating and inaccessible for many, and probably accounts for many of the difficulties that he encountered inside and outside of Iran, notwithstanding his relatively prolific output when compared to other émigré filmmakers. But his mastery of the language of film and the empathy he has for his characters means that his films can speak to all of us, and reward repeated viewings. *Utopia* is such a film. If Renate, Helga, Rosie, Susie and Monika remain trapped by the film's end, prisoners of their own minds as much as they are prisoners of their physical environment, then perhaps, the final shot of the film might suggest, we are partly to blame and perhaps we are the ones that have a responsibility to try to change that situation. Indeed, in the final moments of *Utopia* Shahid Saless seems to turn the gaze of the camera upon the viewer, presenting them with an image of passivity that could also be construed as a critique of their own inertia, as the end credits roll over a shot of the audience at the opera house during the aforementioned performance of *Five Poems for a Female Voice*. Filmed from the perspective of the singer on stage, with the silent, immobile audience staring directly into the camera, in a sense making the viewer the object of the film's gaze, the shot could be regarded as confronting the viewer with their own passivity, and by extension their own complicity in the acceptance of the social status quo, which has enabled the events that they have just witnessed unfold on screen.

NOTE

1. For a more detailed analysis of this scene, see Gow (2011, 169–73).

BIBLIOGRAPHY

Gow, Christopher (2011), *From Iran to Hollywood and Some Places In-Between: Reframing Post-Revolutionary Iranian Cinema*. London and New York: I. B. Tauris.

Jaggi, Maya (2009), 'A Life in Cinema: Abbas Kiarostami', *The Guardian*, 13 June, <https://www.theguardian.com/film/2009/jun/13/abbas-kiarostami-film> (last accessed 30 August 2018).

Naficy, Hamid (2001), *An Accented Cinema: Exilic and Diasporic Filmmaking*. Princeton: Princeton University Press.

Shahid Saless, Sohrab, Mamad Haghighat, Rahgozar and Timothy S. Murphy (1999), 'This Isn't Pessimism: Interview with Sohrab Shahid Saless', *Discourse* 21, 1 (Winter): 175–80.

Wagner, Richard (1904), *Wagner Lyrics for Soprano*, ed. Carl Armbuster, Boston: Oliver Ditson.

CHAPTER 3

The Blind Owls of Modernity: Of Protocols, Mirrors and Grimaces in Sohrab Shahid Saless's Films

Matthias Wittmann

> Of what use are all the revolutions if people are
> not capable of revolutionising themselves?
> *The Last Summer of Grabbe* (1980)

HASHTI (ANTEROOM)[1]

Let me begin by quoting a passage from Siegfried Kracauer's posthumously published book fragment, *History: The Last Things Before the Last* (1969), a text in which he tackles the problem of subjectivity and the restriction to a single perspective in historical interpretation. For the author, the tiniest facts of history can be made accessible only through what he calls a 'micro history' of 'close-ups' (Kracauer 1995, 105), an approach he undoubtedly favours over the distortions of macro histories and their panoramic views, which oversee the details following a synthesising, subsumptive logic.

> As I see it, the vast knowledge we possess should challenge us not to indulge inadequate syntheses but to concentrate on close-ups and from them casually to range over the whole [. . .] This allegedly smallest historical unit itself is an inexhaustible macrocosm. (Kracauer 1995, 137).

This is not tantamount to an immersion in details until complete (self-)extinction. Rather, for Kracauer, this breaking down of macro entities into their smallest elements through close-ups entails a 'minimum distance that must be upheld between the researcher and his material' (Kracauer 1995, 86). The observer has to re-introduce the macrocosm into the microcosm:

'This allegedly smallest historical unit itself is an inexhaustible macrocosm' (Kracauer 1995, 116). But how is it possible for the stalker of close-ups to keep this minimal distance? According to Kracauer, he should penetrate the façade and materials of history with the eyes of an exile who resides in a 'no-man's land': that is, as a silent, emotionally detached observer, similar in this respect to the photographer who is excluded from the field of vision.

> I am thinking of the exile who as an adult person has been forced to leave his country or has left it of his own free will [. . .] his identity is bound to be in a state of flux; and the odds are that he will never fully belong to the community to which he now in a way belongs. (Nor will its members readily think of him as one of theirs.) In fact, he has ceased to 'belong'. Where then does he live? In the near-vacuum of extraterritoriality, the very no-man's-land [. . .] The exile's true mode of existence is that of a stranger. [. . .] There are great historians who owe much of their greatness to the fact that they were expatriates [. . .] It is only in this state of self-effacement or homelessness that the historian can commune with the material of his concern [. . .] A stranger to the world evoked by the sources, he is faced with the task – the exile's task – of penetrating its outward appearance, so that he may learn to understand that world from within. (Kracauer 1995, 134)

Consequently, the image of the witness, which takes the photographer's attitude as a model, stems in Kracauer from the exiled, alienated and expatriated mode of existence. The emotionally detached observer dwells 'in the near-vacuum of extraterritoriality', an area that Kracauer also calls the *anteroom*, and which can be compared to the *hashti* in Iranian architecture, an octagonal space – but it could also be hexagonal, rectangular or square – situated directly beyond the *sar-dar* (doorway). An *anteroom/hashti* perspective oscillates between participation (absorption) and distance, microcosm and macrocosm, activity and passivity, detail and whole, concretion and abstraction, though first and foremost between form and event. The form produces the event and the event produces the form. None the less, a tension remains due to a split between the two. This deficiency of the form to grasp the event can be considered as a kind of traumatic structure.

What I want to suggest is that this emotionally detached perspective of the witness can be encountered in Sohrab Shahid Saless's films.[2] The claustrophobically tight shot compositions in Shahid Saless's movies, the immobile framings, the frequent long takes and long shots, the slow panning camera movements, the slow zooms in and out seem to put us – the spectators – in the 'anteroom' of the diegesis, imposing on us the role of distant witnessing observers. Far from being 'sutured' to the diegetic world, we watch the everyday life and routines of Shahid Saless's subaltern characters like invisible or hidden third persons, like 'guests without a host'('Gäste ohne Gastgeber'), as the Turkish guest-worker played by Umran Ertok in Shahid Saless's *Addressee Unknown* (*Empfänger unbekannt*, 1983) points out.

> One must know how to put form and theme together. I made enough shorts to get over the desire to do acrobatics with the camera, tracking shots, for example. It is possible to show a bottle without using a zoom. Secondly, I learned to remain objective and somewhat cold, like ice, says Chekhov, to be precise. It involves creating a distance whereby I do not participate in the life of the people in the film, where I don't say: 'Cry over this kid's life.' I show them as an observer. That way, I let the audience make their own judgment. (Haghighat et al. 1999, 162–74, 165)

Shahid Saless's style – supported by his cinematographers Houshang Baharlou, Naghi Ma'soomi and Ramin Reza Molai (amongst others) – rejects subjective markers and point-of-view shots almost completely. This hinders our access to the characters' subjectivity. I would consider this stylistic signature as a kind of anticolonial 'epistemic disobedience' (Mignolo 2009, 159–81), set against the epistemic violence of traditional Western cinematic codes of subjectivity: *eyeline matches*, *shot/reverse shot*, *découpage classique*. Even when the characters are actually observing and witnessing something – though most of the time with expressionless faces – it is never certain that a counter-shot would reveal what they are looking at (Figs 3.1–3.3). And they are witnessing quite a lot, from daily life routines to shocking and exceptional events like murders, as in *The Willow Tree* (*Der Weidenbaum*, 1984).

Figure 3.1 Michael looking out of the window. (Source: screen grab from *Time of Maturity* 1976.)

Figure 3.2 The railway guard's wife looking out of the window. (Source: screen grab from *Still Life* 1974.)

Figure 3.3 Rosie (Gundula Petrovka), Helga (Johanna Sophia) and Monika (Birgit Anders) looking out of the window. (Source: screen grab from *Utopia* 1982.)

Even when Shahid Saless seems to employ traditional patterns – *découpage*, *shot/reverse shot* – we almost never get to share the (semi-)point of view of his characters. Instead, the instance of enunciation occupies a third-person position most of the time, in between or in front of the characters, comparable

Figure 3.4 The railway guard and his family having dinner. (Source: screen grab from *Still Life* 1974.)

to a ghostly witness. The space claimed by this invisible guest is in no way a transit zone between subjectivity and objectivity; it is in no way a 'free indirect subjectivity' (Pasolini, in Ghaffary 2013) nor a 'subjectivity without a subject' (Metz 1991, 102) (Fig. 3.4).

Further to the above, this invisible witness (or reporter) does not speak for the characters at all; there is no rhetoric of representation. Above all, we are confronted with a consistent defetishisation of things, gestures and human actions. One could say with Karl Marx that Shahid Saless puts an 'irreducible emphasis on the [. . .] necessity for de-fetishizing the concrete' (Spivak 1998, 271–313, 277). Even when we see close-ups that would suggest a fetishism of details, they have no connection to the expressionless faces of the characters, as if Chekhov's sober and apparently emotionless style of indexing details, facts and data had been translated into image-phrases (Figs 3.5 and 3.6).

At certain moments, the editing is so abrupt and the camera angle so completely side-on with respect to the characters' faces that the shot/reverse shot patterns seem to separate the dialogue partners rather than connect them. Shahid Saless's is a very special technique of editing, which, taking my cue from Sulgi Lie, I suggest we call *lateral montage*.[3] It is here especially that one can see the influence of Shahid Saless on Abbas Kiarostami. As Christopher Gow has shown in his book *From Iran to Hollywood and Some Places In-Between*, there is a deep and intertwined relationship between Shahid Saless and Kiarostami,

Figure 3.5 The cooking pot. (Source: screen grab from *Still Life* 1974.)

Figure 3.6 The railway guard's glasses. (Source: screen grab from *Still Life* 1974.)

whether in their preference for circling structures and the camera's attachment to restless characters, especially busy young boys – as in *A Simple Event* (1974) and *Where Is the Friend's Home?* (1987), for example – or in their rejection of any form of psychological approach (Gow 2011, 183ff.). A fundamental aspect of this exclusion of subjectivity is the peculiar way in which Kiarostami and Shahid Saless make use of the shot/reverse shot technique to isolate and dissociate the dialogue partners from each other. Even if the characters are sitting next to each other, we do not experience any eyeline-matching or any other connection.

Shahid Saless's distantiated views – sometimes reinforced by the camera's architectural attachment to the prison walls of *petit bourgeois interiors* – seem to produce what Gilberto Perez calls 'a deadly space between' (Perez 1998, 123ff.), an epitome of alienation and a prefiguration of the kind of *rhetoric of surveillance* (Levin et al. 2002) that is often found in many contemporary movies.

PROTOCOL STYLE

In light of such distantiated views as the ones just described, I am inclined to call Shahid Saless's style *protocol style*, a term that I borrow from the Austrian writer Albert Drach, who, as a Jewish lawyer in Mödling (near Vienna), was forced to flee from the Nazis in 1939. In books like *The Massive Protocol Against Zwetschkenbaum* (1939), Drach develops a unique technique of *pretended objective writing*, which excludes the subjectivity of both narrator and narrated: a witness perception – assumed to be unbiased – that introduces a maximal distance between form and reported event, thus vigorously opposing the dictates of the emotions, at least at a surface level (Fetz 1995). I would like to use this term to characterise, *mutatis mutandis*, Shahid Saless's style, as he drew great inspiration – as already indicated – from the Russian playwright and short-story writer Chekhov. Let me quote from an 1888 letter from Chekhov to Alexei Suvorin:

> In my opinion it is not the writer's job to solve such problems as God, pessimism, etc; his job is merely to record who, under what conditions, said or thought what about God or pessimism. The artist is not meant to be a judge of his characters and what they say; his only job is to be an impartial witness. I heard two Russians in a muddled conversation about pessimism, a conversation that solved nothing; all I am bound to do is reproduce that conversation exactly as I heard it. Drawing conclusions is up to the jury, that is, the readers. My only job is to be talented, that is, to know how to distinguish important testimony from unimportant, to place my characters in the proper light and speak their language. (Karlinsky 1973, 104)

Once again, we stumble upon the terms *witness* and *testimony*, but Chekhov adds: 'My only job is to [. . .] know how to distinguish important testimony from unimportant'. In this respect, the protocol presiding over the selection turns out to be a Janus-faced device, hovering between description and prescription, as Drach has shown in his own ambiguously constructed protocols. These not only represent a technique for the documenting of testimonies, but also are an institutional instrument, an archival code for the production of facts and the construction of objects. Protocols are based on a pre-defined set of rules and regulations that determine the data to be picked up and the way these are to be transmitted. They imply a grid for the production of truth, knowledge, facts and evidence. And, above all, protocols are means for the (mis)construction of temporality through the discrimination between important and unimportant testimony, to repeat Chekhov's words. Thus, Shahid Saless's *epistemic disobedience* – or should we call it epistemic violence? – bears within itself a certain kind of coldness, a dystopian 'sadomodernism' (Weigel 2013) that confronts us with shocks and prison cells in order to arouse in us the desire for liberation through dialectical intoxication. Also corresponding to the protocol style on a visual level is Shahid Saless's highly selective approach in his inner monologues and voiceover descriptions. The meticulously arranged and tightly composed fragments, details and close-ups can be experienced in both a concrete, material way and an allegorical way – 'allegorical' here in the sense of Fredric Jameson's very Benjaminesque notion of allegory as an *'imperfect* representation or the failure of representation', and in this respect also as an intrinsic traumatic structure (Buchanan 2007, 169).

Let me give two examples: firstly, a short description of Moscow taken from Chekhov's *Vanka* (1886), in which a nine-year-old apprentice is writing a letter to his grandfather, the only relative of his to be taken back to his home village; and secondly, a short perception-based protocol of German behaviour given in voiceover by the Turkish guest-worker in *Addressee Unknown*:

> As for Moscow, it is a large town, there are all gentlemen's houses, lots of horses, no sheep, and the dogs are not vicious. The children don't come round at Christmas with a star, no one is allowed to sing in the choir, and once I saw in a shop window hooks on a line and fishing rods, all for sale, and for every kind of fish, awfully convenient. And there was one hook which would catch a sheat-fish weighing a pound. And there are shops with guns, like the master's, and I am sure they must cost 100 roubles each. And in the meat-shops there are woodcocks, partridges, and hares, but who shot them or where they come from, the shopman won't say. (Chekhov 1886)

Similarly to Chekhov's *Vanka*, who, as an apprentice, is in exile for work purposes, the Turkish guest-worker in *Addressee Unknown* also describes Germany from a *near-vacuum of extraterritoriality* (Kracauer): that is, the ethnographic perspective of the exiled.

Das seltsame an Deutschland ist, dass hier Männer Kinderwagen schieben. Dass Radios so billig und Teppiche so teuer sind. Und dass den ganzen Tag Kirchenglocken bimmeln. In Deutschland dachte ich zu Anfang, hier würden die Menschen Hunde gebären statt Kinder. Denn sie haben viele Hunde und tragen sie auf dem Arm. Hunde und Katzen leben wie Könige in Deutschland. In Deutschland gibt es Leute, die habe Geld. Und sehen trotzdem traurig auf die Erde. Sollen sie doch den Kummer denen überlassen, die kein Geld haben. Die Deutschen sind pünktlich wie die Eisenbahn. Das kommt daher, dass sie nur ein Gleis kennen, nie vom Weg abgehen, kein Unkraut, keine Blumen in den Seitenwegen pflücken. Sie fahren immer geradeaus, sind pünktlich wie die Eisenbahn und nehmen nichts wahr. (00:22:05–00:23:14)

The strange thing about Germany is the fact that men push the pushchairs. That radios are so cheap and carpets so expensive. And that all day long the church bells are ringing. At first, I had the impression that human beings were giving birth to dogs instead of children. Since the Germans have lots of dogs and they carry them in their arms. Cats and dogs live like kings in Germany. In Germany there are people who have money. They nevertheless look sadly at the ground. The Germans are punctual like the train since they only know one rail track, they never lose their way and they never pick flowers or weeds on the side tracks. They go straight ahead and experience nothing.

Though Shahid Saless's protocol style grants us enough time to detect details, gestures and slight rhythm changes, it is nevertheless committed to a rigid set of rules and patterns. According to Adrian Martin, films that have an 'intensively rule bound structure' (Martin 2014, 179–204) can be called *dispositif films*. One could also use the term 'parametric narration', after David Bordwell (Bordwell 1985, 274–310): narration in which the definition of space – the rules of framing and editing – dominates the plot.

I would like to consider the rules and patterns of Shahid Saless's protocol style as an ontological statement about capitalist modernity and its dehumanising effects: isolation and alienation, surveillance and claustrophobia, automatisation and rationalisation, reification and commodification. Worthy of note is the fact that this modernity was experienced by Shahid Saless and many other Iranians first and foremost as a colonial project – an imposed modernisation – and not so much as an intellectual, political or cultural one. According to Ali Mirsepassi, the programme of the Pahlavi state was 'modernization without modernity' (Mirsepassi 2003, 73f.).[4] Shahid Saless was forced to track the colonial matrix of power from Iran to Germany, from the rapid modernisation programme and the *white revolution* imposed dictatorially by Shah Mohammad Reza Pahlavi to

Figure 3.7 The railway guard leaving his home. (Source: screen grab from *Still Life* 1974.)

the cultural logics of late capitalism in Germany, including the class differences produced by the neoliberal era of Helmut Kohl. He followed the technologies of control from the Iranian SAVAK (secret police and intelligence service) to the German *Ausländerpolizei* (immigration authorities) (Langford 2016), from government censorship in Iran to political and commercial forms of censorship in Germany, criticising capitalist modernity by means of an aesthetic modernity without putting forward any anti-enlightenment claim à la Martin Heidegger. It is remarkable that Shahid Saless never imagined any hidden *authentic ground*. He always refrained from developing an alternative vision to modernity that would end up in a totalising call for 'spiritual purity' or a 're-rooted community' (Mirsepassi 2011, 15).[5] In Shahid Saless's conception of capitalist modernity, *home* is defined by work. The loss of work is equal to the loss of home, as shown at the end of *Still Life* (1974), when the dismissed railway guard and his wife have to leave the cottage to their successor (Fig. 3.7).

> I must admit with extreme sadness that I have no nostalgic longing for Iran. When each morning I set foot outside my house, whether it was in Germany, France, Venice, or the Soviet Union – the places where I have lived and made films – I would feel at home, because I had no difficulties. I am essentially not a patriot [. . .]. I think one's homeland is not one's place of birth, but the country that gives one a place to stay, to work, and to make a living [. . .] Germany was my home for a long time. (Naficy 2001, 200)

THE HISTORY OF MODERNITY ACCORDING TO SHAHID SALESS

In assuming that in Shahid Saless's films one can find variations on recurrent audiovisual motifs with a tightly woven intertextuality – motifs that, in a way, constitute a coherent world view – my aim is to extract the short history of capitalist modernity that the director is telling us about. There is one question that implicitly accompanies all of his films: the question of the (im)possibility of liberation – liberation from the prison cells that are inscribed on the characters' bodies through ideological, linguistic, symbolic and physical forces, and first and foremost, through the control of labour time. 'Which freedom and whose freedom are we talking about?', asks the woman from *Addressee Unknown* (Iris von Reppert-Bismarck) in a letter to her divorced husband written before she commits suicide, bemoaning a world made of steel, glass and concrete. 'What help can you get from all the revolutions as long as the people are not able to revolutionize themselves?', asks Christian Dietrich Grabbe (Wilfried Grimpe) in *The Last Summer of Grabbe* (1980). In *Utopia* (1982), the five female prostitutes kill the ruthless pimp, their torturer and exploiter. However, the question remains as to whether the collective murder will prove to be an act of liberation or whether the technologies of continuous surveillance and punishment are so deeply internalised that freedom remains an *ou-tópos*. 'Go to work!' is the final command that Renate (Imke Barnstedt), maybe the new despot of the Arena Club, gives to her future servants. At least the prostitutes are allowed to dance and drink after their revolt.

It is remarkable that the Arena Club's corridors, as well as the prostitutes' health care, seem to echo the institutional school hallways and biopolitical treatment of the schoolboys in *A Simple Event* – not to mention the closed curtains in both films. 'We get a sense that all those people living behind those windows are prisoners of the system,' as Mehrnaz Saeed-Vafa notes in her remarkable documentary *Saless, Far From Home* (1998), especially in connection with the man waiting for his fiancée to return in *Diary of a Lover* (1977).

Shahid Saless's characters are, most of the time, subjects of labour and subjected to the regime of labour time. The quasi-permanent ticking of the clock accompanies the railway guard and his wife in *Still Life*, as well as the son and his mother in *Time of Maturity* (1976). In *Hans – A Young Man in Germany* (1985) we even have three ticking clocks, alternating and interfering with each other in one apartment. The sound of the clock – which Shahid Saless added in post-production – structures and models the everyday. If time is money and the organs of the body are functions of the law of value, spending time on leisure is a waste of time. Outside of moments of sleeping, eating or waiting, we rarely see Shahid Saless's characters wallowing in idleness. Even in their sleep, the characters seem to continue to work: the boy in *A Simple Event* perpetuates his restless activity in his dreams, his imagination offering no way out from the prison of daily life. Other characters repair through 'dream work' what went wrong during the day. Luise (Friederike Brüheim) in *Changeling* (*Wechselbalg*, 1987), for example, who refuses to buy a hat for her adopted daughter, tries to rectify the failure subsequently in her dream. In *The Willow Tree* (1984), the murderer anticipates in his dream his own coming suicide. And we must not forget the nightmare in *Addressee Unknown*, in which the wife, who is having an affair with a Turkish guest-worker, dreams of a black-and-white photograph showing Jews surrounded by soldiers from the Waffen SS in front of a shop window covered with swastikas and a star of David. The only coloured elements that we can see are the yellow badges the Jews were forced to wear. Suddenly, the Jews' faces are bleached out and the faces of Turkish guest-workers are faded in instead. The composite dream image performs a 'telescoping', in Walter Benjamin's sense, 'of the past through the present' (Benjamin 1999, 471): a telescoping of fascism through late capitalism, and vice versa.

Precisely because leisure time is very rare in the clock-structured life of Shahid Saless's characters, moments of blissful idleness are strikingly outstanding. These are the moments in which the characters interrupt their functional being with – or are interrupted by – events that are not part of the social order of purposes: a busy boy who interrupts his restless activity and pauses for a second to exchange short glances with a girl sitting in a courtyard (*A Simple Event*); another who moves aimlessly in circles with his bike (*Time of Maturity*); Hussein (Parviz Sayyad), a Turkish guest-worker, who tries to learn the German words he might need to seduce a German woman, rather than those dictated by the state that relate to regional geography or other modern comforts of the nation (*Far from Home*). Yet another *technology of the self* (Foucault 1988, 18, 27)[6] is applied by Husseyin when he uses the time at night to write a letter to his family, regaining a certain kind of subjectivity and a connection to his hometown, Istanbul.

Let me get back to the regime of labour time and its control over bodies. One reason for the claustrophobic effects of Shahid Saless's protocol style might be the fact that the diegetic *hors-champ* (or out-of-field) is almost irrelevant in his films. The isolating and alienating prison cells do not need an outside-the-frame, since the inside is already completely exhausted and organised by the forces, rules and interests of the outside world. They are comparable in this to what Foucault calls a 'positive unconscious' (Foucault 1970, XXI and 87).[7] It is mainly the character's habitus (Bourdieu) – the system of incorporated dispositions that gives rise to schemes of action, perceptions and so on – that is structured by the internalised dictates of capitalist society and the demands of forced modernisation. What we see and hear is what we get. Everything that can be said and shown is exhaustively presented. Given that we are accustomed to Shahid Saless's protocol style, we never expect a reframing that would reveal something not yet shown, even when the action goes beyond the limits of the frame. And if we witness some ambient noises or other sounds – departing planes, clocks, passing cars, barking dogs, police sirens, the constant noise of the electricity generator (in *A Simple Event*) – we never become over-curious about the sound source and we do not expect a reframing as in the theatre. 'For me the sound of the wind, thunder, or drops of water serve as music' (Gow 2011, 183ff.).

> Sound effects are important. In *A Simple Event*, for example, when the kid is waiting for his father on the seashore. One hears toads, the noise of the wind, the steam of the coast guard ship. One does not see but hears the danger that hangs over him. Or in the school, there is the constant noise of the electric generator, which didn't exist since I always shoot without sound and then I post-synchronize. I often add the sound of departing airplanes, clock sounds, passing cars. And especially, in the films I shot in Germany, the sound of police sirens which are ever present. It's the music of our life. Not the sound of a piano or a fade-in sound between two love declarations! It's brutal, but it has to be done. (Haghighat et al. 1999, 168)

In a way, Shahid Saless's frames form closed and saturated systems organised around one character, who could be moving, resting or waiting. There is no time and space left outside this given, concrete and closed system, not even dream images or memory images, since every emergency exit that might lead elsewhere leads back to the already internalised prison cells. The runaway prostitute in *Utopia* always comes back to the club. At work, she feels 'comfortable, safe and useful – all of which are important aspects of the notion of *home*. At the same time this is also the place of the ultimate alienation since no individual expressions are allowed or even possible here' (Naficy 2001, 33). Accordingly, all the family systems and the (more or less forced) communities in Shahid Saless's films are micrological and topological mirrors of the macrological textures of power.

There is one activity in particular that functions as a kind of *fait social total* (Marcel Mauss) and this is *dictation*, especially school dictation. Scenes of education, alphabetisation, disciplinary actions and school dictations are a recurring motif in Shahid Saless's films: *A Simple Event* and *Time of Maturity* mirror each other in this respect and can be brought into relation with criticism of public education, as one can find it in Kamran Shirdel's *Tehran Is the Capital of Iran* (1966), and later in *The Night It Rained* (1967). Shahid Saless's school scenes also found an afterlife in Abbas Kiarostami's *Where Is the Friend's Home?* and *Homework* (1989), and in Amir Naderi's *The Runner* (1984).

There is a kind of scepticism towards language that is worked out in Shahid Saless's films. Alphabet, language and literacy are shown as tools of control and discipline, abstraction and construction, and especially as an instrument of nation-building. Dictations establish realities. They produce facts through language and rhythms. And they install tensions between the manipulative coherence of national narratives – that is, the success stories of *reforms*[8] – and the contradictory complexity of social life. 'What damage Goethe caused! He always knew the language, but never the reality, the cruel reality and he never saw the crack,' Grabbe says in *The Last Summer of Grabbe* (1980). As the Turkish guest-worker says in *Addressee Unknown*,

> 'Do you know what reality means? Everybody is talking about it. It's just a word. She has been manipulated for such a long time till she began to exist merely as a word. I think reality has to do with emotions. Dead feelings murder reality. What do you feel for me? I have real emotions. I know that you are here and that I know that we can talk in your language.'

Already, in *A Simple Event*, one can experience the alienation that language can induce, as in the scene where the schoolchildren are forced to listen to abstract, ideological stories completely detached from social reality, about Cyrus the Great and 'his people'; in the mean time, the boy is looking outside the window and watching something that has absolutely no relation to the definitions dictated by the teacher. In a country where different fictions are quarrelling for the right to overwrite reality, only forms of fictions and contradictions can approach the lived experience of social reality. This is method that can also be found in Kamran Shirdel's films, especially *Tehran Is the Capital of Iran*, where he juxtaposes contrasting versions of reality in an Eisensteinian manner.

From the rhythms of school dictations in *A Simple Event* and *Time of Maturity* one can draw a connecting line to the rhythms of factory machinery in *Far from Home* and the effects of sex-work instructions in *Utopia* on the bodies of the prostitutes. In *Time of Maturity* not only is the boy forced to listen to clerical–fascistic tales at school, but he also receives shopping requests from the old, blind lady in dictation form, from above: he has to kneel down in front of her in order to write down the shopping list. The railway employee in *Still Life* has to suffer comparable bodily (and simultaneously symbolic) violence when he comes to learn of his dismissal: the official letter is delivered to him like dictation from above, read aloud by a messenger standing on top of a vehicle on the railway track.

The scenes of dictation in Shahid Saless's films are scenes about the inhumanity of an unenlightened belief in progress, (re-)installing subjection as the condition of subjectivation. The striking fact that the boy from *Time of Maturity* has to receive shopping instructions from an old blind lady,[9] who, on top of that, puts a little bell around his neck in order to control his movements – 'Stand still!' – suggests parallels with Max Horkheimer and Theodor W. Adorno's arguments on the blindness of instrumental rationality in *Dialectic of Enlightenment* ([1944] 2002):

> The blindfold over the eyes of Justitia means not only that justice brooks no interference but that it does not originate in freedom.
>
> The more completely the machinery of thought subjugates existence, the more blindly it is satisfied with reproducing it.
>
> This ideology became a blind eulogy of blind life, which imposes a praxis by which everything living is suppressed.
>
> That life goes on at all, that the system, even in its most recent phase, reproduces the lives of those who constitute it instead of doing away with them straight away, is even credited to the system as its meaning and value. The ability to keep going at all becomes the justification for the blind continuation of the system, indeed, for its immutability.
>
> Blindness encompasses everything because it comprehends nothing.
>
> Those blinded by civilization have contact with their own tabooed mimetic traits only through certain gestures and forms of behavior they encounter in others, as isolated, shameful residues in their rationalized environment. What repels them as alien is all too familiar. It lurks in the contagious gestures of an immediacy suppressed by civilization: gestures of touching, nestling, soothing, coaxing.
>
> Despite and because of its obvious deficiency, the system of power has become so preponderant that powerless individuals can avert their fate only through blind compliance. (Horkheimer and Adorno 2002, 12, 20, 36, 119, 141, 149 and 164)

It is remarkable that Adorno considers the protocol as a kind of flipside of the dictate, although, in a hidden way, it performs the same function. The dictate acts out what the protocol does undercover: producing and manipulating social reality. Thus, there is a hidden alliance, a cooperation between dictate and protocol, since the grid of the protocol, its way of producing facts under the veil of positivistic pretentions, is synchronised with the demands of capitalist society.

Nevertheless, according to Adorno, a protocol can be equivocal in another way too, especially when it is used as a style in art and music (Adorno 1975, 61). In this respect, the protocol is not only a technique of manipulation in the service of instrumental rationality, but also an artistic form of accounting for the ephemeral, and a materialist resistance to control and to the bourgeois 'cult of the soul', through intensifying disparities and conflicting realities. Here, the protocol performs a *mimesis of the living*, in contrast to the *mimesis of death* performed by the protocols of capitalist ideology.

> Ideology becomes the emphatic and systematic proclamation of what is. Through its inherent tendency to adopt the tone of the factual report ('Protokollsätze'), the culture industry makes itself the irrefutable prophet of the existing order. With consummate skill it maneuvers between the crags of demonstrable misinformation and obvious truth by faithfully duplicating appearances, the density of which blocks insight. Thus the omnipresent and impenetrable world of appearances is set up as the ideal. Ideology is split between the photographing of brute existence and the blatant lie about its meaning, a lie which is not articulated directly but drummed in by suggestion. (Horkheimer and Adorno 2002, 118)

My claim is that both sorts of protocol can be found in the films of Shahid Saless, as well as various combinations of the two. With a micrological protocolary attentiveness, Shahid Saless shows and constructs a world frozen by the dictates of capitalist society and the compulsion of adaptation, which squeezes the characters into what Adorno (with Marx) would call 'Charaktermaske' (Horkheimer and Adorno 2002, 175)[10] (*character masks*): that is, mimetic protocols and mirror images of the capitalist system of value production, an intrinsically contradictory system implying competing forces and conflicting interests. As shown by Shahid Saless, *character masks* have to mediate between those conflicting interests (and not desires!) in the everyday. At the beginning of *Time of Maturity*, the boy has to be silent in order not to waken his mother while the clock is ticking loudly, reminding him of the necessity to get ready for school. 'Sei ein guter Mensch! Be a good human being! Be a fully functional agent of value!' is the categorical imperative in *Far from Home*. In *The Changeling*, Luise, the main protagonist who is trying to raise her adoptive daughter according to the ideals of the middle-class *German home*, is incapable of interpreting the desires of her daughter since she constantly represses thoughts of possible happiness beyond Protestant self-mortification through work and compulsory exercises. 'How can I show my daughter that I like her? I never learned it,' states Luise in a rare moment of desperate self-awareness, with an inkling of the possibility that she might have learned only how to fulfil expectations. In *Utopia*, the imperative 'be a good human' re-emerges in the form of the pimp's command: 'Be kind to your customer!'

The afore-mentioned dictates and imperatives are very closely intertwined with the recurring mirror scenes in Shahid Saless's films. Shahid Saless shows his characters over and over again in front of mirrors, sometimes training their *character masks*, sometimes trying to efface their masks or, even better, to replace them with others, like the prostitute in *Time of Maturity* (Eva Manhardt), who removes her make-up in the morning in order to change her social role and become a 'good mother'. Most of the time, the characters' gazes in the mirror even seem to exacerbate their deprivation of subjectivity as they come to nothing but an acceptance of 'the law' of value. They are consumed by the necessity of being an optimal agent of the *symbolic order* (Lacan). Consequently, it is the symbolic violence of society that they see reflected in their mirrored faces. Gabi (Katharina Bacarelli), the changeling, is literally and visually constrained into her pre-defined role of exemplary adoptive child from the *petite bourgeoisie*: between her new father and her new mother, the adapted adoptive child finds its place only in the reflection of a mirror image. Even before the girl arrives at her new home, she is already represented in the form of a toothbrush mug with her name written on it.

At the end of *Still Life*, the railway guard not only is expelled from his *character mask* and his function as a railway guard. When he looks in the mirror, 'what he sees is the reality of the face of a defeated old man losing his ground to modernity and to youth'. With Hamid Naficy, one can read this scene as a reverse *mirror phase*: 'the old man's gaze at himself does not produce the misplaced empowered self as the Other or its resultant jubilant smile' (Naficy 2011, 396). As a consequence, the old man erases his face and his history by removing the mirror. In contrast to the bourgeois frameworks of remembering (archives, documents, letters, photos, diaries and so on), no traces are left that could be passed to the next generation (Hoggart 1988, 10f.). There is no subjectivity left after effacement through suspension from work.

The *mimesis of death*, the frozen expression of adaptation borne by Shahid Saless's characters, and at which they stare when they look in the mirror, finds a hypertrophic cinematic form at the beginning of *The Changeling*, when Luise's life is very briefly and elliptically recapitulated in the credit sequence in the form of frame-size photographs. At the end of this montage of portraits, there is a slight transition from stasis to motion, from frozen frame to moving image. Luise seems to be raised from the dead, from *rigor mortis*. She is re-animated, but her face stays expressionless and frozen. In a way, then, she is morphed to a member of the living dead and it is not by chance that Shahid Saless uses Michael Jackson's *Thriller* as a diegetic song during a swimming-pool scene.

Is there an exterior, an outside, to the prison cells of rationalisation? In the end, we should not forget the moments of irony that flash up in Shahid Saless's films.[11] Within all those afore-mentioned mechanisms of reification and technification, one can always find revolutionary moments in which the characters become a distorting mirror of the compulsions they have to bear. The cartoonish masks they put on in those moments, the grimaces they wear, become counter-protocols to the protocols of society. It is precisely these moments that I take to be moments of empowerment and reclamation of subjectivity. Consider, for example, the brief, hysterical laughter of the suspended railway guard at the end of *Still Life*, when he realises that his superiors are more interested in their family photos than in his attempt to find out the reason for his dismissal. Or again, the weird conversation – or better, the mutual incomprehension – between the old lady and the Turkish guest-worker Hussein in *Far from Home*: 'Guter Mensch, sehr guter Mensch! A good man, a very good man!' In these moments, Shahid Saless's characters parody the tragedy of their own lives by exacerbating the masks they have to wear. The grimace is indeed the expression of totally estranged subjectivity; none the less, this moment contains a dialectical twist, a sort of mimesis of the living. The subject seeks to break the spell of reification by reifying itself, by re-enacting the character mask it is forced to put on and exposing the mask as a mask. And in those cartoonish moments of distortion, of mirroring and replaying the imposed constraints, traces of a lost mimesis of the living can be spotted. These partake in the 'social genesis of schizophrenia' (Adorno 1981, 255) and the laughter of the revolution to come.

NOTES

1. The following considerations are part of an ongoing research project on trauma- and memoryscapes in Iranian cinema, funded by the Swiss National Science Foundation (SNF).
2. Incidentally, it is an interesting coincidence that the Islamic term *shahid* (شهيد) – often translated as *martyr* – derives from the Quranic Arabic word for *witness*, as is also the case in Greek, where *martus* – the root word for *martyr* – means 'the one who bears witness'.
3. I would like to thank Sulgi Lie for coining this term during the course of a workshop on Abbas Kiarostami, which we organised together with Joan Copjec (Basel, 2017).
4. 'The modernization programs did not, however, encompass change in the political power structure, nor did they introduce cultural and political modernity. On the contrary, through the modernization process, a more structured and powerful autocratic state power was built. Thus, "modernization in some spheres of life occurred without resulting in *modernity*". The Pahlavi state's vision of social change neglected critical elements of modernity dealing with culture and politics: that is, the very complex process dealing with accommodation of social change in the context of the Iranian cultural and historical experience [. . .] The future of modernization, in its blind and brutal rampage forward, appeared increasingly bewildering and confusing. The economic and social relations of the

society were changing without the participation of the people affected by these changes. In many cases, even the state elite did not have a say in policy making. The Shah viewed the reform programs as "his" plan and "his" policy. Thus, people who were affected by the modernization programs and policies were in large numbers alienated from the process, and in many respects an attitude of resistance to and even hostility toward modernization developed.'
5. 'In contrast to the conservatism of the counter-Enlightenment tradition, Heidegger [. . .] made a call for total and radical change combined paradoxically with a call for absolute authority in tradition. His alternative vision of modernity is thus totalizing in its call for what amounts to a "spiritual purity" and restored "rooted" community. These political ideas of "home", or being and belonging, had very strong resonance in Iran during the rapid modernization program imposed dictatorially by the Shah, and greatly helped to shape the "nativist" philosophy of the revolution in terms of both a "spiritual" sensibility and a defense of "local" culture against universalism grounded in a dangerously conceived "return" to a "pure source" of being or "authentic" identity.'
6. '[T]echnologies of the self, which permit individuals to effect by their own means or with the help of others a certain number of operations on their own bodies and souls, thoughts, conduct, and way of being, so as to transform themselves in order to attain a certain state of happiness, purity, wisdom, perfection, or immortality [. . .] Writing was also important in the culture of taking care of oneself. One of the main features of taking care involved taking notes on oneself to be reread, writing treatises and letters to friends to help them, and keeping notebooks in order to reactivate for oneself the truths one needed.'
7. 'Learning the language of the invisible means first and foremost studying the language, the structures and the grid of what can be said, shown, remembered, and perceived. What is hidden is [. . .] caught in the grid of thought, woven into the very fabric it is unrolling. It is not an exterior effect of thought, but thought itself.' 'Order is, at one and the same time, that which is given in things as their inner law, the hidden network that determines the way they confront one another, and also that which has no existence except in the grid created by a glance, an examination, a language; and it is only in the blank spaces of this grid that order manifests itself in depth as though already there, waiting in silence for the moment of its expression.'
8. On reform discourses and reform criticism in Iranian cinema see Blake Atwood (2015, 33–60). See also Atwood (2016).
9. In comparison, in *A Simple Event* one can find an old man who just pretends to be blind.
10. 'In this country there is no difference between a person and that person's economic fate. No one is anything other than his wealth, his income, his job, his prospects. In the consciousness of everyone, including its wearer, the economic mask coincides exactly with what lies beneath it, even in its smallest wrinkles.'
11. For making me aware of Shahid Saless's sense of humour I would like to thank Mehrnaz Saeed-Vafa and her performance in the Stadtkino Basel, 2016, during the conference *Image under Construction: Revolution of Forms in Iranian Cinema Before and After 1979*, 2–5 November 2016.

BIBLIOGRAPHY

Adorno, Theodor W. (1981), 'Notes on Kafka', in *Prisms*. Cambridge, MA: MIT Press.
— (1975), *Philosophie der neuen Musik: Schönberg und der Fortschritt*. Frankfurt am Main: Suhrkamp.
Atwood, Blake (2016), *Reform Cinema in Iran*. New York: Columbia University Press.

— (2015), 'Re/Form: New Forms in Cinema and Media in Post-Khatami Iran', in Peter Decherney and Blake Atwood (eds), *Iranian Cinema in a Global Context: Policy, Politics, and Form*. London and New York: Routledge.
Benjamin, Walter (1999), *The Arcades Project*. Cambridge, MA, and London: Harvard University Press.
Bordwell, David (1985), *Narration in Fiction Film*. Wisconsin: University of Wisconsin Press.
Buchanan, Ian (ed.) (2007), *Jameson on Jameson: Conversations on Cultural Marxism*. Durham, NC, and London: Duke University Press.
Chekhov, Anton (1886), *Vanka*, <https://en.wikisource.org/wiki/Best_Russian_Short_Stories/Vanka> (last accessed 1 November 2017).
Decherney, Peter, and Blake Atwood (eds) (2015), *Iranian Cinema in a Global Context: Policy, Politics, and Form*. London and New York: Routledge.
Fetz, Bernhard (ed.) (1995), *In Sachen Albert Drach. Sieben Beiträge zum Werk*. Vienna: Vienna University Press.
Foucault, Michel (1988), 'Technologies of the Self' (Lectures at University of Vermont, October 1982), in *Technologies of the Self*. London: University of Massachusetts Press.
— (1970), *The Order of Things: An Archeology of the Human Sciences*. New York: Routledge Classics.
Ghaffary, Mohammad (2013), 'A Poetics of Free Indirect Discourse in Narrative Film', *Rupkatha Journal: On Interdisciplinary Studies in Humanities*, 5, 2, <http://rupkatha.com/V5/n2/24a_Free_Indirect_Discourse_in_Narrative_Film.pdf> (last accessed 17 October 2019).
Gow, Christopher (2011), *From Iran to Hollywood and Some Places In-Between: Reframing Post-Revolutionary Iranian Cinema*. London and New York: I. B. Tauris.
Haghighat, Mamad, Bertrand Augst and Timothy S. Murphy (1999), 'Itinerary, 1944–1983: Interviews with Sohrab Shahid Saless', *Discourse*, 21, 1 (Winter).
Hoggart, Richard (1988), *A Local Habitation: Life and Times 1918–1940*. London: Chatto & Windus, p. 10f.
Horkheimer, Max, and Theodor W. Adorno [1944] (2002), *Dialectic of Enlightenment: Philosophical Fragments*. Stanford: Stanford University Press.
Karlinsky, Simon (1973), *Anton Chekhov's Life and Thought: Selected Letters and Commentary*. Evanston, IL: Northwestern University Press.
Kracauer, Siegfried (1995), *History: The Last Things Before the Last*. Princeton: Markus Wiener.
Langford, Michelle (2016), *Sohrab Shahid Saless: An Iranian Filmmaker in Berlin*, <http://www.screeningthepast.com/2016/12/sohrab-shahid-saless-an-iranian-filmmaker-in-berlin/> (last accessed 1 June 2018).
Levin, Thomas Y., Ursula Frohne and Peter Weibel (eds) (2002), *Ctrl [space]: Rhetorics of Surveillance from Bentham to Big Brother*. Cambridge, MA: MIT Press.
Martin, Adrian (2014), *Mise en Scène and Film Style: From Classical Hollywood to New Media Art*. New York: Palgrave MacMillan.
Metz, Christian (1991), *Impersonal Enunciation, or the Place of Film*. New York: Columbia University Press.
Mignolo, Walter (2009), 'Epistemic Disobedience, Independent Thought and Decolonial Freedom', *Theory, Culture and Society*, 26, 7–8: 159–81.
Mirsepassi, Ali (2011), *Political Islam, Iran, and the Enlightenment: Philosophies of Hope and Despair*. New York: Cambridge University Press.
— (2003), *Intellectual Discourse and the Politics of Modernization: Negotiating Modernity in Iran*. New York: Cambridge University Press.
Naficy, Hamid (2011), *A Social History of Iranian Cinema, Vol. 2: The Industrializing Years 1941–78*. Durham, NC, and London: Duke University Press.

— (2001), *An Accented Cinema: Exilic and Diasporic Filmmaking*. Princeton: Princeton University Press.
Perez, Gilberto (1998), *The Material Ghost: Films and their Medium*. Baltimore: Johns Hopkins University Press.
Spivak, Gayatri Chakravorty (1988), *Can the Subaltern Speak?*, in Cary Nelson and Lawrence Grossberg (eds), *Marxism and the Interpretation of Culture*. Basingstoke: Macmillan.
Weigel, Moira (2013), 'Sadomodernism: Haneke in Furs', <https://nplusonemag.com/issue-16/essays/sadomodernism/> (last accessed 1 June 2018).

CHAPTER 4

A Simple Event from a Historical Perspective: What Do We Talk About When We Talk About Realism?

Majid Eslami

Interestingly, Sohrab Shahid Saless is one of the most significant figures in the history of Iranian cinema, despite him actually having made only a couple of films in Iran. In this chapter, Shahid Saless's film *A Simple Event* (1974) is analysed in terms of its visual elements and stylistic devices, as well as directorial approach. The director's use of non-professional actors and the inspiration he took from Chekhov have already been discussed on several occasions, but this chapter takes a unique historical perspective and applies it specifically to examine the concepts of 'realism' and 'minimalism' in Shahid Saless's work.

Sohrabi Shaid Saless's name is legendary in Iranian cinema. He is one of the few Iranians who studied cinema outside of Iran and succeeded in becoming a great and influential filmmaker. Amongst the other handful of successful Iranian directors who studied abroad are Dariush Mehrjui, who made the highly praised film *The Cow* (1969), and Kamran Shirdel, who made the critically acclaimed *The Night It Rained* (1967). However, Mehrjui studied philosophy and Shirdel was more inclined towards documentaries.

With only two feature films, *A Simple Event* (1974) and *Still Life* (1974), as well as a handful of short films, amongst which *Black and White* (1972) is still recognized, Shahid Saless was yet able to consolidate his reputation as a prominent filmmaker in Iranian cinema history. He also managed to continue making both fictional and documentary films after emigrating, and consequently made a name for himself within German cinema of the 1970s and 1980s. On the other hand, his premature and tragic death in 1998, when he was only 54 and living in isolation and exile, accentuate the dramatic facets of his life.

Perhaps the process of making his first film, *A Simple Event*, is an important contributory factor to Shahid Saless's legendary allure. The fact that he went to Bandar Shah (today renamed Turkman Port) with limited means to make a short film and, instead, came back with a full-on feature film (which was accepted at the Second Tehran International Film Festival in 1974 and won an award there) sounds like an embellished tale to this day. However, the simplicity of the film's sequences, its contained and focused storyline and its limited number of locations all fit within the parameters of this tale. It is noteworthy that Shahid Saless's consequent films also display all of these characteristics. It is, in fact, these very features in his cinema that easily register as his personal style in the audience's mind and prevail in his later work.

This seemingly effortless filmmaking style (which was perhaps partially due to production limitations during the making of *A Simple Event*), the almost static camera, the reluctance to use close-ups or conventional editing, the use of non-professional actors, the embracing of a somewhat mechanical style of acting and, of course, minimal dialogue became in turn an easy trope for young, ambitious filmmakers looking for a quick way to create a recognisable style for themselves. This is especially visible in a number of films made after the revolution, all of which feature the above-mentioned stylistic elements. Rafi Pitts's *It's Winter* (2006) and Babak Payami's *One More Day* (2000) both remind us of Shahid Saless's apparently facile filmmaking style, but fail to incorporate his signature radicalism. Majid Barzegar's acclaimed body of work – *Rainy Season* (2010), *Parviz* (2012) and *A Very Ordinary Citizen* (2015) – is also clearly made under the influence of Shahid Saless's cinematic style. And, of course, the most prominent filmmaker to be greatly influenced by Shahid Saless is Abbas Kiarostami (1940–2016), the only Iranian director to win the Cannes Palme d'Or with his *Taste of Cherry* in 1998. Traces of this influence are clearly visible in Kiarostami's *A Report* (1977), his only feature film to be made before the revolution. However, after the introduction of humour and the now-famous car scenes, Shahid Saless's impact fades considerably in Kiarostami's later work. The main similarities between all of the above-mentioned films and those of Shahid Saless come down to the use of a mechanical acting style, the presence of a large number of people with ordinary appearances (Bresson 1975, 14),[1] a rather slow rhythm to the editing, and the depiction of the cold and distant relationship between characters: a kind of alienation and reluctance to show emotion, as is the case with the male protagonists in both *A Report* and *Parviz*, which are reminiscent of the lead character in Shahid Saless's *A Simple Event*. It is perhaps the insistence on moving the film along through the use of long shots that stays with the audience more than anything else.

Shahid Saless's style itself has a number of elements in common with that of some other renowned filmmakers. Directors such as Aki Kaurismaki (b.1957), Chantal Akerman (1950–2015) and, most significantly, Robert Bresson (1901–99) are amongst these names. The static camera and the phlegmatic, vacant faces of Shahid Saless's non-actors are both reminders of Bresson's well-established directorial style. Bresson intentionally makes his scenes devoid of emotion and allows a somewhat neutral tone to take over his films. For example, in *Pickpocket* (1959), the dramatic content of the robbery scene is in direct and serious contrast with the protagonist's frigid and expressionless face. Or, in *A Man Escaped* (1956), the suspense of the prison escape scenes is not apparent in the lead character's frosty, impassive face. The most obvious difference between the two filmmakers is that Bresson uses dynamic editing and numerous close-ups to move the story forward, while Shahid Saless replaces those techniques with an insistence on long shots, along with long takes. Bresson's unrelenting use of close-up in films like *Pickpocket* evokes Alfred Hitchcock's style in films such as *Notorious* (1946), whereas Shahid Saless's insistent use of long shots brings to mind the work of Michelangelo Antonioni. Certain similarities between Shahid Saless's style and that of Akerman, especially in films such as *Jeanne Dielman* (1975) and *Anna's Meetings* (1978), can also be pointed out. However, both of these were made after Shahid Saless's style was already formed, and the Belgian experimental filmmaker's body of work, both before and after these films, is completely distinct in terms of style. Perhaps it can be said that both Akerman and Shahid Saless were influenced by Bresson and other similarly notable directors in the 1960s.

As already mentioned, another filmmaker whose early films are stylistically similar to those of Shaid Saless is Aki Kaurismaki. A clear example of this resemblance can be found in *The Match Factory Girl* (1990). Kaurismaki's bitter and pessimistic point of view, along with the fixed camera, blank faces and minimal use of dialogue, all feed into this comparison. In his later work, Kaurismaki incorporated dark humour, absurd atmospheres and the use of music, thus distancing himself from this so-called 'Shahid Salessian' vibe and creating a different ambience.

With this introduction complete, the purpose of this chapter is to look at Shahid Saless's first film, *A Simple Event*, to analyse two terms that have been used in relation to his cinematic style: realism and minimalism.

REALISM IN SHAHID SALESS'S CINEMA

Many Iranian critics consider Shahid Saless a 'realist' filmmaker and have often used this term while discussing his various films in their articles. However, just as Kristin Thompson elaborates in the context of Vittoria de Sica's *Bicycle Thieves* (1948) and Jean Renoir's *Rules of the Game* (1939) in her book *Breaking the Glass Armor*, realism is a conventional notion and 'many different styles have been historically justified to their publics as realistic . . . No one set of traits can define realism for all time' (Thompson 1998, 56). In that light, in using the term realist to define his cinema, we first have to see which traits in Shahid Saless's work have contributed to this association.

While discussing *Bicycle Thieves*, Thompson points out that 'realism has often been perceived as a departure from the norm of popular, classical, familiar cinema' (Thompson 1998, 201–2). This statement holds true for Shahid Saless's early work. The bulk of the films made in Iran around the time of *A Simple Event* and *Still Life* were popular commercial works now known as *Filmfarsi*.[2] These, like similar popular films in other countries, were full of unrealistic characters who would work through unbelievable plots in unrealistic settings and geographies. It is only natural that Shahid Saless's films seemed realistic in comparison. His settings were all real and the mere fact that he set his stories in remote but genuine locations (Turkman Port and a train station in the middle of nowhere), his lead characters were all played by non-actors who looked real, and there were no exaggerated twists and turns in his storyline and plot all perfectly justify attributing this quality to his work. Moreover, Shaid Saless's unexpected usage of the non-actors' real voice – in direct contrast with the long-running dubbing tradition in Iran, which was the norm at the time and was even used in films that were supposedly arthouse and non-commercial – heightened the sense of 'realism' in his films. Also, there was no trace of the conventional loud, climactic background music that was heavily featured in other films of the time. Instead, Shahid Saless restricted himself to using a melancholic female voice singing a folk song over the opening and closing credits of *A Simple Event*.

Perhaps this steering away from the conventions of popular cinema manifests itself, more than anything, in a disregard for the Aristotelian unities and dramatic principles; at first glance, Shahid Saless's films seem rather unconcerned with such rules. However, upon closer examination of *A Simple Event*, we notice that the film is anything but devoid of dramatic situations: the boy's encounter with the soldier and loss of the fish, the inspector's quizzing him, his summons to the principal's office and, most importantly, his mother's death. All of these moments combined are more than enough to form a central dramatic core, but the film deliberately avoids tying them together and using them as turning points to heighten the tension and reach a dramatic climax. As such, the tone remains unvarying throughout both dramatic and non-dramatic situations, thus creating a sense of alienation and estrangement that some might associate with 'realism'.[3] In one scene, for example, the boy (Mohammad) is late for class (Fig. 4.1) and when the teacher asks him where he has been, he does not respond. After a few seconds of silence, the teacher instructs him to sit down. That is it. Or in another scene, when the ministry inspector asks Mohammad a few questions, the boy does not answer him. The inspector repeats his questions but Mohammad remains quiet and the scene ends with a silent fade-out.

In another instance, after the incident with the soldier and losing the fish, Mohammad's father slaps him in the face. But even here, the emphasis is not

Figure 4.1 Mohammad in the classroom. (Source: screen grab from *A Simple Event* 1974.)

on the slap as a dramatic action, especially since the boy does not have a significant reaction to it. Mohammad does not shed a tear and the fact that he does not cry is a testament to his estrangement and alienation, much more than it is emblematic of him having a 'realistic' reaction to the situation.

A lot of things in the film are unusual and strange. Examples abound: people do not greet each other, not the boy and the mother as he enters the house, nor the father and mother when the father comes home. Iranians always greet each other when they enter a new place or go home. But in this case, nobody greets anybody. It is not only about saying hello. Nobody nags; there is no small talk and no cracking of jokes. The old vegetable seller who takes the fish and pays for them does not really say anything. The boy does not talk or interact with his classmates. In one scene we see Mohammad smoking with another boy on the street in silence. A man approaches the boy, slaps him, puts dark glasses on and leaves with the boy to beg on the streets. This scene brings to mind the beggar in Buñuel's *The Young and the Damned* (1950). The teacher is a parody of himself when he teaches, or is in the presence of the inspector, and even when he wants to comfort Mohammad after his mother's passing. In stark contrast with the students' worn-out clothes, the teacher seems to come straight out of a Chekhov story with his tie and formal clothes. The students make fun of him during the vaccination scene. The lessons themselves are full of innuendo in their tone. In one lesson, the teacher sets out a maths problem, wherein a number of people are present somewhere, then half of them leave, then from the half that remain, another half leave and so forth. Everyone is in the process of leaving and this has an obvious allegorical meaning, maybe alluding to the fact that everyone (especially intellectuals) somehow is always in the process of leaving Iran. Also, throughout the film, the fact that the lessons taught at school have no relation to or bearing on the children's real life is highly emphasised. The stark contrast between the convoluted language used in the textbooks and the vernacular is also very obvious.

There are other strange things too. For example, everyone enters the house with their shoes on and the father sleeps on a bed, whereas in Iranian culture, especially at that time, people would usually take off their shoes outside, and within that socio-economic class everyone would sleep on the floor. Moreover, people have no discernible accents in the film. Granted, this may be an overreach since, in acclaimed films of the time such as Mehrjui's *The Cow*, the village people have no accents either, whereas in Kiarostami's *The Passenger* (1970), which takes place in Malayer, a small town in central Iran, the townspeople and other characters speak with the local accent. But it is exactly this fact that diminishes the 'realistic' aspects of the depiction of the provincial people in Shahid Saless's film.

It seems as though the picture that Shahid Saless builds of the province is an amalgam of the reality of the place and his mental image of it, which was clearly influenced by Chekhov's stories, set in nineteenth-century Russia. Shahid Saless's realism is akin to Bresson's. The environments and settings are real, and people's appearances look real, but their relationships are highly stylised and unreal.

The solitude of the boy in *A Simple Event* has more in common with the loneliness of the girl in Bresson's *Mouchette* (1967) or the protagonist in *A Man Escaped* (1956) than that of the lead character in De Sica's *Umberto D* (1952). In the same vein, the rift between the father and son and their lack of communication are dissimilar to the relationship in *Bicycle Thieves*, as this is more of an existential solitude than a social one. Shahid Saless creates a world that bears a great resemblance to the world as we know it; some things, however, are essentially different by design. For example, people talk very little in his world, so dialogue is reduced to the bare essentials; greetings, goodbyes and small talk are unnecessary. Also, family members are not accustomed to eating together, as was customary at the time; instead, the boy eats separately, by himself, and we never see the father eat at home. Shahid Saless likes to design relationships in a specific way in order to convey a specific meaning. This meaning is more an outcome of his world view than the result of his observations in the real world; in the case of *A Simple Event*, it can be summarised as something like 'everyone is alone' and 'real connections are impossible between people'. Despite depicting the flawed relationships that prevail in the classroom, the shortcomings of the official textbooks and the unsatisfactory behaviour of the teacher, principal and inspector, then, the film cannot be considered to be a critique of the educational system. By the same token, despite portraying the flawed relationships that govern the household (the relationship between parents and boy, the overall environment prevailing in the household, coercion of the boy to work and so on), the film can hardly be categorised as a critique of family dynamics and the treatment of children. This is noteworthy since a lot of films made through the Institute for the Intellectual Development of Children and Young Adults (Kanoon) during the same era, including Kiarostami's early work, had clear-cut educational and critical purposes. Shahid Saless's film goes beyond all of that, though, as it is more of a critique of the logic of the universe at large, much like the writings of Kafka or Camus, or those of his own favourite author, Chekhov.

The most important element that leads one to draw such a conclusion is the way in which people are characterised. The boy is present in almost every scene, and although the film tries to permeate his solitude and isolation, we do not really come to know him deeply as an individual. Eliminating dialogue and reducing actions to repetitious ones (such as bringing water, getting the fish to the vegetable seller, taking the money to the father and, of course, refusing to study) both help to create a vague and obscure image of the boy. Facial expressions, reactions and, perhaps most importantly, dialogue could have shed some light on him as an individual. In many of Bresson's films, while the dialogue is similarly scarce, the lead character's voiceover narration illuminates a lot of his inner thoughts and ideas. Shahid Saless does not utilise narration, at least not in this film. Neither does he resort to tricks to guide us towards the character's inner world. Consequently, the boy's personality becomes a vessel for delivering an idea or a message, much as in classical allegorical fables. Nor is this limited to the boy, since the father, mother, teacher and vegetable seller are also portrayed in the same way.

If we look at it closely, this film should not be considered realistic at all. Instead, if we define realistic things through their rich and multi-layered texture, this film stands at the opposite end of the spectrum: namely, minimalism – a certain kind of stylised and manipulated minimalism. Look at how the locations are reduced to just a handful (and then shot only from limited angles), how people are defined through just a few simple personality traits, how the students are depicted as a shapeless, indistinguishable mass, and how all other seemingly extraneous elements, such as greetings, small talk and verbal reactions, have been omitted. What remains is an allegorical world more akin to literature, with only a façade that looks like the Turkman Port of 1973. Shahid Saless gets rid of all the additional elements that make that world real, in such a way that even when the boy dreams (before his father wakes him up and sends him for the doctor), that dream is comprised of bits and pieces of his quotidian life (the same running in the streets and taking the fish to the vegetable seller). When the father wakes him up and Mohammad

A SIMPLE EVENT FROM A HISTORICAL PERSPECTIVE 71

Figure 4.2 View from outside the building. (Source: screen grab from *Taste of Cherry* 1997 by Abbas Kiarostami.)

leaves to fetch the doctor, there is a shot that is very similar to the penultimate one in *Taste of Cherry*. In the latter, we see in long shot a light in an apartment that finally goes out, signifying that Badiee, the film's lead character, is all packed up and ready to go and lie in the grave (Fig. 4.2). Here, the boy rings a doorbell at night in long shot; the light comes on and the doctor comes to the door, goes back inside, after a while brings his bag and leaves with the boy to go to the family's house (Fig. 4.3). The scene also shares many similarities with that between the old carpenter and the boy in Kiarostami's *Where Is the Friend's Home?* (1987). However, the key difference is that Kiarostami was a true realist, or at least believed in the concept of realism much more than Shahid Saless did; he thus utilises the scene with the carpenter to create a fascinating dialogue between the old man and the child. Such a thing is not conceivable in Shahid Saless's world, so the duo walk in absolute silence until they reach the boy's home. Once inside, the doctor takes a stethoscope out of his bag and examines the mother. The whole scene takes place in a lengthy long shot, in which the father stands to the right of the frame, the boy is on the left side, and the doctor is at the centre, on his knees with his back to us, as he conducts the examination. This process lasts a long while in absolute silence. Then the doctor gets up and utters a single sentence: 'She is already dead.' In the real world, or at least in a realistic film, one would expect the doctor to move a bit faster when he finds the patient unresponsive, or at least murmur something

Figure 4.3 Mohammad outside the doctor's house. (Source: screen grab from *A Simple Event* 1974.)

under his breath, but in Shahid Saless's world people behave in the way he wants them to behave. This world is a figment of his imagination.

Another scene that can be analysed from a realistic point of view is the one in which the mother is called into school. The boy is taken out of class and brought to the principal's office, where his mother and the principal are present. A heavy silence prevails. The boy lifts his finger to ask for permission but does not utter a word. The principal keeps repeating one sentence: 'Mother, this child will not study.' The mother continually repeats another sentence in response: 'But you know best, Sir!' There is a similar scene in Kiarostami's *The Traveller* (1974) (probably influenced by Shahid Saless), in which the mother is also called into the principal's office, where a trio consisting of the principal, the child and the mother forms. The mother says that the principal is in charge and can do as he sees fit. Subsequently, the principal picks up a stick and punishes the boy in front of his mother, the boy bursting into tears. Therein lies the main difference between a stylised minimalist film and a realist one (Figs 4.4 and 4.5).

Realism has always had a strong following in Iranian film criticism. Iranian cinema, in turn, has been influenced to various degrees by Italian cinema, especially by Italian neorealism. Neorealism deeply affected a new wave of Iranian films, the effect manifesting itself in movies such as *The Cow* and Masoud Kimiai's *Gheisar* (1969), and led to a creation of a genre within Iranian cinema

A SIMPLE EVENT FROM A HISTORICAL PERSPECTIVE   73

Figure 4.4 Mohammad's mother in the school principal's office. (Source: screen grab from *A Simple Event* 1974.)

Figure 4.5 In the school principal's office. (Source: screen grab from *The Traveller* (*Mosafer*) 1974 by Abbas Kiarostami.)

that is now referred to as 'social cinema', recent examples of which include the films of Kianush Ayari (b.1951), Rakhshan Bani-Etemad (b.1954) and Saeed Roustayi (b.1989). Moreover, its profound impact is perceptible in films produced by the Institute for the Intellectual Development of Children and Young Adults, chief amongst which is the work Kiarostami and his followers.

Neorealism's effects can even be detected in Iran's popular commercial cinema. The depiction of poverty and class differences, one of the main topics of many of the mainstream Iranian films often referred to as *Filmfarsi*, is an example. Shahid Saless's films, however, are free of such effects. Instead, he was more greatly influenced by French cinema (Robert Bresson in particular) and by Central Europe's art-house films of the 1960s (perhaps the Czechoslovakian New Wave), as well as modern literature. He made films that were different, in the true sense of the word, as they moved away from all of the conventions that governed the various cinematic genres in Iran, such as the use of professional actors, familiar-looking urban locations and formulaic plots. His cinema is a melange of documentary observations, disregarding complicated or dramatic storylines, and featuring substantial amounts of stagnation and silence, as well as recurring motifs. Some people have tried to label his films as realistic and to classify them in a particular category by highlighting certain of their realistic or documentary-like qualities, but their efforts have been in vain. His films still keep their oddity intact.

Shahid Saless liked to portray the world in the way he saw it, and this portrayal was essentially different from what we saw or what others tried to show us. His goal was to shock his audience, much like a doctor who uses electric shocks on his or her sick patients. From his point of view, his audience were all sick patients who had grown accustomed to the false comforts offered by commercial films over the years. His films were the bitter medicine. *A Simple Event* still maintains its bitterness and estrangement.

NOTES

1. 'No actors. (No directing actors). No parts. (No learning parts). No staging. But the use of working models, taken from life. BEING (models) instead of SEEMING (actors).'
2. *Filmfarsi* is a term first coined by Houshang Kavoosi (1922–2103), one of the most renowned film reviewers in Iran. He used it to define popular films in Iranian mainstream cinema before the Islamic revolution in 1979. These films were often heavily influenced by Indian ones with their diluted storylines of fallen dancers and young and poor lowlifes, who would all eventually find the righteous path, their numerous noisy dance and musical scenes, and their lack of geographical identity; they were replete with moral messages and technically lacking in many areas, and were made with sole purpose of entertaining their uneducated mass audience. The majority of these films were made in large numbers between 1950 and 1970, until the 1978 Islamic revolution brought about their extinction. A few of their characteristics can be detected in the popular mainstream works made after

the revolution; however, the films that were typically associated with *Filmfarsi* do not exist any more. Hence the label has morphed into a derogatory one over the years, and in recent Iranian criticism, a film is called *Filmfarsi* if the author wants to define it as lowbrow and worthless.
3. 'Minimalism is a term often used in analysis of visual arts and music. A style of art, design, music etc that uses only very simple ideas or patterns' [*Longman Dictionary of Contemporary English*, 1978]. I believe its use can be extended to discuss works of literature and cinema as well. For the purposes of this article, I am using minimalism to describe works that intentionally use limited resources to create an effect that, in fact, can be a way of defining Shahid Saless's work.

BIBLIOGRAPHY

Bresson, Robert (1975), *Notes on Cinematography*, trans. Jonathan Griffin. New York: Urizen Books.
Thompson, Kristin (1998), *Breaking the Glass Armor: Neoformalist Film Analysis*. Princeton: Princeton University Press.

PART II

Creative Exiles

This part of the book considers how experiences of displacement and dislocation have, throughout history, shaped cinema and moving image practices more generally, and how creative exiles struggle to re- and deconstruct their identities, both to produce art and reproduce their existence as artists against the complex cultural, political and economic background of their respective 'host' societies. Is there a 'cinema of exile', consisting of certain aesthetic, stylistic, financial and socio-political regularities?

CHAPTER 5

Sohrab Shahid Saless and the Political Economy of the New German Cinema

Michelle Langford

In a 1979 report to the Goethe Institut, the German filmmaker Herbert Achternbusch wrote: 'The name of the Iranian director, who makes the best German films, is Sohrab Shahid Saless' (Achternbusch [1979] 1988, 211). When Sohrab Shahid Saless relocated to Germany in late 1974 he found himself in the midst of one of the most vibrant new filmmaking movements in Europe. Led by the likes of Alexander Kluge, Edgar Reitz, Werner Herzog, Rainer Werner Fassbinder, Helma Sanders Brahms and Volker Schlöndorff, the New German Cinema had reached a high point, garnering recognition and prizes at film festivals around the world. Shahid Saless was no stranger to the power of festivals and prizes to boost the careers of innovative *auteurs*, or *Autoren* as they were called in Germany. Indeed, the first two feature films he produced in Iran – *A Simple Event* (*Yek Ettefaq-e Sadeh*, 1974) and *Still Life* (*Tabi'at-e Bijan*, 1974) – had received many accolades and awards earlier that year at the Berlin Film Festival and this recognition offered him a lifeline when it became clear that he would not be able to continue his career in his homeland due to increasing pressure from the government. After he began making films in Germany, his work continued to be much sought after by international film festivals. However, despite managing to relaunch his career successfully in Germany, he struggled to find himself either professionally or personally 'at home' there. During his first year in Germany, he wrote and directed *Far From Home* (*In der Fremde*, 1975), a film about a Turkish guest-worker living in Berlin. Shahid Saless began to see his own struggles of finding a secure home reflected through Hussein (Parviz Sayyad), the protagonist of that film.[1] As a filmmaker who, back in Iran, had been a founding member of the New Film Group, a collective of Iranian New Wave filmmakers striving to launch a new art-film movement, he was very keen to find a new home and secure his 'membership' of the New German Cinema.

In this chapter, I aim to situate Shahid Saless within the context of the cultural and economic policies of West Germany that enabled the New German Cinema to arise and, for a time at least, to thrive. More specifically, I will consider how the emergence of a 'cultural' mode of production in Germany, which relied heavily on state subsidies and television co-productions, helped Shahid Saless to re-establish his career in exile. I want to show that, despite his veritable absence from histories of the New German Cinema, Shahid Saless was indeed very much a part of that history. In his book *The Use and Abuse of Cinema: German Legacies from the Weimar Era to the Present*, Eric Rentschler writes that 'if one rescans Kohl-era productions, one will find many buried treasures, exemplars of a lesser known and still to be written subterranean history of German cinema'[2] (Rentschler 2015, 9). Rentschler even mentions Shahid Saless's *Utopia* as one such film from this era with which he had a 'vivid encounter' (Rentschler 2015, 10). I offer this chapter as a small contribution to the unearthing of this subterranean history.

THE NEW GERMAN CINEMA

In November 1975, the cover of the German news magazine *Der Spiegel* was emblazoned with the proclamation that the German film is 'back'. Prompted by this headline, we might well ask 'back from where?' Turning to look at the feature article, we see that this 'return' is presented as a triumphant homecoming of the kind that is usually reserved for victorious armies and sporting teams (Anonymous 1975, 182–92). The anonymous author enthuses about the many German films that had recently screened at major international festivals and the numerous prizes and critical accolades they had received. Collectively, the young filmmakers are referred to as '*Wunderkinder*' (prodigies) and they were invested with almost messianic status. The author cites international publications such as *Newsweek* and *The Guardian*, together with festival directors and films scholars like Andrew Sarris and James Monaco. Even the rising stars of New Hollywood, such as Steven Spielberg and Francis Ford Coppola, were apparently singing their praises. In highly sensationalist language, the article celebrates nothing short of the rebirth of German film culture, the likes of which has not been seen since the 'golden age', the Weimar Cinema of the 1920s. The article leaves us in no doubt that this moment in the mid-1970s represented a particularly high point of the New German Cinema. Importantly, however, it appears that success at home was largely contingent on the legitimising effect of international praise. Indeed, as Randall Halle has highlighted, the New German Cinema was initially faced with considerable disinterest at home: 'the real success came only when the films were well received in the USA' (Halle 2016, 732).

It is at precisely this moment that Shahid Saless was attempting to make his own mark on the German film scene while also struggling to secure his residential status in Germany (Langford 2016). His thoughts on the matter were captured in a letter to Ken Wlaschin, director of the London Film Festival, who had personally invited him to attend the festival with his first German-made film, *Far From Home*. His film was scheduled to screen alongside a special programme of recent German films, but in the letter, Shahid Saless bitterly lamented to Wlaschin that neither he nor his film is mentioned in the article in *Der Spiegel*. Shahid Saless writes:

> I have coincidentally noticed an article in the latest issue of Der SPIEGEL about German films. The author speaks proudly of your invitation of the German contingent to the festival. However, there was no mention of me 'as foreigner' (*Ausländer*) or my film.[3]

As I have previously argued, it was perhaps premature of Shahid Saless to expect to be named alongside the New German Cinema directors so soon after his arrival in Germany. However, his comments confirm that he had very clear ambitions to join this filmmaking community and to be counted among its ranks. He would go on to direct another twelve feature, documentary and television films in Germany, and while little recognition of his work can be found in the historical and critical literature on the New German Cinema, it can be argued that, in terms of the political economy of filmmaking in the Federal Republic, he was indeed deeply connected to this vibrant filmmaking movement, particularly for the way that his own modest success in Germany was both hindered and helped by the same rather precarious economic and cultural policies that gave shape to the New German Cinema in the 1970s and 1980s. In this sense, despite his relative absence from the historical record, he was very much a part of the New German Cinema, even though at the time he felt considerably marginalised.

By 1979, there were signs that he was beginning to be recognised as part of the New German Cinema. In October 1979, he appeared at an event hosted by the Goethe Institute in San Francisco, alongside Herbert Achternbusch and several other New German Cinema directors.[4] The panel discussion, 'New Directions in New German Cinema', was moderated by prominent film critic Ronald Holloway and covered a series of questions that are relevant to this chapter, including the origins of the New German Cinema, how it was financed and the role of public television in Germany at the time. Seeing Shahid Saless's name among other filmmakers like Herbert Achternbusch, Uwe Brandner, Michael Günther and Bastian Clevé suggests that, to some extent, he had by this stage been recognised as a member of the New German Cinema, although, as Achternbusch emphasises in his own recollections of this and similar events held in Berkeley and Los Angeles, 'Americans cannot grasp that there isn't simply one New German Cinema.' He continues:

> Of course, we were supposed to be the representatives, against the background of the film festival of the rejects we were meant to be the third line, show that there is lots more territory around the heroes and stars, prove that the German cinema has unlimited potential, we, the two nihilists [referring to himself and Shahid Saless], who every time we make a film barely break free from the slimy embraces of all the forward-looking assholes, those know-it-alls without a spark. (Elsaesser 1983, 102)

The event at the Goethe Institute coincided with what appears to have been a considerable rise in interest in German and European film financing among film critics and scholars in the USA. Articles published in prominent film journals *Film Comment* and *Quarterly Review of Film and Video* in 1979 and 1980, respectively (Eidsvik 1979, 60–6; Deutelbaum 1980, 130–1), provide an insight into the situation at the exact moment that Shahid Saless was discussing these matters at events in the USA, and also during the time when he was attempting to get his production of *Utopia* (1982) off the ground. These publications, together with some of Shahid Saless's own writings and archival materials, therefore allow us greater insight into the experience of a relatively marginal proponent of the New German Cinema. Before moving on to look more specifically at Shahid Saless's experience, I shall provide a brief overview of the emergence of the New German Cinema.

ORIGINS OF THE NEW GERMAN CINEMA

The New German Cinema emerged at a time of great cultural and social change in Germany. In the early 1960s, a generation born around the end of World War Two was beginning to come of age, among them a number of aspiring young filmmakers. In 1962, a group of emerging filmmakers took the opportunity afforded by the Oberhausen Short Film Festival to author and sign a manifesto that would plant the seeds for what would eventually become the New German Cinema. The Oberhausen Manifesto, which was signed by 26 filmmakers, was born out of a critique of the state of the post-war German film industry – largely for the way it privileged commercial imperatives over the artistic capacities of cinema. In demanding a break from the cinema of the past, they adopted the catchphrase *Papas Kino ist tod!* (Daddy's cinema is dead) and began lobbying for support to establish a new kind of film with new freedoms. In short, they called for freedom from the usual industry standards, freedom from commercial interests and freedom from special interest groups. This new kind of film would be founded according to new formal, economic and intellectual conceptions of film production, and should ideally be supported by the state. The manifesto was effectively a call to action for young filmmakers to start lobbying the government for access to film subsidies that would not be based on commercial criteria alone, but would recognise film as an art form alongside other, more established art forms such as opera and theatre. This gave rise to what Thomas Elsaesser has called a 'cultural mode of production' that was characterised primarily by a heavy reliance on state subsidies that relegated filmmakers to 'artisanal' conditions, subjecting them to a high degree of precariousness, even though it also granted them the status of *Autoren* (Elsaesser 1983, 40).

The 'Young German Film', as this loose collective that grew out of the Oberhausen event initially came to be known, emerged at a time of significant crisis in the German film landscape. Not only had the quality of German productions diminished significantly after filmmaking recommenced in the postwar era, but also the market was severely affected by the influx of popular films from Hollywood. For example, as Moeller highlights, 43 per cent of the box office in 1976 went 'into American coffers' (Moeller 1980, 158). Added to this, the sharp rise of home television ownership in the early 1960s caused the theatrical exhibition market to diminish considerably. The lobbying efforts of the young German filmmakers therefore came at the right time to have some impact, particularly since commercial producers were also keen to see the introduction of government subsidies to support the flailing industry.

This lobbying led to several concrete outcomes. The first was the establishment of the Kuratorium Junger Deutscher Film in 1967. This organisation was designed specifically to support young, first-time filmmakers rather than established commercial producers. In its first three years, the Kuratorium received direct funding from the federal government, through which filmmakers could apply for interest-free loans that had to be paid back only when and if the films made a profit. With funding of 5 million Deutschmark (DM) over three years, the Kuratorium financed some twenty feature films, as well as numerous shorts and documentaries (Elsaesser 1983, 22). This situation would not last, however, for counter-lobbying by commercial producers led to the introduction of a new policy framework, the *Filmförderungsgesetz* (FFG) (Film Support Act), which laid the groundwork for the establishment of the Filmförderungsanstalt (FFA) (Federal Film Board) in early 1968 (Halle 2016, 725). The FFA, which was funded by a levy on cinema admissions, did not apply any quality criteria in its assessment of applications and did not fund first-time filmmakers. Rather, a subsidy, known as *Referenzförderung*, was awarded to producers whose previous film (a *Referenzfilm*) had met a certain target at the box office. A gross of 500,000 DM at the box office over two years could provide a return of up to

50 per cent of the production costs that could be invested in a new film. For films that had won a major international award or a German Film Prize, or had received a quality rating from the Filmbewertungsstelle Wiesbaden (FBW), the box office requirement was reduced to 300,000 DM (Moeller 1980, 159). Obviously, even with provision for awards, this arrangement privileged established, commercial producers who had strong links with distributors. There was also no compulsion for producers to re-invest the subsidy in the work of the same director, which meant that filmmakers were often at the mercy of unscrupulous producers who had the power to decide how they used the *Referenz* funding. Despite these difficulties, many of the more prominent New German Cinema directors were able to benefit from FFA subsidies, particularly after various amendments were made to the policy. In 1974, an amendment to the FFG added provisions for project subsidies for new productions without the need for the so-called *Referenzfilm*; however, these subsidies, of between 100,000 and 300,000 DM, were paid in the form of a loan that would have to be paid back out of any profits (Moeller 1980, 159).

For independent filmmakers like Shahid Saless, whose films struggled to find wide distribution, awards were often the only way they might even hope to become eligible for a subsidy from the FFA. Thus, there was potentially a lot riding on his entry of *Far From Home* into competition at the 1975 Berlin Film Festival, even if it was permitted to compete only as an Iranian entry. A win would certainly have increased his chances of securing funding for his next project. This made his 'loss' to the Hungarian film *Adoption* (*Örökbefogadás*, Márta Mészáros, 1975) all the more bitter.[5] His frustrations would have been even more acute, given that, as an Iranian–German co-production, the film was also deemed ineligible to be considered for the German Film Prize (Bongers 1975). Over the next eight years, he would make another six feature and documentary films in Germany before finally gaining government support for *Utopia*, both directly in the form of a loan from the Berliner Filmförderung (BFF) and indirectly through FFA *Referenzförderung*, although this was not for one of his own films[6] (Ortkemper 1983, 172). *Utopia*, which also relied on the unique interdependence between film and television in West Germany (and which I discuss in more detail below), was typical of many works of the New German Cinema in the sense that funding was frequently cobbled together from a variety of sources. Hamid Naficy has highlighted the fact that this is a characteristic of the intersitial mode of production under which many exilic filmmakers such as Shahid Saless worked (Naficy 2001, 46–55); however, it was also a symptom of what Moeller refers to as the 'precarious' nature of financing for the New German Cinema more generally. Shahid Saless's exilic precariousness was compounded, then, by the instability and complexity of the German financing systems. This becomes clear as we trace the production history of *Utopia*.

UTOPIA AND THE VAGARIES OF GERMAN FILM FUNDING

Shahid Saless had written a treatment for *Utopia* in 1977, while he was still living in Berlin, and it would be almost seven years before the completed film finally premiered at the Berlin Film Festival in February 1983. A brief synopsis of the completed film allows us to see how its controversial subject matter would have contributed to the difficulties he faced in getting the film produced. *Utopia* is a dark drama of human power, control and oppression set in a brothel in West Berlin. The establishment is run by Heinz (Manfred Zapatka), a misogynistic and controlling pimp who demands absolute conformity to his rules on the part of the five women who work for him. The minimally decorated rooms of the converted apartment provide for a claustrophobic atmosphere that intensifies the women's sense of entrapment, which eventually reaches a point where they finally resist Heinz's tyrannical rules, killing him. Ironically, however, the women do not take this as an opportunity to escape. Instead, they choose to stay on and run the brothel themselves. It seems that their confinement has rendered them unable to break free of their role as commodities in a cruel and inhuman capitalist system. This very simple story unfolds over an epic duration of three and a quarter hours in a series of often excruciating long takes, mostly occurring inside the brothel. While the topic of *Utopia* is perhaps no more controversial than that of some of Rainer Werner Fassbinder's more radical works like *Fox and His Friends* (*Faustrecht der Freiheit*, 1975) or *Querelle* (*Querelle: Ein Pakt mit dem Teufel*, 1982), the subject matter, style and the fact that the ending does not culminate in the women's liberation from the system that oppresses them meant that both funding organisations and television producers were reluctant to support the film.

Archival documents reveal that Shahid Saless applied unsuccessfully for a script development grant from the Bundesarchiv (Federal Archive) in February 1978 after he had relocated to Munich.[7] The screenplay was co-authored with Manfred Grunert, a novelist, screenwriter and director, who had fled East Germany in 1955. In early 1979, he began the long process of applying to the FFA for *Projektförderung*, a project loan.[8] The struggle to secure a producer, funding and distribution would lead to many delays and disappointments before the shoot finally commenced in January 1982. It would take another year before it would eventually premiere in competition at the Berlin Film Festival on 20 February 1983, and even then, its release would be marred by technical issues affecting the quality of the film print and subtitles. I shall now try to trace the film's journey through the complex and protracted production process.[9]

Shahid Saless's first challenge in his epic journey to make *Utopia* was finding a producer who would support the project and assist with funding applications, negotiate with distributors and seek out all-important television co-producers. While many of the New German Cinema filmmakers had established their own production companies, according to Shahid Saless, this option was not open to him since he was not a German citizen. In an article published in the German film journal *Medium* in 1983, shortly after the release of *Utopia*, he wrote: 'Because I am a foreigner (*Ausländer*), I am not allowed to be a producer. I have to find a producer who will grant me the honour of working with me'[10] (Shahid Saless 1988, 56). In the case of *Utopia*, archival material indicates that, initially, Shahid Saless was working with Hamburg-based Provobis Gesellschaft für Film und Fernsehen, the company that had already produced three of his German films: *Far From Home*, *Time of Maturity* (*Reifezeit*, 1976) and *Diary of a Lover* (*Tagebuch eines Liebenden*, 1977). However, on 10 July 1978, Shahid Saless approached Wolfgang Ersterer at another larger production company, Multimedia Gesellschaft für Audiovisuelle Information mbH, asking if he would be interested in producing *Utopia*.[11] It is likely that Shahid Saless parted company with Provobis because the subject matter of *Utopia* was considered too risqué for Provobis's parent company, Tellux Group, which was majority-owned by the Catholic Church.[12] On 14 December 1978, he was offered a contract by Multimedia that provided him with a loan of 7,000 DM in exchange for the temporary rights to the screenplay of *Utopia*.[13]

Much later in the process, an additional Berlin-based co-producer, Ullstein Tele Video, was brought on to the project and it appears that Shahid Saless may have had no say in this decision. Shortly after the completion of *Utopia* he wrote: 'It sometimes happens overnight that a second independent coproducer for whatever reason invests a small bit of money in your film. You don't even have the chance to choose your own coproducer or to turn him down' (Shahid Saless 1988, 57). While it is unclear whether Shahid Saless is referring to Ullstein Tele Video here, Shahid Saless complained elsewhere: 'a private producer, I am told, invested 200,000 DM. This point, by the way, is also the object of a lawsuit' (Shahid Saless 1999, 172).

With the backing of Multimedia, Shahid Saless was able to pursue the rather frustrating process of applying for *Produktionsförderung* from the FFA. The initial application was submitted by Shahid Saless himself on 12 January 1979, very soon after signing with Multimedia. However, further correspondence with the FFA indicates that he was asked on several occasions to provide additional documentation. At one point, he remarks on his status as a foreigner. In a letter, dated 7 February 1979, to Robert Backheuer, a founding board member of the FFA, he wrote: 'Please do not allow me, a foreigner [*in der Fremde*], to become a victim of bureaucracy. I am not responsible for the oil crisis!'[14] This is a fleeting reminder that he was planning this new project just as the Iranian revolution was reaching a climax back home, and also of the continuing sense of self-consciousness he felt as a foreigner. The application for *Produktionsförderung* was ultimately unsuccessful, and later, he would reflect rather bitterly on his experiences with the FFA. In a provocatively titled article, 'Notizen im Exil' (notes in exile), which was published posthumously, he provides some indication of the FFA's negative response to his application. He complains that the officials at the FFA are not governed by any particular rules or standards when assessing screenplays for funding, apparently describing the screenplay he had written with Grunert as a 'macabre story', labelling it as 'stuffy' and 'uncinematic'. He goes on to accuse the FFA assessors, who he characterises as mere bureaucrats with little understanding of the art of film, of being incapable of reading a screenplay 'filmically' (Shahid Saless 1999, 16). This appears to align with Thomas Elsaesser's description of the main approach of the FFA, which was to 'dispense economic aid' rather than 'discriminate on criteria of quality' (Elsaesser 1983, 22).

The commercial imperatives of the FFA were not lost on Shahid Saless or his producer. In late 1978, Shahid Saless approached the prominent Italian actor Gian Maria Volontè to take on the lead role of Heinz. Initially, Volontè asked for a fee of 250,000 DM; however, with a projected budget of only 700,000 DM, this was far too high and Volontè eventually agreed to play the role of the sadistic and dictatorial pimp for the much more modest sum of 60,000 DM. The contract was signed on 16 January 1979; it specified that filming was scheduled to commence in Munich around 26 or 27 March and would continue for approximately three weeks.[15] As part of the negotiations, Esterer at Multimedia also offered Volontè the television rights to the film in Italy.[16] It was not unusual for producers to farm out various extra-territorial exhibition and broadcast rights, particularly if it could help to fund the project directly or indirectly. It is likely that Volontè's European star power would attract interest from other investors or funding bodies, such as the FFA, because a star might help to secure a return on the investment.

During this time, negotiations were also under way for alternative funding and other cast members. On 12 November 1978, Shahid Saless sent Esterer the draft of a letter to Gitty Djamal, a German–Iranian actress who was based in Switzerland. It appears that Shahid Saless may have already discussed the project with Djamal, for he suggests to Esterer that she might consider taking on the main female role of Renate if she were also brought on as a co-producer. Esterer reacted promptly, writing to Djamal three days later with a slightly reworked and corrected version of Shahid Saless's draft, offering her the role and indicating that he would welcome her coming on board as a co-producer. He also explains that Volontè was to play the part of the male lead, that the shoot was planned for late February 1979 and that they were hoping to have the film ready in time for the Cannes Film Festival, which was to take place in May. It appears that Djamal may have initially responded favourably, for in further correspondence dated 29 November 1978, Esterer provides more concrete details of the proposed co-production agreement. He explains that he was looking for an investment of around 150,000 DM, reinforcing the fact that he was looking not for a loan, but for a co-production partner willing to take on a portion of the risk. He adds that, in agreement with the distributor, it may be possible for her, as a co-production partner, to receive the television and possibly even the theatrical rights in Switzerland.[17] It is unclear whether these negotiations went any further, but neither Volontè nor Djamal took part in the film.

Without funding, the shoot could not commence as planned in early 1979. In fact, on 15 January 1979, Esterer wrote to Shahid Saless, advising him that his timeline for the project was unrealistic and asking him to prepare a more workable schedule. Esterer cites a number of very concrete factors that would prevent the shoot from commencing, including the fact that the FFA would not make a decision until at least late February. In addition, Multimedia would need at least eight weeks to negotiate with a television partner, and they were still awaiting a decision from the Berlin credit committee (Berliner Kreditausschusses), which was not due until 15 March. Without that, emphasises Esterer, nothing could go ahead! Esterer further advised Shahid Saless that a minimum of two months would be needed to make preparations after the finance was finally in place.[18] This would mean that nothing could go ahead at least until mid-May. Shahid Saless responded on 24 January and appeared to be positive, despite these delays. In this letter, we get a sense of the great trust he placed in Esterer, writing, 'The project UTOPIA is in good hands. I will wai.....................t.' And he continues, 'I will keep working to ensure that our UTOPIA does not fall under the table.'[19]

As I have already indicated, the FFA application was ultimately unsuccessful. This forced Shahid Saless and his producer to look for alterative avenues, and this caused significant delays to the planned production schedule, proposed cast and even the location of the shoot. Filming finally commenced in January 1982, almost three years after originally planned. By that stage, Volontè had been replaced by Manfred Zapatka, a prominent West German stage actor who had also appeared in several film and television projects, and Imke Barnstedt was cast in the role of Renate, which had originally been offered to Gitty Djamal. In place of Munich, West Berlin was chosen as the filming location, a decision that was a condition of gaining a 350,000 DM production loan from the Berliner Filmförderung (Shahid Saless 1999, 172).

The Berliner Filmförderung, which was established in 1978, was the first of several regional film boards that emerged in the 1970s and 1980s.[20] According to Halle, these 'did not so much nullify the national system as add a layer of regional and local specificity to film policy' (Halle 2016, 727). The Berliner Filmförderung was established with the explicit mandate to attract film production to West Berlin, which was, at the time, a small slice of West

Germany sequestered within the communist East. The first great success of the programme was Volker Schlöndorff's *The Tin Drum* (*Die Bleichtrommel*, 1979), which won the Palme d'Or at the 1979 Cannes Film Festival, the 1979 German Film Award and also the Academy Award for Best Foreign Film in 1980. The Berliner Filmförderung provided support to filmmakers by granting loans of up to 30 per cent of a film's budget, with the stipulation that at least 50 per cent of the film's production costs must be spent in Berlin (Ortkemper 1983, 8). In many cases however, rather than merely 'attracting' projects to the city, filmmakers needed at times simply to go wherever they could secure finding. *Utopia* is a case in point. The production received a 350,000 DM loan from the Berliner Filmförderung and so the necessary relocation was perhaps a small price to pay (Shahid Saless 1999, 172).

With the success of the Berlin scheme, other German states established their own film development boards in the years that followed. But, as Halle has emphasised, the 'disadvantage is that for filmmakers to raise a significant set of funds [. . .] they often have to spend years moving through a decentralized system' (Halle 2016, 728). This was certainly the case for Shahid Saless, for, throughout his career, he remained something of a nomad, never able to settle down in one place, moving from city to city in search of the next opportunity. This sense of decentralisation was further exacerbated by the crucial role played by television in the development of the New German Cinema, and is of particular importance for *Utopia* and Shahid Saless's career in Germany more broadly.

UTOPIA AND THE ROLE OF PUBLIC TELEVISION IN THE NEW GERMAN CINEMA

Perhaps the most important piece of the complex funding puzzle was the role played by Germany's national and regional public television stations. Sheila Johnson once wrote that 'the New German Cinema owes its existence to the munificence of television' (Johnston 1982, 60). In fact, the importance of German television more generally for the establishment and survival of the New German Cinema cannot be underestimated. Outside of the federal and regional film subsidy system, the meagre loans provided by the Kuratorium and distribution advances, television offered more, and sometimes more flexible, opportunities for both emerging and more established filmmakers. As publicly funded institutions, German television stations were obligated to commit funds to support the production of feature and documentary films. This would help them not only to fill airtime but also to meet a legal requirement under Article 5 of the *Grundgesetz* (West Germany's preliminary constitution) to 'provide a forum for different socially relevant groups' (Collins and Porter 1981, 21–2).

The social consciousness and diversity of perspectives that the New German Cinema directors brought to their filmmaking helped the television stations to meet this requirement. Germany's national and regional stations had been commissioning works for decades; however, a formal framework for such film/television co-productions was established in 1974 with the signing of the *Film/Fernseh-Abkommen*, an agreement between the two national stations – ARD and ZDF – and the FFA.

The agreement, which came about partly due to fierce lobbying undertaken by Alexander Kluge, who was also a lawyer, was a step in the right direction, for it guaranteed a substantial investment in feature filmmaking by the television stations. Article 2 of the agreement specified that 'DM 34 million would be made available over five years from 1974–1978 for the part-funding of co-productions with film industry partners who were to provide at least 25% of a project's budget.' Importantly, Article 3 specified a 'holdback' period of two years, allowing time for films produced under the co-production agreement to obtain a theatrical release and circulate on the festival circuit before being broadcast on television (Blaney 1992, 197–8). In addition to the formal arrangements of the *Abkommen*, individual directors continued to enter into informal co-production agreements with television stations. Elsaesser highlights how many 'West German film-makers developed close working relationships with individual executive editors' at one of the national or regional stations (Elsaesser 1983, 113). The impact of television support for the New German Cinema was profound. For example, as Moeller points out, '[a]ll seven films which won the 1978 German national film awards were supported at least in part by television monies' (Moeller 1980, 160).

This unique interdependence between film and television was also crucial to Shahid Saless's career in Germany, a fact that serves to align him even further with the New German Cinema. After *Far From Home*, all of his films were either produced or co-produced by German television stations; however, of those twelve films, only four were premiered at a major film festival or had a theatrical release prior to their television broadcast. This suggests that the majority of his films were co-produced under individual contracts, rather than via the *Film/Fernsehen-Abkommen*, which would mean that they were not subject to a holdback period, or that he was simply unable to secure theatrical distribution. Despite his dependence on television funding, Shahid Saless never considered himself as a television director, but rather always insisted that his films were being made with cinema exhibition in mind. This was a common attitude among the New German Cinema filmmakers, and one of the reasons why the two-year holdback period was negotiated into the *Abkommen*. *Utopia* benefited directly from the *Abkommen*, which was renewed for a further five years from 1979 to 1983; however, this came only after a long and arduous process of finding a supportive *Redakteur* (commissioning editor). Archival records give us some indication of the considerable effort needed to balance his cinematic vision with the requirements of television funding, including underlying assumptions about the tastes and expectations of television audiences.

Records show that, in parallel to seeking a production company, Shahid Saless approached a number of Germany's public television stations looking for a co-production deal. These included the regional broadcasters Bayerischer Rundfunk (BR) and Hessischer Rundfunk (HR), as well as Radio Bremen, Germany's smallest broadcaster, based in the northern city of Bremen. Over the course of 1978, Shahid Saless faced rejections from each of them. In most instances, they could not reconcile Shahid Saless's uncompromising cinematic vision and the challenging content of the film with their views of audience expectations. For example, on 10 April 1978, Hellmut Haffner from BR wrote to say that while the exposé of *Utopia* might be suitable for the cinema, it was far too radical a theme for the small screen.[21] Much later in 1978, Shahid Saless approached HR. In his cover letter to Hans Prescher at HR dated 24 November 1978, Shahid Saless opens by dropping the name of the prominent German actor Eberhard Fechner, with whom he had struck up a friendship. It is obvious that, by this stage, he had already received numerous rejections, for he prefaces his request by saying that *Utopia* will be misunderstood by most and labelled a 'pornographic film'. He goes on to explain that his method is one of 'shock therapy for my viewers'. He contrasts the kind of film he wishes to make with television commercials: 'Absolute beauty exists in commercials. Let us make a hideous [*häßlichen*] film!' Eventually, after quite a lengthy discussion of the philosophical approach he intended to take with his film, he gets to his concrete request by asking if HR would agree to contribute two-thirds of the production costs.[22] The response from HR arrived just two weeks later in a letter signed both by Prescher and Dietmar Schings, another commissioning editor at HR who would later produce Shahid Saless's *Hans – A Young Man in Germany* (1985). In the letter, Prescher and Schings replied thoughtfully to Shahid Saless's outline of his vision; for them, however, the decision came down to the fact that they did not think that their audience would be able to grasp the critical aspects of the film and might instead react aggressively against the portrayal of the female characters.[23] About a week later, Shahid Saless received yet another rejection from Jürgen Brest at Radio Bremen. Although Brest appeared to be much more sympathetic to the film's challenging topic, he explained that it was particularly difficult for Radio Bremen to engage in film–television co-productions, and also advised that a film like *Utopia* would inevitably be relegated to a late-night time slot, suggesting that it would be too risky for an earlier screening and echoing the assumptions about audience responses raised by HR.[24]

Utopia was eventually co-produced by the second national television station Zweites Deutsches Fernsehen (ZDF) under the *Film/Fernseh-Abkommen* and as part of its *Das kleine Fernsehspiel* programme (Ortkemper 1983, 78 and 172). In Shahid Saless's recollection, ZDF contributed 700,000 DM, more than half of the total budget of 1.25 million DM (Shahid Saless 1999, 172). *Das kleine Fernsehspiel*, which translates literally as 'the little television play', was crucial to the careers of many New German Cinema directors as it was committed to fostering experimentation in fiction and documentary, and did not shy away from challenging content. Conceived initially in 1963 as a twenty-five-minute slot for experimental work, *Das kleine Fernsehspiel* moved in 1970 to a regular late-night time slot of 10 p.m. on Thursday evenings, allowing for the broadcast of feature films. This new time slot helped to build a loyal cinephile audience and was late enough to avoid offending the sensibilities of prime-time viewers. Long-time department head Eckart Stein emphasised that the underlying philosophy of *Das kleine Fernsehspiel* was never to try to maximise audiences through the production of popular content; rather, it deliberately embraced challenging and discomfiting projects (Blaney 1992, 255). This meant that *Das kleine Fernsehspiel* would have seemed like the natural home for Shahid Saless. Indeed, his second German feature film, *Time of Maturity* (*Reifezeit*, 1976), had been co-produced by ZDF for *Das kleine Fernsehspiel*, as was *Order* (*Ordnung*, 1980), which Shahid Saless made while he was waiting for the many pieces to fall in place for *Utopia*. *Order* is a good example of a television co-production making it to the international film festival circuit first: it premiered in 1980 during Directors' Fortnight at the Cannes Film Festival, in good company alongside *The Female Patriot* (*Die Patriotin*, 1979), yet another ZDF co-production by one of the most important proponents of the New German Cinema, Alexander Kluge. In fact, while it was common for projects made under the banner of *Das kleine Fernsehspiel* to premiere on television, exceptions were occasionally made for projects that had the potential to make an impact on the festival and art-house circuits. In fact, as Martin Blaney asserts, by 1980, 'over 90% of the films appearing in the *Das kleine Fernsehspiel* slot had been given a theatrical release' (Blaney 1992, 257–8). This provides some indication of the cinematic aesthetic promoted by this department.

Indeed, it appears that ZDF may have been one of the first television channels that Shahid Saless approached, for on 8 February 1978 he wrote a long and rather acerbic letter to Hans Kutnewsky, a commissioning editor there. It seems that Kutnewsky may not have been so keen on the treatment for *Utopia*, leading Shahid Saless to express his frustration in a series of rhetorical questions that indicate that the two men had a significant difference of opinion over the project. But Shahid Saless was not about to give up. Some seven months later, he wrote using the Provobis letterhead to Christoph Holch, another commissioning editor at ZDF's *Das kleine Fernsehspiel* programme. In the letter, dated

15 September 1978, Shahid Saless mentions that Ron Holloway – the American film critic – had advised that he should send his treatment for *Utopia* to Holch. He mentions his previous communication with Kutnewsky, stating that 'your colleague Mr Kutnewsky read the exposé some time ago and was neither fascinated nor convinced'. He asks that Holch reconsider the possibility of ZDF co-producing the film and explains his method as a kind of 'shock therapy', designed to 'awaken the viewer from a deep, numb slumber'. While the archival record does not furnish us with any further insight into the negotiations with ZDF, the fact that the film was eventually co-produced with *Das kleine Fernsehspiel* suggests that, in Holch, Shahid Saless may have found a more supportive perspective; in the end, however, Willi Segler would be appointed as ZDFs commissioning editor on the project. Segler already had a long line of credits to his name, including Werner Herzog's *Strozek* (1976/7), *Nosferatu – Phantom der Nacht* (1978), *Woyzeck* (1978/9) and *Fitzcarraldo* (1981/2), and works by other prominent New German Cinema directors such as Alexander Kluge, Reinhard Hauff and Hans-Jürgen Syberberg. He would also serve later as ZDFs commissioning editor for Shahid Saless's last film, *Roses for Africa* (*Rosen für Afrika*, 1992).

A short time after the release of *Utopia*, Shahid Saless would write that his recognition as a proponent of the 'new young German film' may be credited to a single man at ZDF and four German film critics, none of which he mentions by name. 'For the rest', he proclaims, 'I am superfluous, boring' (Shahid Saless 1999, 15). Elsewhere, he repeats his praise for ZDF and the German television landscape's contributions to the German film scene more generally by saying there are a few cultural editors (*Redakteure*) who are courageous enough to fight for a project, and go to the barricades so that a realistic film can be made. Two of these cultural editors, it becomes clear in the production of *Utopia*, work for ZDF (Shahid Saless 1988, 58).

DISTRIBUTION

By far the most contentious and problematic aspect of the film industry for the New German Cinema directors was the lack of government support for distribution. In his ironically titled article, 'The State as Movie Mogul', which provides a comparative study of government support for filmmaking across Europe in the late 1970s, Charles Eidsvik highlights the German government's neglect of exhibition and distribution. He writes: 'As a result, the *majority* of New German films never play in commercial release: most merely run in festivals, spend time on a small art house circuit, and disappear – often without a commercial distributor of any kind' (Eidsvik 1979, 64). This certainly describes the fate of the majority of Shahid Saless's films, which remained highly sought after by major festivals but struggled to reach wider audiences through theatrical distribution. Both distribution and exhibition in the German market had been cornered by the big, vertically integrated Hollywood studios, which had embarked on a vast project to capture international markets in the post-war period through the control of distribution and investment in theatres. Furthermore, according to Randal Halle, Hollywood companies established subsidiaries in Germany, such as Deutsche Columbia Filmproduktion. This 'allowed access to the various national production mechanisms' (Halle 2016, 729), meaning that, by entering into co-productions, they could reap the benefits of the German film subsidy system managed by the FFA, as well as the regional film boards. This has a mostly negative impact on the New German Cinema filmmakers, as they would have to face the added competition from Hollywood-backed co-productions. However, some of the New German Cinema directors managed to turn this to their advantage. For example, Volker Schlöndorff's *The Tin Drum* (1979) received about 'one million marks from United Artists subsidiary Artemis', which was significantly more than the 700,000 marks secured through government subsidies (Moeller 1980, 162). Shahid Saless appears to have been keenly aware of this situation, for even before he secured the production contract with Multimedia for *Utopia* and long before he submitted an application to the FFA, we see evidence of attempts to secure a distribution contract. Not only would a distribution contract help the completed film reach an audience, it could also provide some direct funding in the form of a distribution guarantee. Additionally, it would also increase the likelihood of a funding application being successful and might help to attract additional private investment.

On 28 September 1978, Roswitha Frankenheimer from Provobis wrote identical letters to three international distributors on behalf of Shahid Saless. One of these, Frankfurt-based United Artists Corporation GmbH, was the distributor of Rainer Werner Fassbinder's *The Marriage of Maria Braun* (1978), which had premiered at the Cannes Film Festival earlier in the year. They had been actively distributing German films since 1949.[25] Another, Warner–Columbia Film Verleih, based in Munich, began distributing German films in 1971. One of the more radical proponents of the New German Cinema, Hans-Jürgen Syberberg was perhaps lucky to have them distribute his 1974 film, *Karl May*, based on the life of the famous German adventure writer and starring veteran German actor and director Helmut Käutner in the title role. The third distributor approached by Frankenheimer was Gaumont, France's largest vertically integrated film company. Warner–Columbia responded in the negative within a couple of weeks and it is likely that no response was forthcoming from Gaumont, for on 21 November Shahid Saless himself wrote directly to Daniel Toscan du Plantier, Director General at Gaumont, dropping the names of his friends, Paris-based German film critic Lotte Eisner and fellow New German Cinema director Werner Herzog. He even goes so far as to suggest that the Filmverlag der Autoren had agreed to handle the domestic distribution of the film. Shahid Saless may have been jumping the gun in this regard, for ultimately, the Filmverlag der Autoren did not distribute the film and neither did Gaumont, Warner–Columbia nor United Artists. Importantly, Shahid Saless was actively seeking distribution very early in the process, not only signalling that he was well aware of the crucial role that distribution played in ensuring that films could be seen by the public, but also indicating that he recognised that distribution was an integral part of building a budget from multiple sources.

The Filmverlag der Autoren, mentioned by Shahid Saless in his letter to Toscan du Plantier, was another important piece in the New German Cinema puzzle, as it was inspired by the spirit of the Oberhausen Manifesto and was founded in 1971 by a group of young directors that included Hark Bohm, Wim Wenders and Peter Lilienthal, specifically for the purpose of distributing their films. Throughout the 1970s, the Filmverlag der Autoren distributed many of the most successful films of the New German Cinema directors, including Shahid Saless's own *Far from Home*. However, by the time he was working on *Utopia*, the company had been purchased by Rudolf Augstein, publisher of *Der Spiegel*, and had become much more oriented towards commercial projects.

In the end, it was not until the film was reaching the final stages of completion in late 1982 that Basis-Film, a small firm committed to supporting the distribution of art-house films, agreed to take on its national distribution. Basis-Film had handled the distribution of numerous cutting-edge works by New German Cinema directors, and can be credited for almost single-handedly promoting Germany's emerging feminist filmmakers like Ulrike Ottinger, Helke Sander, Jutta Brückner and Helma Sanders Brahms. Documentation also shows that Cine-International had agreed to take on international distribution.

After a long and arduous journey, the premiere of *Utopia* in competition at the 33rd Berlin International Film Festival on 20 January 1983 might be seen as the triumph of a struggling artist against the tyranny of an unwieldy system. However, Shahid Saless's struggles were far from over, with the much-anticipated premiere marred by substandard prints. A comprehensive account of the event was recorded by Shahid Saless's attorney, D. E. Ralle, in an affidavit submitted to the Munich civil court on 14 April 1983.[26] From this document we learn that the afternoon premiere was scheduled to commence at 2 p.m. on 20 January. At about 4.15 p.m., Shahid Saless entered the theatre and after a minute or so was startled by the inferior quality of the print. Also appalled by the poor quality of the print, actress Imke Barnstedt, an unnamed technical assistant and the film's cinematographer, Ramin Molai, who had been present for the duration of the screening, urged Shahid Saless to ensure that the inferior print was not used again for the second screening, scheduled for 9.30 p.m. that same evening. At around 5 p.m., Basis-Film confirmed that a copy with English subtitles was held in Berlin and could be made available for the evening screening at the Zoo-Palast Cinema.

Concerned that the second, subtitled print might also be of poor quality, Shahid Saless requested that it be checked at the cinema prior to the scheduled screening. Arrangements were made for Shahid Saless, Molai and Multimedia's attorney, Mayershofer, to meet the head projectionist, Klaus Kutschek, at the Zoo-Palast, where they proceeded to check a reel of the subtitled print. All parties agreed that this was brighter than the print used for the afternoon session, but to be on the safe side, decided to select a second reel randomly to check against the print screened earlier. This was also deemed more suitable and a decision was made to go ahead with the subtitled print for the evening screening. Unfortunately, time constraints prevented the checking of any further reels, and it appears that the randomly selected reels were in much better condition than the rest of the print. By all accounts, the evening screening was an even greater disaster. As Ralle describes in his affidavit, the subtitles did not appear neatly at the bottom of the screen but wandered all over the image, which was also marked by scratches, flashes of light and dust. In some places, the image was infused with a reddish light and occasionally became blurred. Mayershofer remarked that the flaws made the film look like the work of an amateur and noted that this was particularly damaging, given that the film's run-time was three hours and twenty minutes; such disturbances would have a great impact on the viewing experience.

At the press conference the next day, the moderator felt compelled to remind journalists to focus their questions on the film itself, rather than on the inadequate print. This approach appears to have worked, for among the many reviews and short notices that appeared in newspapers across the country in the days immediately after the screening, none of them commented directly on the quality of the print, although their assessment of the film was not overwhelmingly positive, some even remarking that the film seemed like the work of an amateur.

About a week after the ill-fated premiere of *Utopia*, Shahid Saless reached out to the one person he felt would understand not only the struggles he had faced during the production of the film but also the significance of the disastrous premiere. On 28 February, he wrote to Willi Segler, his commissioning editor at ZDF. He opens with the same phrase he had used in a letter to his producer after *Far From Home* failed to take home the Golden Bear at the 1975 Berlin Film Festival: 'And now the party is over!' He continues with a vivid metaphor:

> The child was born by caesarean section. But at least it was born. We participated in a contest for the most beautiful child! But the poor child was ill, his nose was constantly running, he had diarrhoea and screamed incessantly.[27]

Shahid Saless had evidently read some of the reviews that had appeared since the premiere. The one that seems to have caught his attention was written by the highly respected West German film critic Wolfram Schütte and published in the *Frankfurter Rundschau* newspaper on 25 February (Schütte 1983). Shahid Saless remarked to Segler: 'Has Mr Schütte lost his mind?' Schütte opens his review of Shahid Saless's *Utopia* and *Addressee Unknown* (*Empfänger unbekannt*, 1983), and some other German films in the programme, by remarking that the death of Rainer Werner Fassbinder in June 1982 had cast a deep shadow over this year's event, particularly since Fassbinder had taken home the Golden Bear for *Veronika Voss* exactly one year ago. In fact, while he notes that the programme had rarely seen so many German films, he says, 'I have not seen anyone who has done justice to his artistic material.' Although Schütte is heavily critical of both of Shahid Saless's films, his lengthy review provides substantial analysis and assessment of them, showing a considered understanding of what Shahid Saless had tried to do, but ultimately finding the execution overburdened with dialogue, filled with clichés, and infused with heavy-handed polemic and ideological messages. Lamenting that the two films lacked the artistic dimensions of Shahid Saless's earlier films made in Iran, Schütte describes them as 'stillbirths of creativity' (Schütte 1983). Shahid Saless appears to have taken this critique in his stride, remarking that at least Schütte 'respectfully panned' his films.

In the letter to Segler, we also see Shahid Saless preparing to move on to the next phase in the life of *Utopia*, listing the interviews he had given to a broad contingent of the international press and mentioning that the film had already been invited to festivals in Chicago, Montreal, Toronto and Lisbon. He also remarked that the Goethe Institute in London was in the process of arranging a retrospective of his work and that *Utopia* was due to open in London on 3 March. If he had learned anything during his time in Germany, it was not to take the opinions of German film critics too seriously. He had probably also learned that, as a 'German' filmmaker, he must seek out international praise before he could make a triumphant 'homecoming'.

CONCLUSION

There is, of course, much more to say about the reception of *Utopia*, and this is something I aim to explore further in future work. In this current chapter, I hope to have constructed a detailed and complex account of how Shahid Saless went about funding and producing his films in Germany. While *Utopia* is perhaps the most extreme example, taking much longer to bring to fruition than most, we can see the degree to which it was both helped and hindered by the very same cultural and economic policies that brought the New German Cinema into being. In his ability to navigate his way through this complex and haphazard system, Shahid Saless certainly earned the right to figure among the ranks of the New German Cinema. Only now is this part of the subterranean history of German cinema beginning to come to light.

NOTES

1. For an account of Shahid Saless's first year in Germany see Michelle Langford (2016).
2. Rentschler is referring to Helmut Kohl, German Chancellor from 1982 to 1998 (Eric Rentschler 2015, 9).
3. Shahid Saless to Ken Wlaschin, letter, n.d. The letter is undated but must have been written shortly after 17 November 1975. Unless otherwise stated, all correspondence cited in this chapter is held by the Dokumentationsstelle Sohrab Shahid Saless/Farschid Ali Zahedi, Oldenburg, Germany, which I visited in July 2014.
4. The event took place on 22 October 1979.
5. For a discussion of this 'incident' see Langford (2016).
6. Many thanks to Ann-Malen Witt at the FFA for clarifying that the film never received *Projektförderung*. Instead, the film appears to have benefited indirectly from the FFA via the *Referenzfilmförderung* scheme, although the FFA does not retain records of how *Referenzförderung* was distributed. It is possible that Shahid Saless's main production company, Multimedia Gesellschaft für Audiovisuelle Information mbH, may have used some of the *Referenzförderung* received automatically from another film they had produced, or that a second production company, Ullstein Tele Video, may have invested in the project in this way. I would also like to thank Martin Blaney for pointing out that this was common practice.
7. Sohrab Shahid Saless to Bundesarchiv Koblenz, letter, 13 Febuary 1978.
8. Sohrab Shahid Saless to Filmförderungsanstalt, letter, Berlin, 12 January 1979.
9. The archival record is rich but incomplete. I construct this account from information gleaned from correspondence held in the Dokumentationsstelle Sohrab Shahid Saless/Farschid Ali Zahedi, Oldenburg, Germany and from relevant publications on German film and television policy and history, as cited throughout this chapter.
10. This statement may not be technically true. For example, French-born duo Jean-Marie Straub and Danièle Huillet had established their own production company in the early 1960s, and Turkish-born Tewfik Baser set up his production company around 1982.
11. Sohrab Shahid Saless to Wolfgang Esterer, letter, 10 July 1978. The company was founded in 1974 by brothers Fritz and Helmut Rothschild, together with Wolfgang Ersterer (Anonymous 2004a).

12. Roswitha Frankenhauser to Sohrab Shahid Saless, letter, 17 November 1978. The letter is typed on Tellux letterheaded paper; it acknowledges that he is seeking other partners and wishes him luck.
13. Wolfgang Esterer and H. Rothschild to Sohrab Shahid Saless, letter, 14 December 1978.
14. The Iranian revolution had been under way throughout most of 1978 and the turmoil led to an international oil crisis. On 1 February, Ayatollah Khomeini returned to Iran soon after the ruling monarch, Mohammad Reza Shah, fled on 16 January 1979. Shahid Saless uses the title of his first film made in Germany, *In der Fremde*, to refer to his foreignness.
15. Sohrab Shahid Saless to Fausto Ferzetti, letter, 12 October 1978; Sohrab Shahid Saless to Fausto Ferzetti, letter, 4 December 1978; Wolfgang Esterer to Gian Maria Volontè c/o Fausto Ferzetti, letter, 7 December 1978; Fausto Ferzetti to Wolfgang Esterer, letter, 16 January 1979.
16. Wolfgang Esterer to Gian Maria Volontè c/o Fausto Ferzetti, letter, 7 December 1978.
17. Sohrab Shahid Saless to Wolfgang Esterer, letter, 12 November 1978; Wolfgang Esterer to Gitty Djamal, letter, 29 November 1978; Wolfgang Esterer to Gitty Djamal, letter, 15 January 1979.
18. Wolfgang Esterer to Sohrab Shahid Saless, letter, 15 January 1979.
19. Sohrab Shahid Saless to Wolfgang Esterer, letter, 24 January 1979.
20. In 1994 the Berliner Filmförderung was replaced by the Filmboard Berlin-Brandenburg GmbH, to encompass the newly reunified East and West sectors of Berlin.
21. Hellmut Haffner, Bayerischer Rundfunk to H. Farazi/CINE 3, letter, 10 April 1978. It appears that Farazi had approached BR on behalf of Shahid Saless. Farazi is a Persian name but I have been unable to unearth any further information on him. This may be Homayoufar Farazi, an Iranian student and anti-Shah campaigner, who had been threatened with deportation for refusing to leave Munich during the Shah's visit. His case inspired solidarity from German students, who mounted a teach-in on 19 December 1967. See Quinn Slobodian (2012, 132) and Alexander Clarkson, who writes that '[i]n Munich scores of Iranians were ordered to register with the police and temporarily leave their districts' (Clarkson 2013, 161).
22. Sohrab Shahid Saless to Dr Hans Prescher, letter, Hessischer Rundfunk, 24 November 1978.
23. Hans Prescher and Dietmar Schings, Hessischer Rundfunk to Shahid Saless, letter, 12 December 1978.
24. Jürgen Brest, Radio Bremen to Shahid Saless, letter, 20 December 1978.
25. Online Film Portal Database: see Anonymous (2004b).
26. D. E. Ralle to Munich civil court, affidavit, 14 April 1983. Dokumentationsstelle Sohrab Shahid Saless.
27. Sohrab Shahid Saless to Willi Segler, letter, 28 February 1983.

BIBLIOGRAPHY

Achternbusch, Herbert (1988), 'Amerika: Report to the Goethe Institute (1979)', in Eric Rentschler (ed.), *West German Filmmakers on Film: Visions and Voices*. New York and London: Holmes & Meier.
Anonymous (1975), 'Lorbeer für die Wunderkinder', *Der Spiegel*, 47, 17 November, pp. 182–92.
Anonymous (2004a), '30 Jahre Multimedia', *Hamburger Abendblatt*, 4 November, <https://www.abendblatt.de/kultur-live/article106924330/30-Jahre-Multimedia.html> (last accessed 2 October 2018).

Anonymous (2004b), 'United Artists Corporation GmbH', *Filmportal.de*, <https://www.filmportal.de/institution/united-artists-corporation-gmbh-frankfurt-am-main_fe9319f28a214ccb8ddada4bdacb245e> (last accessed 6 July 2018).

Blaney, Martin (1992), *Symbiosis or Confrontation: The Relationship Between the Film Industry and Television in the Federal Republic of Germany from 1950 to 1985*. Berlin: Sigma.

Bongers, Inge (1975), 'Es ist doch vieles Gold, was glänz', *Der Abend*, 9 July.

Clarkson, Alexander (2013), *Fragmented Fatherland: Immigration and Cold War Conflict in the Federal Republic of Germany, 1945–1980*. Oxford: Berghahn.

Collins, Richard, and Vincent Porter (1981), *WDR and the Arbeiterfilm: Fassbinder, Ziewer and Others*. London: British Film Institute.

Deutelbaum, Marshall (ed.)(1980), 'Some Recent Publications from European Film Archives', *Quarterly Review of Film Studies*, 5, 1: 130–1.

Dokumentationsstelle Sohrab Shahid Saless/Farschid Ali Zahedi, Oldenburg, Germany.

Eidsvik, Charles (1979), 'The State as Movie Mogul', *Film Comment*, 15, 2: 60–6.

Elsaesser, Thomas (1983), 'Achternbusch and the German Avant-Garde', *Discourse*, 6: 91–112.

Halle, Randall (2016), 'German Film Policy's New Horizons', *International Journal of Cultural Policy*, 22, 5: 724–42.

Johnston, Sheila (1982), 'The Radical Film Funding of ZDF: An Introduction to an Interview with Eckhart Stein of ZDF German Television', *Screen*, 23, 1: 60–73.

Langford, Michelle (2016), 'Sohrab Shahid Saless: An Iranian Filmmaker in Berlin', *Screening the Past*, <http://www.screeningthepast.com/2016/12/sohrab-shahid-saless-an-iranian-filmmaker-in-berlin/> (last accessed 6 June 2018).

Moeller, Hans-Bernard (1980), 'New German Cinema and its Precarious Subsidy and Finance System', *Quarterly Review of Film & Video*, 5, 2: 157–68.

Naficy, Hamid (2001), *Accented Cinema: Exilic and Diasporic Filmmaking*. Princeton: Princeton University Press.

Ortkemper, Hubert (ed.) (1983), *Film in Berlin: 5 Jahre Berliner Filmförderung*. Berlin: Colloquium.

Rentschler, Eric (2015), *The Use and Abuse of Cinema: German Legacies from the Weimar Era to the Present*. New York: Columbia University Press.

Schütte, Wolfram (1983), 'Monstren und monströse Ambitionen', *Frankfurter Rundschau*, Feuilleton, 47, 25 February.

Shahid Saless, Sohrab (1999), 'Notizen im Exil', in Farshid Ali Zahedi (ed.), *Sohrab Shahid Saless: Bericht über ein abgekürztes Leben*. Oldenburg: Werkstattfilm, pp. 11–20.

— (1988), 'Culture as Hard Currency or: Hollywood in Germany', in Eric Rentschler, (ed.), in *West German Filmmakers on Film: Visions and Voices*. New York and London: Holmes & Meier.

Slobodian, Quinn (2012), *Foreign Front: Third World Politics in Sixties West Germany*. Durham, NC, and London: Duke University Press.

CHAPTER 6

The Aesthetic of Diaspora in Moving Image Practice

Azadeh Fatehrad

'The Aesthetic of Diaspora in Moving Image Practice' reflects on the representation of diaspora and double agency within the medium of moving image. Engaging with socio-cultural factors, the chapter considers the notion of the individual struggle to navigate through complex social relations and the diverse negotiations of agency within artistic practice. Focusing on Sohrab Shahid Saless and selected scenes from his film *Time of Maturity* (1976), it explores the notion of 'in-betweenness' in the Iranian–German filmmaker's work. Shahid Saless's aesthetic and stylistic approach, which masterfully takes the viewer from one uncomfortable scene to the next, is thus the central part of this chapter, but a parallel is drawn with Belgian film director Chantal Akerman's work, as well as that of Romuald Karmakar: in particular, selected scenes from Akerman's *Jeanne Dielman, 23 quai du Commerce, 1080 Bruxelles* (1975) and Karmakar's *Nightsongs (Die Nacht singt ihre Lieder*, 2004) are analysed.

WEST BERLIN'S KREUZBERG: THE DISTRICT OF 'IN-BETWEENNESS'

By way of background on Sohrab Shahid Saless and the time he spent in creative exile in Germany, it is important to note that Berlin was not historically a popular travel destination in Europe. In comparison to Paris or Rome, which attracted most of the elite or bourgeois travellers in search of the roots of classical or modern civilisation, Berlin did not have much to offer. In particular, Kreuzberg, the district Shahid Saless lived in, emerged from its post-World War Two history as one of the poorest quarters in West Berlin – until things started to change for the city as a whole (Hochscherf et al. 2013, 105–6).

The entry of many immigrants to Germany was based on bilateral agreements that the government of Chancellor Konrad Adenauer (1949–63) signed with Italy, Greece and Spain, as well as Turkey and the former Yugoslavia, to encourage *Gastarbeiter* (guest-workers) to arrive to provide the unskilled labour (Wilke 2014, 191) that was needed in post-war Germany (Taras 2012, 169).[1]

Berlin suddenly became an international meeting point not only for West and East Germany but for the whole world. It was promoted as a 'bulwark of freedom' (Hochscherf et al. 2013, 107) – a fascinating metropolis from which to view the capitalist and communist world side by side due to the separation of the city. It was promoted with the slogan 'Visit the City of the Freedom Bell', the bell being a gift from the US government, inspired by the American Liberty Bell.

Things were looking up for Berlin but it did not take long before the split city became problematic. For security reasons arising from the Cold War, '[by] late August 1960, citizens of West Berlin required special approval to pass through border crossings to East Berlin, and the rules for West Berliners travelling to and through the GDR changed as well' (Hochscherf et al. 2013, 109). The following year, Walter Ulbricht (East Germany) had the Berlin Wall built, of course, triggering a diplomatic crisis and cutting off immigration between the two sides of the divide completely (Nijhoff 1997, 301).[2]

The guest-worker programme introduced by Adenauer nevertheless continued, attracting a large number of foreigners to West Berlin, which, over time, became a lively, cosmopolitan urban hotspot with a vibrant, mixed culture. By the 1970s, the city had completely transformed itself.

Many creative foreigners (artists, poets, writers) gathered in West Berlin, and in Kreuzberg in particular, during this time, to share ideas and experiences and to be inspired. The seemingly more open, liberal ways that the city promised were undoubtedly appealing. Aside from Sohrab Shahid Saless, there were other fascinating people like Günter Brus, the Austrian painter; Romy Haag, the Dutch performer; Anne Jud, the Swiss visual artist; and Marwan, the Syrian painter.

The increasing number of immigrants during this period alarmed the German government, though – by 1973, more than 4 million were living in West Germany. This caused the introduction of various restrictions, and guest-workers were forced to renew their permission to stay continuously to ensure that they were not able to settle. They were returned to their home country immediately after the end of their work contract or if they were simply no longer needed. The situation was even worse in East Germany.

The living conditions of those in Kreuzberg were greatly affected by these new measures, and the creatives who had gathered there faced many challenges and limitations. However, they remained there for many years, if not for the rest of their lives, and today Kreuzberg is one of reunified Berlin's greatest cultural centres and is known around the world for its alternative scene and counter-culture, which have been greatly shaped by immigration, especially from Turkey (Wilke 2014, 197); as of 2006, 31.6 per cent of Kreuzberg's inhabitants were non-German.[3]

Colloquially also known as X-Berg (derived from the German word *kreuz* (cross)), Kreuzberg is often said to consist of two distinctive parts: the SO 36, home to many immigrants; and SW 61, roughly co-terminous with the old postcodes for these two areas of West Berlin. Indeed, they have a distinct Middle Eastern feel, which adds a certain vibrancy to the area, although it is also characterised by high unemployment and low wages. Despite this 'Middle Easternness', Kreuzberg is obviously German – hence that state of in-betweenness.

French philosopher Georges Didi-Huberman, in a recent publication, refers to the notion of in-betweenness as an uncertain transformation of identity. He notes that

> You feel less here, and more there. Where 'here'? Where 'there'? In dozens of 'heres', in dozens of 'theres', that you didn't know, that you didn't recognise. Dark zones that used to be bright. Light zones that used to be heavy. You no longer end up in yourself, and reality, even objects, lose their mass and stiffness and no longer put up any serious resistance to the ever-present transforming mobility. (Didi-Huberman 2018, 8)

To return to Sohrab Shahid Saless, the director moved to West Berlin in 1974 in the hope of finding a more nourishing platform for his new-wave style of filmmaking. City life was, indeed, cosmopolitan and colourful but, due to the change in the government's attitude towards immigration, Shahid Saless continued to struggle to obtain a residence permit, even after living in Berlin for more than 30 years. In voluntary exile, Shahid Saless navigated a journey of in-betweenness – a contradiction between the growth and development of his work, and the state of homelessness and misery in his personal life.

Shahid Saless never really felt that he fitted in or belonged in society, remaining an outsider in his adopted city. The notion of an individual struggle to navigate through complex social relations is primarily a negative one of isolation, loneliness and anxiety. However, that position also provided Shahid Saless with a different perspective on his surroundings - a critical viewpoint of an outsider within – and this allowed him to evaluate the value of human life in a unique and often ironic way.

The slow and minimalist/eventless portrayal of the everyday life of marginalised people (Turkish guest-workers, prostitutes) is a fascinating but uneasy experience for the viewer. The social history that is captured in Shahid Saless's films undoubtedly serves as an outstanding record of the life of the poor during 1970s West Berlin, which will be addressed in depth later in this chapter.

Shahid Saless's work not only offers an individual viewpoint on West Berlin life during this period but also serves as a representation of diasporic experience that can be captured in visual art – in this case, moving image practice. French writer Antoni Casas Ros notes that 'an autobiography appears to be the tale of a full life. A succession of acts. The displacements of body in space-time. Adventures, misdeeds, joys, unending suffering'. At the same time, he says, 'my true life starts with an end' (Casas Ros 2007, 13). The 'end' here represents the end of your life in your home country and your departure for an unfamiliar adopted land; even though it has become common practice these days to move abroad, the challenges remain unknown.

Avtar Brah contextualises the position of the adopted home as a 'diasporic space', which is inhabited not only by those who have immigrated into it (and their descendants) but equally by those who are constructed and represented as indigenous. Even though the word 'diaspora', according to *Webster's Dictionary*, derives from the Greek *diaspeirein* (disperse), which comes in turn from *dia*, meaning 'across' and *speirein* meaning 'to scatter', there must be a centre, locus or 'home' from which this dispersion can occur - fragmented and ununited (Brah 1999, 614).

At the same time, the 'diasporic space' brings together a shared experience as a united form different from its origin - a new unified being. It thus represents the intersectionality of diaspora, borders and dis/location as a point of confluence of economic, political, cultural and psychic processes. In other words, the destruction (to be a moment of unknown, to be a new homeland) has its own sculpting tools. It is in a way the 'deserting of subjectivity, the distancing of the individual who becomes a stranger to herself/ himself, who no longer recognizes anyone, who no longer recognizes herself/ himself, who no longer remembers herself/ himself' (Didi-Huberman 2018, 6) that allows other things to happen. The life of a creative in diaspora carries the potentiality of 'becoming', becoming a new being that is in constant transformation; hence the experience shifts from an ordinary dichotomy to a shifting pattern of exclusion and inclusion, old and new (Didi-Huberman 2018, 3).

A space between departure from one's homeland and arrival in a new land, a non-graspable experience of being, becoming and being suspended in a dark unknown: this is not simply about being visible or invisible, rather about being neither just one thing or another at any given moment in time, about being both things at the same time.

Regarding those immigrants in 1970s West Berlin, their new land embraced them in an unknown darkness; they were suspended somewhere in between the identity of their abandoned home country and their new adopted land. They were neither German nor Turkish/American/Pakistani and so on; rather, they were a combination of both, a form of being that is invisible yet substantive, non-descriptive yet fully sensational, reshaping who they are and shaping a new home for themselves in their adopted homeland, continuously moving through different stages of temporality.

In terms of Sohrab Shahid Saless's position as a creative exile, this is vividly reflected in his practice: his unique creative style, the notion of time that is played out in an inspirational yet disorientating manner in his work. His black-and-white films with limited dialogue actually have some parallel with the early silent films of the likes of American–Austrian–German Fritz Lang. Additionally, Shahid Saless's stylistic use of the camera, which pans out into a panoramic view in an exterior space and closes in in the interior, adds to the unease.

Shahid Saless's work reminds us once again that the world is a form of spectacle, stage or performance; it is, in a way, a panoptical stance in itself, which takes a position to observe. It is as if we are watching through a form of panoptic technology (surveillance) - a fetishistic principle of collection, display and the figure of panoramic time as a commodity spectacle (McClintock 1995, 123).

The following pages refer to Shahid Saless's *Time of Maturity* (*Reifezeit*, 1976) as a poignant example of film through which we can reflect on the notion of in-betweenness in creative exile, captured so well in the director's work generally.

THE SENSE OF HOPELESSNESS IN *TIME OF MATURITY*

Sohrab Shahid Saless's *Time of Maturity* patiently details the domestic coexistence of a mother and her son (Michael) in a desolate urban environment, inviting us to share in the boy's perception of their monotonous daily rituals and routines. There is little in the way of plot development - the action is circular, bordering on stasis - yet the film's inexorable rhythm draws us ever closer into this confined and unforgiving world, towards the son's slowly dawning understanding of his mother's nightly comings and goings – his coming of age. In fact, this chapter was mainly inspired by a single scene in the film (Michael on the staircase).

Shahid Saless, in an interview with Mamad Haghighat and Rahgozar, notes that 'the problem that always preoccupies me, whether I film in Germany or Iran, is precisely the antagonism between man and society' (Shahid Saless et al. 1999, 175). Not surprisingly, given this concern, Michael lives on the margins of society. He has no father but Shahid Saless notes that 'it wouldn't be any different if he had one. His mother is a prostitute who sells her body on a daily basis. No relationship exists between this mother and her child' (Shahid Saless et al. 1999, 176). There is a sense of hopelessness; Michael cannot be saved.

Figure 6.1 Michael hiding outside the neighbour's apartment. (Source: screen grab from *Time of Maturity* 1976.)

Shahid Saless says in the interview that he imagines Michael growing up to be a 'schizophrenic' (Shahid Saless et al. 1999, 175), like the character in his film *Diary of a Lover* (1977).

One of Michael's few activities is to do the shopping for an elderly blind woman in his neighbourhood and there is obviously no malice intended in one scene where he is shown playing an innocent 'ring and run' prank on the woman. In fact, we witness Michael in a rare playful scene, arriving at the woman's building, walking up the stairs, ringing the doorbell to the woman's flat and immediately hiding around the corner (Fig. 6.1). The woman opens the door but there is no one there; Michael stays hidden. Shahid Saless's camera all the time captures the scene from the staircase above. The woman closes the door, confused, and Michael makes his way down the stairs again, as quietly as possible, the camera following him and continuing to capture his mischievous joy. The most interesting aspect of the scene is that the camera remains at the bottom of the stairs until Michael disappears and then continues to capture the empty staircase without Michael on it for quite a long time. It is as if we, the viewers, need to remain to observe the empty scene devoid of characters or action.

The scene eventually fades into a different staircase, showing Michael again, walking up the staircase on the right-hand side. The interior is obviously different and we know this is not the woman's building. We do not see him

Figure 6.2 Michael arrives home. (Source: screen grab from *Time of Maturity* 1976.)

travelling between the two buildings; one minute we see him on a staircase in one building and the next he is on another staircase in another building. Finally, after seemingly walking up the stairs for an inordinate amount of time, he arrives home – he is in his own building.

This long, slow walk up the stairs is a technique used by Shahid Saless to let us (the viewers) closely follow and observe the minutiae of the journey of arriving at the door of Michael's apartment (Fig. 6.2). We believe that something exciting or surprising is bound to happen at any minute, as the scene is staged/filmed as if it is capturing an important moment.

Whilst nothing happens during Michael's ascent up the staircase, everything changes once he arrives at the front door and enters the flat he shares with his mother, for he finds her performing oral sex on a stranger in the corner of the room. The camera zooms in, showing the shock on Michael's face as he slowly puts his bag down without saying anything. He immediately leaves the apartment. Every step down the staircase is yet again masterfully captured, the dark staircase seemingly going on interminably as if Michael is making his way deep down into the depths of the building. The fact that the descent is so slow means that we are with Michael every step of the way; we feel close to him rather than being mere observers. In the basement, he sits down and puts his hands on his knees. He is scared and feels utterly alone. He desperately wants to feel safe. We acutely feel his pain.

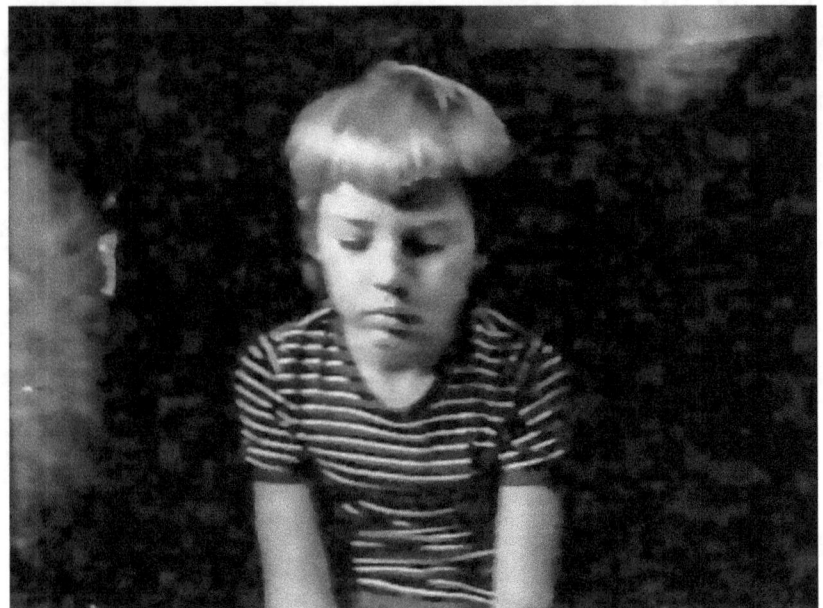

Figure 6.3 Michael sitting alone at the foot of the staircase. (Source: screen grab from *Time of Maturity* 1976.)

It seems as if, for Shahid Saless, the staircase is everything here. He captures it from different angles twelve times during the film for a duration of 28 minutes in total. At the end of this powerful scene with Michael, the camera patiently stays with the boy at the foot of the staircase for what feels like ages (Fig. 6.3). We are forced, by the position of the camera, to remain watching only minimal gestures from Michael, who is looking up the staircase and then looking down. The image fades out into darkness and that is the end of the film; the last image in the viewer's head is that of Michael's sad face as he finally understands the reality of his mother's life – his pain, his loneliness and his suffering.

Shahid Saless explains this devastating moment:

> [T]he viewer who leaves a screening of *Time of Maturity* falls prey to an obscure feeling. The film has affected him deeply and he ends up asking himself why. Why is it thus and not otherwise? The viewer must reflect and decide for himself upon leaving. (Shahid Saless et al. 1999, 177)

The director does not want to tell people what to think; he leaves it up to them to try to decipher their feelings.

It is apparent that there is a parallel between how Michael feels in *Time of Maturity* (also known as *Coming of Age*) and how Shahid Saless himself felt during his time in West Berlin in the 1970s, and various questions arise from the film for both of them. How is it possible to be at home in the literal sense of the word, yet feel lonely and excluded at the same time? How can one feel truly at home, feel a sense of belonging and of being safe (Michael)? What does creative exile mean for a filmmaker like Shahid Saless? How many locations need to be called home before one really believes one has found one? Within the current crisis in relation to borders and migration, could the transitory and ephemeral medium of the moving image be used to present a diasporic lived space? Shahid Saless's work certainly seems to capture this. What is it about his filmmaking that is so successful in this respect? Is it the length/duration of the film, the long shots, the silence? Is it perhaps the images appearing and disappearing on the screen in unexpected sequences (for example, Michael being in one building one moment and in another the next)? Perhaps it is through skilled storytelling that the viewer is made to wonder about what happens next for as long as their imagination will allow, as in the last scene where we witness Michael's profound sadness.

To analyse the question better, a good parallel or comparison would perhaps be Belgian director Chantal Akerman. Shahid Saless (originally from Tehran) was, as we know, part of the film diaspora in 1970s Berlin. His films typically depict poor and marginalised people, often immigrants. Akerman's work, on the other hand, was greatly inspired by the Jewish Eastern European diaspora, she herself being born to Polish Holocaust survivors in Brussels.[4]

Both Akerman's and Shahid Saless's cinematography is characterised by minimal, simplistic conversations which, together with a lack of metaphorical associations, create a very intense moment between what is (not) happening now and what is about to happen. The viewer remains caught in seemingly endless suspense, believing that something is surely about to happen. Both Akerman's and Shahid Saless's films are typically long (over two hours) and the experience is, therefore, excruciating. In fact, one ultimately realises that nothing is about to happen. Instead, a highly intimate voyeuristic dimension is created where the viewer feels that they are inside the film, closely watching the protagonists but not being seen by them.

Jeanne Dielman, 23 quai du Commerce, 1080 Bruxelles (1975) is one of Akerman's best-known films and chronicles a middle-aged widow's stifling routine of domestic chores - and prostitution. The film's constant long takes make the viewer experience the protagonist's drudgery in real time: from one uncomfortable slow-paced scene to another, from one routine moment of domestic activity to another, the storyline does not shift beyond the home and, in fact, remains mainly in the kitchen (Fig. 6.4). The amount of focus or emphasis that Akerman gives the story, though, makes it seem as though there is nothing more important than the mundane life of a lonely woman.

Shahid Saless, of course, also refers to prostitution in *Time of Maturity*, but through the eyes of a young boy (Michael) who witnesses his mother's comings

Figure 6.4 Domestic setting. (Source: screen grab from *Jeanne Dielman, 23 quai du Commerce, 1080 Bruxelles* 1975, by Chantal Akerman.)

and goings late at night. The family lives on the fringes of society, trapped in their poor domestic interior (mainly kitchen and living room), with a monotonous daily routine. The only exit from the building to the world outside is the long staircase that the boy walks up to go to school; the ascent seems interminable, as previously mentioned, and is repeated forty-two times in the film.

Shahid Saless's poetic depiction of the young boy's journey refers to a transitory moment on the staircase between the interior (home, hell) and exterior (the outside world, also a lonely, isolated place). Whether at home or outside, the boy is an outsider, never really present in or connected to his surroundings. He belongs (he is at home after all) and yet does not (he is simply 'there'), echoing Shahid Saless's own experience in Berlin: he was attracted by the avant-garde multicultural promise of the city and the New Wave Cinema in particular, but always struggled to fit in and did not enjoy the professional or financial success for which he had hoped.

Interestingly, in both Akerman's and Shahid Saless's films, the kitchen acts as a domestic theatre to showcase life at home. However, despite being a stage, suggesting some kind of show or spectacle, it actually displays the dullest of activities – waking up, getting up, having breakfast, getting dressed, eating, sleeping and so on, with some minor interaction in between. The interior of the house becomes extremely fetishised – but why, when it seems to depict such unremarkable events? The repetition of the same shots of the home shows how important it is, not just for the marginalised prostitute or widow but for the filmmakers too. The films start and end with a scene in the home and there are constant long takes of it throughout; this suggests a special relation or connection for the film directors, I believe.

Life as depicted in Shahid Saless's films is absolutely brutal, devoid of any intimacy or joy. His characters are typically struggling just to survive. It is not only the single mother working as a prostitute to provide for herself and her son (*Time of Maturity*). There is also the civil servant going through a mid-life crisis in *Order* (1980), and many other similarly hapless characters. As previously mentioned, the director's films are often long and so are uncomfortable for the viewer, who has to endure a sustained sense of pain, misery and suffering. In Akerman's films, human life is similarly full of isolation, sadness and loneliness.

In *I, You, He, She* (1974), Akerman refers to a woman (the 'I' in the title) who is dealing with a painful break-up and languishing in a small room with a single bed and a little table (Fig. 6.5). The film is very slow, uncomfortably so for the viewer (like *Jeanne Dielman, 23 quai du Commerce, 1080 Bruxelles*), as the woman does little other than move her furniture around the room, write letters to her lover and eat granulated sugar. Long shots pan from one side of the room to the other, capturing every excruciating moment of the woman's struggle. 'You' is

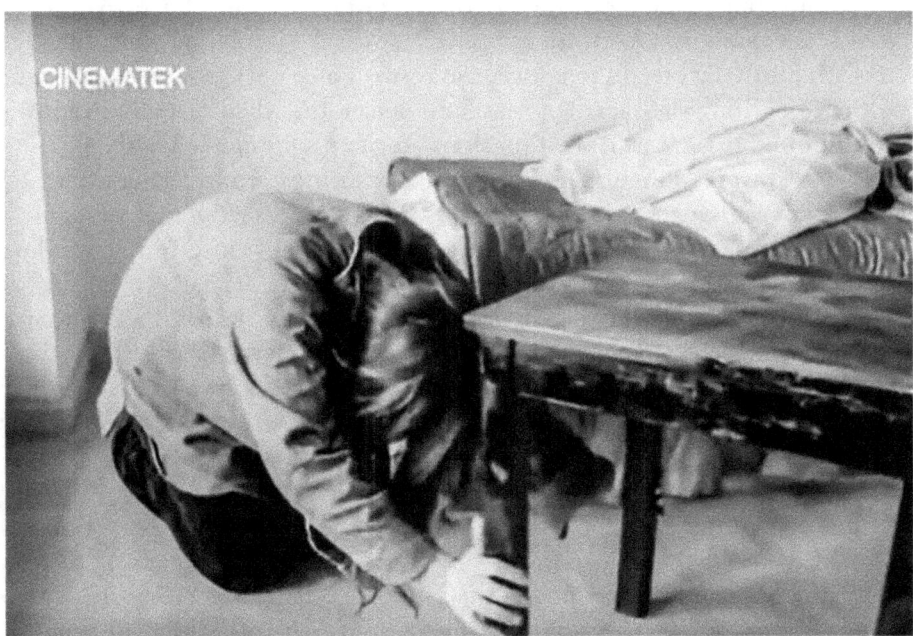

Figure 6.5 The lonely woman and her room. (Source: screen grab from *I, You, He, She* 1974, by Chantal Akerman.)

essentially the script; a voiceover narrates the woman's thoughts and inner turmoil. Her sugar exhausted, the woman finally leaves the flat. She meets 'He', a lorry driver she performs a sexual act on, who shares details of his marriage and sex life with her. 'He' takes her to the house of her lover (a woman, 'She'), who at first sends her away but later relents, feeds her and allows her to stay the night. The two make love. The title perfectly explains the plot of the film; there is nothing more to it than the long, slow depiction of a lonely woman's time, spent in self-inflicted solitary confinement and followed by her encounter with two individuals.

The simple interior of the room in *I, You, He, She*, with minimal furniture and decoration, is very similar to the homes depicted in Shahid Saless's films. *Still Life* (*Tabi'at-e Bijan*, 1974), for instance, portrays the simple life of an elderly man (and his wife), who has spent his life working as a railway guard at a quiet train station. The two are stopped in their tracks when a letter arrives, informing them of the man's impending compulsory retirement. *Still Life* is a powerful meditation on a life lived at the margins of a fast-modernising Iran, on a fragile old age and its disruption by modernity – and a broadside against Mohammad Reza Shah's grandiose rhetoric of economic development.[5] What is interesting here, and in keeping with the tone of Akerman's films, is how simple the interior of the husband and wife's house is; in particular, a single bed suggests a lack of intimacy and a brutal sadness arising from two people living together close to the poverty line.

Despite falling outside the 1970s framework set out above, *No Home Movie* (2015) is also worth mentioning, as it is a fascinating documentary consisting of conversations between Akerman and her Auschwitz survivor mother; the film was Akerman's last and her mother died just a few months after filming. It is clear in the film that Akerman's mother's health is failing and their conversations are largely mundane, boring even. Akerman spurned labels such as 'female', 'Jewish' and 'lesbian', and instead chose to identify herself very much as a daughter. She was extremely close to her mother, and *No Home Movie* is, not surprisingly, extremely intimate and personal (again, it becomes highly fetishised) – a homage to her mother perhaps. Akerman chooses to focus on domestic life centred on the kitchen (Fig. 6.6); there is a scene in which she shares potatoes she has prepared with her mother (domestic skill).[6] Her mother is obviously her creator; she gave her life. Beyond that, however, her mother gives her a sense of belonging and togetherness. As a traditional woman of her time, Akerman remembers her mother in the kitchen. When Akerman cannot be with her mother, she stays in touch with her by Skype from wherever she is in the world, these calls also being captured in the film. In this way, she retains that connection with home, despite being geographically far from it, which is the reality of life in exile. Akerman is trying to say that, even with distance, you know you belong to home (mentally, emotionally, biologically).

Figure 6.6 Conversation in the kitchen. (Source: screen grab from *No Home Movie* 2015, by Chantal Akerman.)

Returning to the questions posed earlier, by way of 'exiles' (plural), I am referring to the different displacements that Akerman (as well as Shahid Saless) went through. Born in Brussels, Akerman spent most of her adult life in Paris, where, in fact, she died. There were also periods spent in New York in the early 1970s and, again, in the early 2010s, when she worked as part of the faculty at City College of New York. These times spent away from home perhaps led to some reflection and evaluation, causing Akerman to redefine the meaning of identity, belonging and so on. It must have been challenging to have a strong sense of these concepts during these constant periods of adjustment and readjustment. Watching Akerman's films, I am constantly asking myself, what is 'home' exactly? For many of us in creative exile, telephone calls, Skype, photographs, images and so on often amount to a home of sorts. Akerman's films can be seen as a kind of vulnerable investigation of the link between private and public realms. It is not a happy place to be in, between the private and the public, acting as eye witness what is going on; in fact, it is a sad, lonely and isolated place.

Similarly, Shahid Saless studied in both Vienna and Paris. He then returned to Tehran, where he made documentaries for the Ministry of Culture. At the same time, he was one of the founding members of Iranian New Wave Cinema, and made *A Simple Event* (*Yek Ettefaq-e Sadeh*, 1974) and *Still Life* (1974). As mentioned above, he fled Iran in 1974, settling in West Berlin and expecting it to provide a more flourishing platform for his work. He did enjoy some success there, but continued to struggle to fund his projects and achieve any significant acclaim. He remained in Berlin until 1994, when he moved to Chicago for what turned out to be the last few years of his life. He died there, aged 54, from a chronic lifelong illness.

Shahid Saless's films are primarily inspired by his favourite writer, Chekhov, and poetically capture the life of marginalised groups of people. The typical eye-witness, simplistic and minimalist narration in Shahid Saless's films allows the viewer a close experience of the life of outsiders who have been shunned by society. The filmmaker's work does not seek to pass comment or judge; rather, it simply presents people and situations as they are, warts and all. In this somewhat detached way, we encounter colourful and fascinating characters: among others, the manipulative pimp in *Utopia* (1982) and the prostitutes in his brothel, whom he pits against each other to keep them dependent on him; the Turkish 'guest-workers' leading a grim life in Berlin in *Far from Home* (*Dar Ghorbat*) (1975); and the apathetic railway guard in *Still Life*, who has worked at the same desolate train station for decades. Akerman's filming style similarly relies on capturing ordinary life, as previously mentioned. By encouraging viewers to have patience and tolerate the at times painfully slow pace, both the work of film directors emphasises the humanity of the everyday.

Before ending this chapter, I would like to take the opportunity to reflect on the work of a third filmmaker, the Frenchman Romuald Karmakar, as I believe the continuation of Shahid Saless's work is profoundly evident in Karmakar's films.

POST-MIGRANT URBANITY IN ROMUALD KARMAKAR'S FILMS

Romuald Karmakar (Mandelbaum 2013, 108) was one of four artists (alongside Ai Weiwei, Santu Mofokeng and Dayanita Singh) to be invited to represent the German Pavilion at the fifty-fifth Venice Biennale in 2013.[7] Notably, none of the artists invited to represent Germany are, in fact, German (although Karmakar is German-born). Georg Fahrenschon, President of the German Savings Banks Association (the main sponsor of the German Pavilion), explained that the line-up reflected the complex and diverse cultural realities of today's Germany, a country shaped by international collaboration and intercultural exchange (Mandelbaum 2013, 51). Similarly, the curator of the German Pavilion, Susanne Gaensheimer, noted that 'on the cultural as well as social level, national affiliation and "Germanness" have become less than unequivocal in today's Germany, an immigration country' (Schiltenwolf and Müller 2013, 52).[8]

On the current complex question of identity and global migration, German journalist Mark Terkessidis has coined the interesting term 'post-migrant urbanity'. 'Cities have always been places of transit, junctions in an international texture,' he says (Schiltenwolf and Müller 2013, 56). Immigration has been happening for many decades already and any cultural articulation nowadays is naturally a consequence of this 'post-migration' or 'intricate history of striving for expansion, zones of influence, semi-dependencies, movement of population, and forced displacement' (Schiltenwolf and Müller 2013, 57). This echoes Avtar Brah's point, mentioned earlier, on diasporic spaces representing the interconnectivity of all these travellers coming from their respective homelands.

Born in 1965 in Wiesbaden (a small city near Frankfurt) to a French mother and Iranian father, Karmakar was raised by an adoptive Indian father. Karmakar moved to Munich in 1982, after a short time spent in Athens. He has been living in Berlin since 2000 (Schiltenwolf and Müller 2013, 108). Even though he was born in Germany, he retains his French nationality and refuses to take German citizenship, unlike Sohrab Shahid Saless, whose primary goal during his stay in Berlin was to secure permanent residence.

There are many similarities between the work of Shahid Saless and that of Karmakar, as is elaborated on in the next few pages. Crucially, whilst not an outsider as such, Karmakar skilfully employed the 'observer' look – the same fetishised quality of witnessing social reality that Shahid Saless possessed – and this is evident in his work. 'Karmakar fetches the apparent distance into immediate proximity and nonetheless lets distance develop again' (Schiltenwolf and Müller 2013, 60), accommodating multiple viewpoints to demonstrate that 'biographical, cultural, or political identity is related to larger, transnational conditions and circumstances' (Schiltenwolf and Müller 2013, 108).

Karmakar established himself as a filmmaker with a series of amateur Super 8 mm short films in 1984. His singular style became more pronounced when he produced his first feature-length film, *A Friendship in Germany* (*Eine Freundschaft in Deutschland*, 1985). The film was a prime response to the history of Germany, capturing a young Hitler (played by Karmakar himself) sharing a dull Sunday meal with a group of friends. The film is an homage to the filmmaker's adopted city, shifting between the contemporary view of the city of Munich and its nostalgic, dark history. It is narrated by one of Hitler's childhood friends (from Munich) and includes snapshots by Heinrich Hoffmann (Hitler's personal photographer). The soundtrack is an 'unbearable litany of German marches that endlessly fill the silence of repetitive eventless scenes of the film' (Schiltenwolf and Müller 2013, 109).

As clearly projected in *A Friendship in Germany*, Karmakar's main concern is 'a tireless evocation of violence as sickness that is simultaneously social and individual, such as that which resonates tragically in German history, and the subtle searching, between proximity and distance, for the link needed to represent this history justly' (Schiltenwolf and Müller 2013, 108). This, of course, is very much in line with Shahid Saless's work that captures life in Berlin in the 1970s, an eventless portrayal of isolated individuals in their slow process of everyday life.

Interestingly, Karmakar's work has been poorly received in Germany. In 2004, he produced his third feature-length film, which was lambasted by the German press. *Nightsongs* (*Die Nacht singt ihre Lieder*, 2004) is a depiction of an 'intimate and poisonous *huis clos* about a couple's separation, comprised of a perverse adult baby and a dangerous hysteric, adapted from a play by the Norwegian playwright Jon Fosse' (Schiltenwolf and Müller 2013, 112).

It had much political relevance. As French journalist Jacques Mandelbaum notes, 'minimal intuition would allow one to think that it was a precise dissection of political breakdown' (Schiltenwolf and Müller 2013, 113). Karmakar responded to the poor reception of his work at the Berlin Film Festival, saying he expected it as he was not German.

> I very quickly emancipated myself from my family's care and moreover I did not seek to adopt German nationality. Nor did I attend film school, which explains why I am not considered an insider. And yet, in Germany, a country that claims to be tolerant, criticism that comes from people who are considered foreigners is very poorly received. (Schiltenwolf and Müller 2013, 108)

Nightsongs is filmed in a middle-class apartment in Berlin. A failing marriage heading for divorce is captured in slow, minimalist exchanges, as if the film had been influenced by Shahid Saless's productions; the long shots of the staircase certainly resonate with Shahid Saless's style of filmmaking. A melancholic rhythm is created by the broken character of the husband, an unsuccessful writer who spends most of his days on the couch reading (Figs 6.7 and 6.8). There is a sense of hopelessness, that his life and his relationship with his wife cannot be saved. In contrast, the wife, obviously a more vibrant, outgoing person who desperately wants more from life, takes us outside the apartment, on a wild night out, every detail being enhanced through close-ups.

Silence is the overarching tone of the film, broken on occasion by the anger of the wife or the crying of the couple's baby. The impending separation is obviously a large part of the drama but there is also the miserable suffering of the two characters; we share their thoughts and this makes us similarly feel melancholy. The pause, silence, gestures of the wife, upset from the argument with her husband, in her taxi to the nightclub, echo the viewer's experience with Michael in Shahid Saless's *Time of Maturity*. Like Shahid Saless, Karmakar invites us to share in the couple's perception of their monotonous daily rituals and routines, conflicts, sadness, belonging, separation and failures.

THE AESTHETIC OF DIASPORA 117

Figure 6.7 The couple on the sofa. (Source: screen grab from *Nightsongs* (*Die Nacht singt ihre Lieder*), 2004, by Romuald Karmakar.)

Figure 6.8 The lonely man on the sofa. (Source: screen grab from *Nightsongs* (*Die Nacht singt ihre Lieder*), 2004, by Romuald Karmakar.)

Also like that of Shahid Saless, Karmakar's work, 'through its *mise en scène*, contains a desire to capture the power and fascination attached to the violence whose mastery, at the same time, it endlessly wants to puncture, analyse, dissect, and naturalize in its mechanisms' (Schiltenwolf and Müller 2013, 111). One might wonder what sort of violence could be portrayed in a Sunday meal or the separation of a couple behind closed doors, but the violence does not relate to fighting or screaming; rather, it occurs in the slowest of gestures floating in silence, the painful experience of witnessing an eventless life of isolation, and the portrayal of 'bodies and words, of gestures and languages that is brutal, ritualized, redirected, sophisticated, to the point that, subliminal, it exerts itself by pretending not to be there' (Schiltenwolf and Müller 2013, 108).

Karmakar can switch between genres, formats and media but his singular style of filmmaking remains evident in all his work. 'His objective seems to be to exhaust the approach, to multiply the ways into the unfathomable kingdom of violence' (Schiltenwolf and Müller 2013, 114). This is also the case with both Akerman and Shahid Saless, their unique imprint clearly on everything that they produce.

One might say that this preoccupation with violence and a sense of hopelessness or not belonging may have been the effect of many exiles or moves. Akerman, Karmakar and Shahid Saless obviously had to go through a number of transformations as they moved to various places around the world. Each time, they had to adapt to new people, surroundings, perspectives and so on. They became outsiders or strangers in their home countries, leaving behind customs, values and traditions, and adopting – or at least witnessing and being influenced – by new ones. The slow-paced, minimalist evocations of the everyday in their films speak forcefully to the traumas of displacement and migration, as mentioned above. I believe that the medium of the moving image here creates a form of temporary home; as the image appears on the screen and disappears, accompanied by a simple narration of everyday life, the viewer gets to experience, almost seemingly first-hand, everything that Karmakar, Akerman and Shahid Saless endeavoured to do - and suffered - through their exiles. My question remains unanswered – what is really a home and how does one know when one has found one?

NOTES

1. It was envisaged that this new workforce would contribute to what came to be known as the *Wirtschaftswunder* (Miracle on the Rhine), the rapid reconstruction and development of the economies in West Germany and Austria after World War Two. For more information see Manfred Wilke (2014, 191).

2. The whole of Europe, in fact, became more concerned with controlling immigration around this time. In 1957, the thirteen member states of the Council of Europe entered into an agreement regulating the movement of people between their countries, in particular tightening up what forms of identification would be accepted (R. Plender (ed.), in association with the AIRE Centre, 1997). For more information see Plender (1997, 301).
3. The Turkish presence in Germany actually dates back to the time of Fredrick the Great in the mid-eighteenth century, but it was after the guest-worker programme was established in the 1960s that Turks became the country's largest ethnic majority. Turks in Germany came to be defined as *ausländische Mitbürger* (fellow citizens) around this time but, for many, post-unification developments resulted in their demotion from co-citizens to third-class citizens (Taras 2012, 171).
4. For the sake of simplicity and to use the same socio-political timeframe for comparison, this text refers to works produced by Akerman and Shahid Saless in the 1970s.
5. For Mohammad Reza Shah's grandiose rhetoric of economic development see Suzanne Maloney (2018).
6. This echoes a potato-peeling scene in *Jeanne Dielman, 23 quai du Commerce, 1080 Bruxelles*.
7. Romuald Karmakar is actually French. There was an agreement at the 2013 Venice Biennale for France and Germany to swap and exhibit in each other's pavilions. Karmakar was joined by Albanian Anri Sala, for instance, exhibiting in the German pavilion as a French artist. Susanne Gaensheimer, Director of MMK Museum of Modern Art (Frankfurt), and Christine Macel, Chief Curator of the Musée National d'Art Moderne – Centre Pompidou, orchestrated this elegant card trick, designed to confuse nationalist attributions (Mandelbaum 2013, 108).
8. For decades, artists like Dayanita Singh from India and Santu Mofokeng from South Africa, to name just two of many examples, have worked with German publishing houses, printers and media technologies, collaborated with German collections and art institutions, and accepted offers to teach in Germany. No less remarkable is the fact that Germany has become a country in which artists like Ai Weiwei, who are victims of political persecution in their home countries, might find refuge. For more information see Schiltenwolf, Barbara and Müller, Markus (2013). *Deutscher Pavillon 55th International Art Exhibition Catalogue La Biennale di Venezia*. Berlin: Die Gestalten Verlag.

BIBLIOGRAPHY

Brah, Avtar (1999), 'Diaspora, Border and Transnational Identities', in R. Lewis (ed.), *Feminist Postcolonial Theory: A Reader*. London: Routledge.
Casas Ros, A. (2007), *Le Théorème d'Almodóvar*. Paris: Gallimard.
Didi-Huberman, Georges (2018), *The Eye of History: When Images Take Positions*. London: MIT Press.
Hochscherf, Tobias, Christoph Laucht and Andrew Plowman (2013), *Divided, But Not Disconnected: German Experiences of the Cold War*. Oxford: Berghahn.
McClintock, Anne (1995), *Imperial Leather: Race, Gender and Sexuality in the Imperial Contest*. London: Routledge.
Maloney, Suzanne (2018), 'The Revolutionary Economy', *The Iran Primer*, United States Institute of Peace, <https://iranprimer.usip.org/resource/revolutionary-economy> (last accessed 1 June 2019).

Mandelbaum, Jacques (2013), 'Romuald Karmakar', in Barbara Schiltenwolf and Markus Müller (eds), *Deutscher Pavillon 55th International Art Exhibition Catalogue La Biennale di Venezia*. Berlin: Die Gestalten.

Plender, R., in association with the AIRE Centre (1997), *Basic Documents on International Migration Law*. London: Martinus Nijhoff.

Schiltenwolf, Barbara, and Markus Müller (eds) (2013), *Deutscher Pavillon 55th International Art Exhibition Catalogue La Biennale di Venezia*. Berlin: Die Gestalten.

Shahid Saless, S., M. Haghighat, Rahgozar and T. S. Murphy (1999), 'This Isn't Pessimism: Interview with Sohrab Shahid Saless', *Discourse*, 21, 1, *Middle Eastern Films Before Thy Gaze Returns to Thee* (Winter), p. 175.

Taras, Raymond (2012), *Xenophobia and Islamophobia in Europe*. Edinburgh: Edinburgh University Press.

Wilke, Manfred (2014), *The Path to the Berlin Wall: Critical Stages in the History of Divided Germany*. Oxford: Berghahn.

PART III

The Stateless Moving Image

This part of the book confronts persistent problems concerning the archiving and transmission of transnational film, Shahid Saless's work being a case in point. 'Stateless' films – that is, moving-image works that belong to no single nation – present particular challenges for curators, archivists, researchers and film programmers, something that this section seeks to address.

CHAPTER 7

Curating the Nomadic: Film and Video at Ambika P3

Michael Mazière

I would maintain that art spaces have a duty to be demonstrably different from the kinds of public spaces dedicated to consumption that have invaded the centres of our cities. There, the displays take on some of the aspects of visual art in their seductive, tempting and luscious attraction. However, as presentations dedicated to a single end – individual purchase – there is a limit to their possible effect on our imagination and thinking. They are aesthetic devices at the service of a predetermined motivation and therefore at odds with any idea of artistic freedom, however compromised that now may be. (Esche 2004)

Ambika P3 was developed specifically as an experimental project space. Unlike venues such as museums, galleries and cinemas, the site had a multidisciplinary and industrial nature that enabled the research to operate at arm's length from both the physical boundaries of the white cube and the black box, and their ideological constraints. Ambika P3 opened in 2007, as the University of Westminster's space for international contemporary art and architecture, presenting a public programme of solo and group exhibitions, education projects, talks and events. It encourages a form of research through the development of new forms of content creation, and this is underpinned and evidenced by the multiple roles assigned to the space: for example, as a hybrid studio/production, space/exhibition environment, form of architectural screen, immersive environment, space of narrative encounters, site of discourse and site of pedagogy. Between 2007 and 2017, I commissioned and collaborated on a series of exhibitions that aimed to bring the distinctive elements of film and video installation to Ambika P3's project space in order to explore the form, theme and processes inherent to artists' film and video as a defined field of practice. In physical terms, the constituent parts of artists' film and video installation are the screen, time, space, image, projection and audience, which, added to the elements of the space, such as walls, height, light, scale and floor, provide the basic building blocks of these projects. Running in parallel and equally important is the curatorial engagement with identity, history and theory – which translates into an attention to the presentation of artists whose work was difficult to locate and had been often omitted by institutions because it defied dominant categories, slipped between the cultural nets or could not be easily monetised.

CURATING THE 'OTHER'

> At its best, the curatorial is a viral presence that strives to create friction and push new ideas, whether from curators or artists, educators or editors. This proposition demands that we continue to renegotiate the conventions of curating. (Lind 2009, 15–16)

Curation is a broad field, and in the contemporary context has become a catch-all phrase to encompass almost any aspect of life that involves some form of considered organisation. Evolving from the field of museology, curation was characteristically seen as a scholarly activity and/or an administrative concern. With the development of experimental forms of art, in the post-war period we see a shift away from museology towards the development of more specialist forms of curatorial practice, evolving to account for new forms of art such as performance, site-specific installation, public art and media-specific practice.

The process of producing an exhibition is usually divided into clear areas of commission and curation, design, production, delivery, installation and exhibition. Yet a substantial part of the exhibition programme at Ambika P3 has been developed through a variety of partnerships that question these boundaries. From the outset, Ambika P3 has been open to proposals and has actively sought individuals and organisations with which to collaborate from inside and outside the University of Westminster. Each of these relationships has been unique and tailor-made to suit the projects involved. From hosting and producing to curating, the degrees of cooperation have been broad and flexible. Examples range from partnerships with education institutions on PhD by practice (*AV PhD*, 2009)[1], and Art and Science Projects with the University of Cambridge (*Casebooks*, 2017),[2] to work with agencies such as Film London (Martina Amati's *Under*, 2015),[3] and collaborations with commercial galleries, such as Anthony McCall's *Vertical Works*[4] with Sprüth Magers Gallery (2011), and Chantal Akerman's *Now*[5] with Marian Goodman Gallery (2015) (Figs 7.1 and 7.2). These

FILM AND VIDEO AT AMBIKA P3   125

Figure 7.1 Seven-channel HD video installation of *Chantal Akerman, Now*. (Source: installation photo at Ambika P3 London, by Michael Mazière, University of Westminster 2015.)

Figure 7.2 Seven-channel HD video installation of *Chantal Akerman, Now*. (Source: installation photo at Ambika P3 London, by Michael Mazière, University of Westminster 2015.)

selected examples of Ambika P3's diverse and flexible partnerships were developed through both opportunity and planning, and delivered innovative and immersive exhibitions where space, site, material and collaboration operated as a matrix to be explored and tested.

FILM AND VIDEO

Ambika P3 is an effective site for the development of installation works in film and video specifically because of its physical qualities as a giant underground black box. Curating film and video work has been my field of practice/ expertise for over thirty years and one of the major strands of the curated programme at Ambika P3. During diverse curatorial projects I have interrogated artists' film and video and their relationship with installation art, experimental film, video art, expanded and narrative cinema, television and traditional fine art practices.

These curated exhibitions involved either commissioning new site-specific work for the space or adapting and developing existing artists' film and video projects. In separate exhibitions by Ward (*Rink*, 2009)[6] and McCall (*Vertical Works*, 2011), the cinematic apparatus of projection is scrutinised through its displacement to a specific experimental site. The manner in which *Rink* displaced the geometry of the cinematic apparatus by using the floor as a screen subverted the traditional architecture of the cinema and opened both a conceptual and a physical immersive space, within which audiences could experience the work. This developed the critical issues at play: namely, the construct of perspective, the illusion of identification and the lyrical possibilities of a non-linear abstract set of compositions. In *Vertical Works*, the only space defined is that of the projection beam, luring the viewer to engage with the work as pure material light. The works created a poetic world out of light photons and transformed the industrial space into a site of contemplation. Both works were experiential and provided a variety of forms of engagement for the audience – from visual pleasure and contemplation to more specific understanding of projection and its effect.

In Hall's *End Piece* (2012),[7] the different facets of site are explored through the sculptural aspects of video installation and the participatory context of broadcast television as social phenomenon. The commission was a contemporary reworking of Hall's early work, *1,001 TV Sets*, and formed the centrepiece of the exhibition featuring 1,001 cathode-ray tube TV sets of all ages and conditions (Fig. 7.3). The TVs were tuned to the five analogue stations playing randomly, which gradually ceased broadcasting between 4 and 8 April 2012 as the analogue signals broadcast from London's Crystal Palace were finally closed down. As the broadcasts ended, we were left with only the white noise of

Figure 7.3 David Hall's *1,001 TV Sets (End Piece)*. (Source: installation photo at Ambika P3 London, by Michael Mazière, University of Westminster 2012.)

a past order, now replaced with the dizzying and multi-platform, pay-as-you-go consumption of the contemporary moving image.

The curation/installation of film and video, alongside other art practices such as sculpture, performance, mixed media and interactive art, is examined in *Casebooks* (2017), questioning both its specificity and its ability to be curated alongside other media. This exhibition confirmed that while artists' film and video was previously a distinct practice, it is now firmly part of the ecology of contemporary art practice.

Victor Burgin's solo retrospective exhibition, *A Sense of Place* (2013),[8] enabled an examination of the relations between photography and video with particular emphasis on curating a trajectory through the body of his work. Through the building of nine separate gallery spaces, the exhibition mapped out a series of physical propositions for the interpretation of his work. Amati's *Under* (2014) provided design strategies on how to develop and transform a single screen work through the architecture of installation. *Under*'s layout created distinct spaces for the projection of art, studio and documentation material, guiding the audience through the distinct contexts of the project.

Now by Chantal Akerman (2015) focused on how curation can be used to configure the spatial manifestation of personal and political identity. In the mezzanine entrance was her earliest work, *In the Mirror* (1971/2007), a portrait of a woman looking at herself naked in the mirror. In the lower side of the space we fitted five works, and in the main space the new piece *Now* became the centrepiece of the exhibition and would be accessed last. This layout had the advantage of allowing the audience to have a beginning and end point, as well as a more open territory that they could navigate in a non-hierarchical manner. The architecture of the exhibition, designed in close consultation with Akerman, reflected her nomadic life experience and art strategies.

The approaches described above allowed the development of new plastic and installation languages particular to each project. Characteristically, this enabled a less object-centred form of exhibition in favour of interpretative itineraries for the work's reception. These prioritised the experimental, reflective and collaborative, many being open to the serendipity of the curatorial process, ad hoc solutions and the iterative development of ideas. The exhibitions also engaged with and were open to many voices, in particular those of the participating artists, curators and other stakeholders. For example, embedded in many of the projects and exhibitions was a form of critical practice that extended the curatorial into other educational and public platforms, which, through art, touches on social, political and historical issues.

The affiliations to academic institutions (the University of Westminster in this case) provide further opportunities for the curation of new contexts for the dissemination and explanation of creative practice, which other independent or commercial spaces might not be able to. These forms of site-specific project are not just confined to the commissioning of artworks and production, but extended by their placement within an academic institution, around which it was possible to develop further networks of collaboration and discourse through conferences, symposia, publications and other public events.

Examples of this engagement with research and critical practice can be seen in the various conferences and symposia attached to these projects. 'Exhibiting Video', a three-day event, brought together international artists, curators and writers – including Stuart Comer, Museum of Modern Art, New York City; Sean Cubitt, Goldsmiths, University of London; Shezad Dawood, Artist; Catherine Elwes, University of the Arts London (UAL); Solange Oliveira Farkas, Videobrasil, São Paulo; Marquard Smith, Royal College of Art, London; Stephen Partridge, Duncan of Jordanstone College of Art and Design; and Lori Zippay, Electronic Arts Intermix, New York City – to consider on what terms the rise of video in contemporary arts had taken place, how notions of medium specificity and site specificity shaped the exhibition of video art, and how museums and galleries understood video art.

Elizabeth Ogilvie's *Out of Ice* (2014)[9] exhibition was itself followed by the International Conference 'Reading and Exhibiting Nature', planned in association with the University of Westminster and co-hosted by the Universities of Aberdeen and Edinburgh, and Anchorage Museum, Alaska. This conference examined how people become attentive to nature in the world around them and how it is being understood in contemporary cultural and artistic production. With a focus both in and beyond the polar regions, it explored how people read nature, find meaning in nature, incorporate nature into social relations, and work with nature through art. Speakers included Tim Ingold, University of Aberdeen; Julie Decker, Anchorage Museum; Ronald Binnie, Edinburgh College of Art; David Dernie, University of Westminster; Dominic Hodgson, British Antarctic Survey; Jeremy Pataky, Anchorage Museum; and Geoffrey E. Petts, University of Westminster.

These works together represent a sustained curatorial engagement with the raw elements of film, video and installation, such as screen, projection, audience, light and object, as well as with the operations of site, projection, immersion, subject, the body, itinerary and identity. They remain the operatives that guide our relationship with the both the artist and their work.

NOTES

1. *Viva Viva – AV PhD*, 8–14 December 2008, Ambika P3. An exhibition of over a decade of completed audiovisual practice-based doctorates from all of the UK. In partnership with Goldsmiths, University of London, University of Westminster, Brunel University, Birkbeck College, Royal College of Art, Royal Holloway, Manchester Metropolitan University and University of Ulster.
2. *Casebooks*, 17 March–23 April 2017, Ambika P3. Six contemporary artists and an extraordinary medical archive, Jasmina Cibic, Federico Díaz, Lynn Hershman Leeson, Rémy Markowitsch, Lindsay Seers and Tunga. Produced in partnership with the University of Cambridge and supported by the Bodleian Libraries, University of Oxford and the Wellcome Trust.
3. Martina Amati - *Under: A Multi-Screen Film Installation on the Art of Freediving*, 26 September–11 October 2015. Exhibition produced in partnership with Film London and the Wellcome Trust.
4. Anthony McCall – *Vertical Works* (*Breath*, 2004; *Breath III*, 2005; *Meeting You Halfway*, 2009; and *You*, 2010), 1–27 March 2011.
5. Chantal Akerman – *Now*, 30 October–6 December 2015. The first large-scale exhibition in the English-speaking world of Akerman's installation work. In partnerships with A Nos Amours and Marian Goodman Gallery.
6. David Ward – *Rink*, 4–22 November 2009.
7. David Hall – *End Piece*, 16 March–22 April 2012, including *1,001 TV Sets* (*End Piece*), 1972–2012; *Progressive Recession*, 1974, and *TV Interruptions* (seven TV pieces).
8. Victor Burgin – *A Sense of Place*, 1 November–1 December 2013, including *Voyage to Italy* (*Basilica I & II*) (2006); *Olympia* (1982); *Solito Posto* (2008); *The Little House* (2005); *Mirror Lake* (2013); *A Place to Read* (2010), *UK76* (1976); *Zoo78* (1978); *Portia* (1984); *In Grenoble* (1982); *Hotel Latone* (1983); *Gradiva* (1982).
9. Elizabeth Ogilvie - *Out of Ice*, 17 January–9 February 2014. Scottish environmental artist Elizabeth Ogilvie portrays the psychological, physical and poetic dimensions of ice and water in *Out of Ice*, a vast immersive installation specially created for the subterranean spaces of Ambika P3.

BIBLIOGRAPHY

Esche, Charles (2004), 'What's the point of art centres anyway?', *Possibility, Art and Democratic Deviance*, <http://transform.eipcp.net/transversal/0504/esche/en.html> (last accessed 17 October 2019).

Lind, Maria (2009), 'The Curatorial', in Liam Gillick (ed.), *Art Forum International*, <https://virt-sem-app.fbkultur.uni-hamburg.de/VSA-SS13/Lind_The%20Curatorial%2057-66.pdf> (last accessed 1 June 2019).

CHAPTER 8

A Certain Tenderness

Gareth Evans

It is widely appreciated now that curation, to do justice fully to its concerns, must remind itself, at all stations on the journey from idea to auditorium, of its etymological origins in the Latin, *curare*, to care. A certain tenderness needs to accompany its aesthetic–historical–philosophical research. The attention one gives must be not only academically and culturally active but also humane. The forms that this might take cross the borders of encounter, between the work selected and its renewed home in the world, amongst all of those required to enable such a passage, and between the work and its expectant audience.

While there should never be a lack of ambition in this undertaking, in terms of desired reach, it feels appropriate to retain a modesty in presentation, a humility, a lived acknowledgement of one's own 'care-taking', at a given moment, for a particular purpose, event, venue and assembly. In other words, expectations around scale, finance, institutional and promotional considerations should not be assessed as the determinants of 'success'. Rather, rigour, a precise passion, a grace and honesty in the showing and support – whether to forty people in a studio cinema or speaking with five over post-screening drinks – seem more reliable indicators in enabling a lasting resonance, a committed passing of the baton of enthusiasm to those new to the films, artworks and ideas presented.

Such an approach feels particularly relevant when considering how the works of Sohrab Shahid Saless might circulate now. Acclaimed within festival networks for his features and, with his German public television films inevitably very widely viewed (in comparison to attendances for world cinema) at the time of broadcast, it is nevertheless true that Shahid Saless remained properly known in any larger sense only to a few. The importance, therefore, of the 'Exiles' retrospective and this volume is self-evident.

However, the image culture in which his œuvre now finds itself, one so radically transformed from the period of its making in terms of production, distribution and exhibition, does not automatically *guarantee* a wider or more enduring reception, regardless of the numerous platforms available. The fact of its survival and retrieval is the first and absolute achievement. Without that, nothing is possible. The longer struggle to secure Shahid Saless within a lineage of Iranian, German and international cinema – at a time when canons (against or within which one might be placed) of any hue are turning deltaic, losing their singularity and branching into multiple tributaries – and when the very medium itself is losing its cultural significance as a central informant, is an altogether different enterprise.

For this writer, the 'statelessness' of Shahid Saless's life and work is much less of a curatorial or archival challenge than others might feel. The experiential reality for a great majority of people globally now is almost entirely in alignment with the spirit and sensibility of the maker and the made. Ours is an era of mass statelessness, exile and displacement, whether topographically, politically or psychologically, among much else.

In this sense, all who feel or have become like this are kindred spirits, fellow travellers, comrades to Shahid Saless, perhaps more in number now than ever, whether they know his films or not. Works that might be 'marginal' in the 'official' estimation are core to an understanding of our times. Their importance is hiding in plain sight. 'Minority' makers, nomadic or refugee or otherwise forced into mobility, are the carriers of the signal tales, lighters of the beacon fires. *The edge is where the centre is.*

It is two writers – ardent internationalists – who come most acutely and relevantly to mind here, with their signature solidarity to such populations and such individuals as Shahid Saless. *A Seventh Man*, written by John Berger (and with photographs by Jean Mohr) from inside exactly the Germany of Shahid Saless's own arrival, is a praise song of resilience and resistance for the *Gastarbeiter*, the non-European arrivee, scored with the same angry melancholy (Figs 8.1 and 8.2).

And, in that vein, how can we not also think of W. G. Sebald? Born a month earlier but in the same year as Shahid Saless, himself in creative exile from his birth nation and destined to die far too young, also in his fifties, Sebald speaks to the emigrant sensibility so profoundly, and with the same shared eye for the telling detail and a pitch of apparent calm and engaged depth, that one can only wonder if he ever saw any of Shahid Saless's films. They would both have turned seventy-five in the summer of 2019.

Finally, and in light of the above, we appreciate that life, when tested, turns (or turns into) poetry, towards a lyric density, a compacting of experience into an expression that encompasses sorrow and joy at once, twin sides of the same blade. In that spirit, and informed by a record of the Berlin that Shahid Saless would have known, the following is offered, in gratitude and appreciation, for

A CERTAIN TENDERNESS 133

Figure 8.1 *Gastarbeiter*. (Source: photograph by Jean Mohr 1975.)

Figure 8.2 *Gastarbeiter*. (Source: photograph by Jean Mohr 1975.)

all his work has given us, and to all those involved in bringing it back off the shelves and gifting it to the light.

RENDEZVOUS

>From the milk pale body of curtained rooms

to the body in its labour
clown-face in coal
in oil and steam
in a terrible kiln
on the exhausted bench
making and unmaking the known
looming
on knees
cleaning
emptying
cleaning
emptying
unending as the bricks

between work and the wall lies the wall
walls everywhere the walls

why must we decide ourselves by wounds?

Sunday light
on other days

is a burnished sack of air
we carry to the furthest yard
we can
before it spills

sometimes Sunday light
on Monday still

a still in secret
distilling
the ways out

the earth beneath the ground and then the earth
above it

press

but let us

let us now repair

what do they mean

the things we found and found again

while we waited for the years

to do their worst and then
so tired
to try and do their best

really how

what do they mean

let us repair them while we can

the little bright angel waiting by the gate to the derelict garden

the little dazed angel we carried back on splints of broom

the hand urging us that way not this

the knot of a face

the dog on three legs trying to scent its way in

the rubble and the war buried under it

the wind between the blocks

one or two thin trees

the guilt in the eyes and the joy
in the laced fingers

the abandoned caravan – oh its amputated wheels

the car that turned into a wall and
the wall that turned into a child

the face that searched for directions for
a way out for
the man and the other man who
actually lived

the trolley piled with scraps of the future

the two women who stopped
and are still there

the little girl who inherited her
eyes from a time long before

the razor still sharp after everything
they had seen

the fellow whose cuffs didn't work and whose hair wanted to leave

the wall that stared at another wall

the working until the lamp gave up and gave
out
and then more
work
this time
the labour of the dark

the sitting right down in a bath of smoke

the holding a dog to the chest like a heart that just happened to
live outside the body

the almost not being able to breathe

the way the hoardings faded but the memories didn't
the way the memories faded but the hoardings didn't

the little man who could just reach the keys

play me something

the shadow of this house on that house

the bed that is never made or unmade

the reflection of the mirror in a shard of water

the thing in the eye no tissue can remove

the place where the road is the destination

the trying to sleep in real night

the drum of one stick waiting for the other

the glass that does not end

the feet that have stopped dancing

the frozen kiss in the wasted alley

the shape of someone sleeping in the bottles

the headless embrace

the mouth that finds the laughing breast

everything one has and nothing
in return

the cosmos of a body on the collapsed sofa

the large tongue that seeks and is found

the stick figures on the door and the stick figures on the street

the cart race without corners

the fading price of silver and of gold

the harvest of crosses in the shadow of the wall

the entire history of a glance
and the sight the century fashions out of tears

the gun barrel luminous as tar

the play gun in the mouth of a cellar

the boys who will always be boys

another gun or the same gun

the leg in the sun-drained window

more smoke building itself
floor
by
floor
out of the ruins

the man and his hat together
on a bench in all the leaves
of the year

the little inky dark angel in its colonnade of lights

a bottle woman gazing at a bottle woman

hands that can touch the past

the coffin of *not yet ready*
of one last
       look
              back

the old Order car with ash on its tyres

a man made faceless with his urge

something like desire emerging out of plaster

'the origin of the world'

semaphore of a dancing arm in air

the wooden horse of landfill slowly rocking
to a stop

* * *

If we ever leave

on the last train out
past the frayed end of the clock
it is for flood-fields
and the solitude of a single bed somewhere between sky
and sky

while trees whisper their beginning
to the fire
and brush their rings
against the mist

and all the things that are
find themselves as close as skin
across the sunken pastures

and while
in the harvested grain of the uncoloured months
a figure from snow approaches a house
stacked out of winter

* * *

so always
and
again
from the milk pale body of curtained rooms

to the body in its labour
clownface in coal
in oil and steam
in a terrible kiln

on the exhausted bench
making and unmaking the known
looming
on knees
cleaning
emptying
cleaning
emptying
unending as the bricks

and as passing

and as strong[1]

NOTE

1. A response to photographs from Gundula Schulze Eldowy (2011).

BIBIOGRAPHY

Eldowy, Gundula Schulze (2011), *Berlin in einer Hundenacht/Berlin on a Dog's Night*. Leipzig: Lehmstedt.

CHAPTER 9

Statelessness as Practice: Sohrab Shahid Saless and the Work of Exile

Pierre d'Alancaisez

'Statelessness as Practice' is based on a fundamental question: would Sohrab Shahid Saless see his work succeed or fail in the cultural landscape of media, galleries and commentary today? By exploring ways in which contemporary practitioners have situated themselves in and against the lived reality and ideas of statelessness and displacement, and how the reception of such constructions by the art world and cultural society has developed since Shahid Saless's time, this chapter offers a new perspective for contemporary debate of archive, moving image and curatorial practice. Considering the cultural gap between the audiences that Shahid Saless found in Germany and his own heritage, this essay suggests possible motifs in some of the major trends in curatorial practice over the last decade that have led to the foregrounding of statelessness in public displays such as screenings and exhibitions. Bringing these ideas together, this chapter concludes by considering how curatorial strategies play out against the creative production considering a constant need for 'new', or the ongoing activity of national or regional promoters. The text looks at some developments in distribution channels such as galleries and digital platforms that were not available to Shahid Saless.

SHAHID SALESS'S HISTORY

In the early 1970s, Sohrab Shahid Saless was internationally recognised as a pioneer of a new wave of Iranian cinema. However, as a filmmaker who had joined the ranks of the European filmmaking avant-garde, he turned his attention to German society, producing films that focused on the lives of outsiders and outcasts. The 1976 *Time of Maturity* (*Reifezeit*), the story of a boy coming of age next to his prostitute mother, marks a turning point in the young director's ascendant career.

A desire for mainstream success would hardly mark Shahid Saless out, were he a German-born filmmaker. By the early 1980s, even a number of the signatories of the radical 1962 Oberhausen Manifesto were beginning to enjoy international recognition, with the likes of Volker Schlöndorff and Wim Wenders eventually establishing Hollywood practices. In a sense perhaps best symbolised by the phrase *Film ist Kultur* - which could well have attracted a capital *K* even without German orthographic rules - the German cinematic avant-garde became the mainstream.

With time, Shahid Shaless's personal mythology came out of alignment with his filmic interests. Recognised initially for work that brought images of Iran or Turkey on to the European screen, his later œuvre divorced itself from nationality and assumed an insider's view on German society. Deciding to be a *filmmaker* and not an *Iranian filmmaker in exile* meant that Shahid Saless had to forego the reputation and support he had enjoyed as an *Ausländer*.

THE ART WORLD SINCE THE 1990S

The tensions in the film career of Sohrab Shahid Saless have some parallels in the more recent histories of visual artists since the early 2000s, including those whose practices involve the moving image. The increased currency of contemporary art within mainstream Western culture (here *culture* with both a lower-case and capital *c*) has rendered space and created intellectual demand for work that approaches issues of displacement, statelessness and exile. Not only has a desire for news from elsewhere made it possible for artists to develop transnational careers in a mode analogous to Shahid Saless's early experience, but the proliferation of art institutions and the unstoppable expansion of the art markets have made some of these practices commercially viable and integral to the mainstream.

At its inception, contemporary art's regard for 'foreign' art practices was market-driven. In the 1980s and 1990s, European auction houses tried to develop demand for Russian art, and soon after shifted their import focus to South Asia. These attempts were met with limited success, as domestic European and American artistic production was still only freshly fulfilling the expectation of *the shock of the new*. Conceptual practices like those of Young British Artists did not need to look far past the local or personal to secure a place in the newspaper headlines or to break sales records.

After the end of the Cold War, Western democracies indulged in narratives of a unipolar international stage: conflicts and changes sweeping through parts of the Middle East did not palpably mix with domestic news agendas preoccupied by the evolution of neoliberal capitalism. In a dramatic rift, the 2001 terrorist attacks on New York played themselves out as though specifically for the media, and the advent of rolling news and internet communication focused the attention of Western audiences on the international. These tools allowed society to observe and critique the effects and complexities of globalisation in real time – and contemporary art practice followed suit.

In the past two decades, the Western European art world's appetite for this idea of otherness and alternative modes of expression has been almost inexhaustible, with world events regulating both supply and demand. For example, the twentieth anniversary of the 1989 fall of the Berlin Wall saw coordinated efforts by cultural funders on both sides of the Iron Curtain to facilitate engagement with twentieth- and twenty-first-century art from the post-Soviet block. Marketplaces like Vienna reinforced their position linking Western European collections with Eastern European artists and their legacies, while the expansion of the European Union in 2004 gave rise to countless spotlight exhibitions in old Europe's art institutions, which were 'discovering' the art of previously isolated nations. Later, the events of the Arab Spring, combined with the growing importance of the affluent parts of Middle East as markets for contemporary art, shifted the attention of art institutions on to those geographies. Most recently, the academically driven attempts to decolonise Western tools for understanding non-Western cultures, and public attention to Europe's migration crisis have given rise to deeper visibility of the contemporary art practices of Africa, the Indian subcontinent and Asia. This rapidly developing demand has allowed artists, whether practising in their non-Western domicile or in the 'exile' of the international art world, to devise structural techniques for sharing narratives of cross-border peril or nostalgia.

Artists have made work commenting on displacement with a range of motivations. For some, such practice reflects on their own lived experience of exile and the circumstances leading up to it: for example, in Mounira al Solh's *I Want to Be a Party* series of drawings and embroideries, which collect family anecdotes from the Lebanese war. For others, like Bouchra Khalili in her 2008–11 *Mapping Journey Project*, which tracks the geographical movements of individual migrants trying to settle in Europe from North Africa, observation of statelessness and its conditions is an intellectual or political exercise. For others still, migration and exile offer opportunities for a particular type of voyeurism or sensation - arguably so in the monumental 2017 *Law of the Journey* by Ai Weiwei, which renders a dinghy, such as those seen on the Mediterranean, together with a dozen faceless figures, as an oversized rubber inflatable. The boundaries between these types of practice are not always clear, and in the interlocking discourses of post-colonial theory, identity politics and market trends they can become further blurred. Despite this complexity, galleries and museums have been increasingly keen on displaying works that pay attention to the troubled idea of the nation-state and the individual caught in or out of its boundaries. Alongside, contemporary art has adopted the documentary as a mode of expression, and this has helped moving image media to enter exhibition spaces and to receive attention from audiences. A glance at institutional exhibition programmes announced on the platform *e-flux* reveals a plethora of titles like *No Place - Like Home* (Argos, Brussels, 2008), *Asylum* (Bielefelder Kunstverein, 2016) or *It is Obvious from the Map* (Redcar, Los Angeles, 2017), all creating platforms for artists' film. Experimental and participatory practices are also growing in institutional acceptance and at points have found their ways into commercial structures. The refugee mutual-support network Silent University, initiated by Ahmet Öğüt, has attracted support from multiple institutions, including Tate Modern, and received recognition from the Visible Award. For the artist Christoph Büchel, it was a commercial gallery that brought some of his most ambitious projects - for example, turning a space in London's Piccadilly into a community centre - to fruition where museums have struggled.

MOTIVATIONS

The following examples of artistic practices map out some of the ways in which the ecosystem of galleries, museums and collections have been prepared to support intellectual, research and production attitudes to issues of exile or migration, and also indicate a range of artists' motivation for engaging with such work. To draw fast links between conceptual desires and market or institutional success may be cynical, but certain patterns make themselves apparent.

The artist drawing on personal experience of exile or conflict has at their disposal an emotional and intellectual genuineness, and this offers an opportunity for audiences to engage intimately with first-hand experience. Rabih Mroué's work, for example, has been deeply affecting to its viewers, combining, as it does, theatrical proximity and intellectual rigour. Mroué has been deliberate in the choice of platforms for his practice, aligning himself with research institutions and avant-garde festivals. Characteristic of such an approach is an absence of reference to otherness and resistance to exoticisation. Through their personhood, the artist transcends geographies and brings a subjective experience that sits on a par with that of his or her viewers.

Artists can take on statelessness as a social cause, directing their work as indictment or call to action. In documentary mode, as in the example of Oliver Ressler, artist film and video tend to expand in long form on stories and images already familiar to their audiences from the news. But where, in reportage, a news camera's presumed impartiality enforces distance, here the artist's subjectivity welcomes a viewer's own. The same subject matter is rendered more universal still through a prism of abstraction: Libia Castro and Ólafur Ólafsson, for example, quite literally translate political maxims into graphic shapes or music. A broad range of art institutions (except for the most commercial outposts) have been supportive of such work, and in recent years a conviction that art practice can overcome the limitations of other political action has prevailed.

The most problematic to situate are practices that use notions of statelessness or exile for their intrinsic otherness or conceptual appeal. As individuals, Slavs and Tatars can claim some limited personal experience of life in the turbulent international political arena, but in their practice they take on ideas representing a range of ethnic and national groups to which they have only a tangential connection. It could be claimed that the work profits from emphasising the otherness of its subjects, while at the same time proclaiming the unity of cultures or drawing attention to under-represented narratives. In more extreme examples, Artur Żmijewski's filmic visits to refugee camps could be seen as exploitative, while Ai Weiwei's Kurdi photograph resulted in a significant backlash (see below). Nevertheless, these artistic approaches attract attention and commercial success, arguably by creating spectacle and inviting audiences to participate from a comfortable distance.

RABIH MROUÉ

The Beirut-born artist Rabih Mroué began his career as an actor, playwright and director. In the aftermath of the Lebanese civil war in the 1990s, Mroué's early experimental work in theatre, film and installation combined political urgency and intellectual innovation, and quickly gained recognition from international theatre, film and art institutions. To audiences outside Lebanon, Mroué's works, like *Three Posters* (an evolving lecture performance that examines the role of the body in political and religious martyrdom) or *The Pixelated Revolution* (a participatory installation composed of first-hand mobile phone images of fighting and death in Homs, Syria), offered an insight into societies torn apart by conflict by means that are at once intimate and voyeuristic. The 2008 *Je veux voir*, a collaboration with artist–filmmakers Joana Hadjithomas and Khalil Joreige, in which Mroué stars alongside Catherine Deneuve, is perhaps the starkest example of the economies of exile (Fig. 9.1). In the film, the French star (playing herself) tours war-torn Lebanon with Mroué (playing himself) as guide. By 2012, Mroué's work was exhibited at Documenta, in *Manifesta*, at HAU 2, Berlin, as well as myriad independent arts institutions, and is represented by a commercial gallery in landmark events like Frieze Art Fair.

Figure 9.1 Rabih Mroué and Catherine Deneuve in *Je veux voir*. (Source: Joana Hadjithomas and Khalil Joreige, photograph by Patric Swirc 2008.)

Mroué's practice has consistently attracted engagement from its audiences. Given the complexity of the Arab world that the work depicts, this is testament to the sincere approach that the artist deploys towards his subjects. A degree of solidarity is implied in both the making and the reception of the work. Installations like *I, The Undersigned*, 2007, in which Mroué publicly apologises for his role in the civil war, show the artist connected to his place and people.

CASTRO AND ÓLAFSSON

The very notion of statelessness itself drives the practice of artists Libia Castro and Ólafur Ólafsson, whose manifesto campaign, *Your Country Doesn't Exist*, has taken the form of film, performance, publishing, billboards and murals, as well political action, resonating with local sentiment wherever staged. Castro (Spanish) and Ólafsson (Icelandic) are in no way stateless themselves, but had an opportunity to develop their conceptual approach to issues of migration in the early 2000s while settled in the Netherlands. At the time, the Netherlands seemed a cultural land of plenty that boasted 'open' borders and enviable funding opportunities for artists of all provenances. Key to the artists was their participation in Van Abbemuseum's 2008 research and exhibition project, *Becoming Dutch*, which placed questions of geographical privilege and nationhood at the centre.

Figure 9.2 *Your Country Doesn't Exist*. (Source: Libia Castro and Ólafur Ólafsson, *Do It Yourself*, 2015.)

Castro and Ólafsson's works combine first-hand accounts by refugees, as, for example, in the *Bosbolobosboco* series (amorphous sculptural structures composed of rags and packaging tape that serve as listening posts for oral histories), and abstract iterative political thinking in the *Do It Yourself* projects (inviting Icelandic state ambassadors to execute a painting-by-numbers to reveal the slogan 'your country doesn't exist') (Fig. 9.2). The artists presented *Your Country Doesn't Exist* as an operatic performance on a gondola at the 2011 Venice Biennale, a public-realm campaign at the 2012 Liverpool Biennial, and in multiple further manifestations in dozens of institutional exhibitions across Europe. Their film works, like *Caregivers* (2008), highlight the exploitation of Southern Europeans by labour markets in the service of the economies of the north. These have been featured on the art-film festival circuit, and have also gained the support of museum and private collections.

Castro and Ólafsson's political stance may appear unusual: at first glance, their works do not sympathise with the individual, but instead call out the notion of the state as bogus. As action, their stylised and often aesthetically humourous works have not been without wider impact: a project that the artists created in collaboration with Australia's refugee communities for the 2014 Sydney Biennale contributed to the resignation of the event's chair, whose business interests were implicated in human rights abuses at the Manus Island refugee detention camps.

SLAVS AND TATARS

The collective practice Slavs and Tatars describes itself as a 'faction of polemics and intimacies devoted to an area east of the former Berlin Wall and west of the Great Wall of China known as Eurasia'. The group's output comprises visually appealing objects that often incorporate multilingual slogans or visual puns, performance lectures on geopolitical and cultural events, and publishing with distinctive graphic design qualities. At the group's core are a Pole and an Iranian–American, and the contentious histories of their 'home' regions have nourished the practice as much as the linguistic diversity and untranslatability of the cultures.

Slavs and Tatars' work is not rooted per se in personal experience of exile, but explores the meta-fictions of nationhood or regional or ethnic identity. Many of their works point to the glibness of prevailing narratives, as, for example, in the series of mirrors and etched text *Nations* (2012) (with slogans like 'Nice tan, Turkmenistan' or 'Men are from Murmansk, Women are from Vilnius'), or to the insuppressible desire to be marked out as 'particular' that is active in these cultures (*Make Mongolia Great Again*, 2016). At the basis of the practice is a question of the usefulness of nationalistic or culturally exclusionary boundaries to anything other than hegemonic control.

The combination of accessibility of the visual works and the charisma of the theoretical arguments put forward by Slavs and Tatars has won them substantial international recognition, and the artists have participated in numerous biennials (Sharjah in 2011, Venice in 2013), and held solo exhibitions across much of Western and Eastern Europe and the Middle East (from Trondheim Kunstmuseum and CAC Vilnius to SALT Istanbul). Their work was subject of a special project, *Love Me, Love Me Not*, at the 2013 Venice Biennale, was shown in Art Basel's signature section *Statements* in 2012, and continues to attract the attention of art institutions and private collections across the regions.

Slavs and Tatars' practice brings together meme-making and intellectual discourse, and seeks opportunities both to emphasise and to collapse notions of the exotic or foreign. The work appears driven by exhibitionism, as, for example, in *Monobrow Manifesto*, 2010–11, which contrasts the facial hair of a Persian prophet (hot) with that of *Sesame Street*'s Bert (not). The strategy of presenting highly polished and surface-level treatment of histories, cultures and conflicts in the exhibition practice gives the work instant recognition and creates access to platforms for deeper engagement in parallel.

OTHER ARTISTS

Plenty of other visual artists have chosen statelessness as a subject in perhaps reactive or opportunistic fashions. Europe's recent migration crisis has provided ample opportunity for observation and mediation of humanity in displacement, and this has aroused the interest of the continent's art institutions.

The Polish social provocateur Artur Żmijewski created *Glimpse* in 2017. The series of video portraits was filmed in the Calais 'Jungle' and Berlin Tempelhof refugee camps, presented at Documenta 14 in Athens. In 2016, Ai Weiwei, renowned for his own dissidence and forced exile, recreated a press photograph depicting the death of the three year-old Alan Kurdi on a beach near Bodrum. More traditionally filmic or documentary practices, such as that of Austrian video artist Oliver Ressler, take on migration in works like *There are No Syrian Refugees in Turkey* (2016), and gain audiences just as readily as the artist's investigations into issues of climate change or financial markets.

FILM IN GALLERY CIRCLES

In parallel with a sustained appetite for work of and on exile, the infrastructure of galleries and museums has significantly expanded its support for artist film and video, and has sought ways to incorporate moving-image work into public programmes and collections. By the 1990s, specialist institutions supporting artist video work were prolific around Europe. In Germany, festivals like Videonale pioneered the distribution of artists' work within contemporary art structures, while ZKM, the centre for art and media in Karlsruhe, established itself as a 'Mecca for media arts'. In the UK, organisations like London Filmmakers Co-operative and its successor, LUX, have worked to carve out a productive space for artists working outside traditional cinematic funding structures. The past decade has seen strong representation of film practices on mainstream platforms: flagship events like biennials now routinely include substantial amounts of moving image on a par with other media.

With this proliferation of opportunities for screen-based work to reach contemporary art audiences, public acceptance of film in museums and galleries has been developing steadily, although not uniformly. The most commercial of circles, like art fairs, have not found sustained ways to promote film or video art, but this has not stopped galleries from trading in the material.

The relationship between film and art film has also become more bilateral. Artists working with film have found it possible to break into mainstream cinema: Steve McQueen, the Turner Prize-winning artist represented by high-profile commercial galleries in New York and London, made his big-screen mark with films like *Hunger* and *12 Years a Slave*. Conversely, contemporary art platforms have looked to traditional cinema for content: for example, the feature-film work of a leading figure of New German Cinema, Alexander Kluge, was featured prominently in a landmark exhibition *The Boat is Leaking. The Captain Lied* at Venice's Fondazione Prada in 2017, and the 2018 Turner

Prize shortlist included the documentary and feature filmmaker Naeem Mohaiemen alongside three other artists working with film and video. Overall, the conceptual space for film work has expanded significantly, with boundaries between documentary, feature and experimental film eroding, while artists and filmmakers have been able to move with new ease between funding structures and distribution channels.

IF SHAHID SALESS WERE WORKING NOW

To imagine a career path for Sohrab Shahid Saless in the cultural markets of today is at best idle fancy, but the filmmaker's struggle in the realities of 1970s and 1980s Germany is at considerable odds with the breadth of opportunities his work could have been met with now.

Shahid Saless's signature treatment and choice of subject matter were not controversial: personal and psychological drama, and society in the shadow of World War Two fall in line with other filmmakers' preoccupations at the time. There is little in his films that would have marked him out as 'other' or *Ausländer*, and still less that could have been incomprehensible to German audiences. In reality, however, Shahid Saless's films had little chance of resonating with popular German audiences or building the commercial success the director desired. *The Long Vacation of Lotte H. Eisner* (1979), for example, is a series of interviews with film critic and co-founder of Cinémathèque Française Lotte Eisner, a project whose cinema-on-cinema insularity is inescapable. The later *Utopia* (1982) is a compelling human drama that is none the less demanding of viewers with its 200-minute running time and the inescapable emotional suffering of its characters. While lacking market appeal, these works were, in a sense, perfectly orthodox, and a couple of decades later their forms could have found comfortable homes at the crossing of film and visual art. Indeed, the recent revival of interest in Shahid Saless's œuvre has been driven by research that spans film, media and art histories.

The success gap between Shahid Saless and his fellow filmmakers is therefore perhaps more indicative of the director's personal motivations and attitudes than his work per se. Shahid Saless appears to have struggled with the expectation that he would continue his thematic associations with Iran and take on the role of an exiled Iranian artist, a brand that, ironically, could have gained in relevance alongside Iran's troubled role in international politics. The desire to assimilate into the German *Kultur* rather than the cult and to abandon his Iranian associations may well have cost Shahid Saless his rightful place in the history of cinema.

CHAPTER 10

Screening Sohrab Shahid Saless's Work: Contemporary Perspectives

Dario Marchiori

This chapter deals with the topic of curatorship, applied to the case study of Sohrab Shahid Saless. It explores specific issues at stake when working on a transnational author, from an economic, geopolitical and ideological point of view. Possibly, the general frame of the art of curatorship happens to be film history as such, so that a strong articulation between academic work and cultural policy has to be made to understand the significance of screening the films made by Sohrab Shahid Saless.

Among the tasks of a film curator, one of the main issues is to allow people to discover or rediscover great movies that have been forgotten or repressed, and to share them with a larger audience. Such a mission may seem to be obvious, but it can be overshadowed by different drives as well as by topical trends or institutional constraints. While he/she is always and necessarily negotiating with existing institutions and between various demands, even a freelance curator tries to maintain an independence from them. Working on a single filmmaker is rather common in institutions like *cinémathèques*, in the tradition of Henri Langlois retrospectives, huge programmes showing the largest number of films by an individual filmmaker (according to the *politique des auteurs*). But curators need to face another issue, linked to his/her very reason to exist: the making of a programme as a hermeneutic proposal – another path that is very important if we are to understand, for instance, Langlois's work. Programming as a gesture – that is, film curatorship – will be based on ideas, feelings and even chance, which allow the audience to establish links between various films. In a word, making a programme may be a form of 'montage', from the curatorial point of view and/or from the point of view of the audience. When working on a single author, the active role of curator seems to disappear but another risk arises, which needs to be confronted. I could call it the 'identifying temptation': that is, the tendency to appropriate the author's œuvre, at best because of a strong theoretical idea of it or an outstanding knowledge of it. No matter how justified this is, because that temptation may be a strong drive to fight for a retrospective to exist, it may preclude an effective share of the interest in and appreciation of lesser-known authors. That risk is most real when working on rare filmmakers.

We may establish a parallelism here with contemporary art curatorship, in which the creativity of the curator has often been misunderstood as challenging an artist's authorship. For sure, the art world has provided some models to define the curator's work, according to the sociological position of the curator, to his/her links to contemporary artists, to the way he/she intends the activity of a curatorship as a creative one. Such an issue has provoked debates in curatorship, among curators, and between curators and artists: for instance, the French artist Daniel Buren differentiated curators as being *authors* or *interpreters*, thus underlining the various places for creativity. Some conflicts arose – in the 1960s and 1970s, for example – when curators-as-authors emerged who were no artists, like Lucy Lippard or Harald Szeemann (who qualified himself as an *Ausstellungsmacher*, or 'art exhibition-maker'). Therefore, in the field of art as well as in the domain of film screening, there is a paradox in the curatorial approach. He/She may be considered too intrusive or, on the contrary, too self-effacing and unstimulating. The art field is a model in questioning the relationship between the artist and the curator, while the institutional and economic network is quite different from film curatorship. From our point of view, it allows us to understand the work of programming films as – potentially – an art: the art of film curatorship, a complex gesture negotiating with various issues and constraints.

Such opening remarks may seem strange to introduce a short contribution to a book that enshrines contemporary interest in a great filmmaker like Sohrab Shahid Saless. Nevertheless, they are important for understanding the issues involved in screening his work, and beyond that, for considering the questions at stake for contemporary scholars in reconsidering his work just now. In fact, there are quite a lot of similarities between different cultural and socio-economic areas such as critical activity, academic research or screening practices, which the example of Shahid Saless permits us to explore. The perspective here will be a dual one: on the one hand, the author of these lines is writing as a scholar[1]; on the other side, he is speaking as an episodic curator, having screened, introduced and discussed some of Shahid Saless's films.[2] Beyond such institutional duality, the correlation and the common issues within contemporary practices of rediscovery in research *and* in curatorship will be studied here. While contradicting traditional divides, such a link also constitutes a new sociological approach because some curators are now working as teachers and scholars, and a few scholars make film programmes.

Some personal remarks seem to be necessary here, to explore the subjective drive towards Shahid Saless, establishing a third, non-institutional dimension of my approach to his work. The discovery of his films comes from cinephilia and an urge to collect films and curiosities, akin to the one studied by Walter Benjamin through, for instance, Edward Fuchs. Exploring lesser-known domains of film history, I developed an interest in cinema as a whole, beyond any typological or chronological boundaries, and due to the way ideas circulate beyond those boundaries. Shahid Saless's work has particular aesthetic qualities for me, while claiming it to be realist and anti-formalist. His poetics shows a forgotten path to film aesthetics, one that challenges preconceived notions in film theory and criticism. The film form in his work, from both a narrative and a stylistic point of view, is strongly coherent, introducing a huge range of variations on the same themes: his mix of tenderness and roughness, his general attention to rhythm, his original way of shooting essential aspects of everyday life – a place, a body, a look, a simple gesture. The most interesting paradox, to me, is the fact that the more simple, realist and impersonal you are, the more peculiar, formally engaging and perhaps personal you may be. A small detail alienates me through its formal qualities and focuses my attention on the concrete world, while stimulating my imagination, which surrounds and supports the images and sounds I experience. Ultimately, the director shows the viewer the very potential of film as a medium and intensifies our perception of reality. None of these aspects is linked to a specific cultural or sociological context, but their concrete materialisation in films is historically determined within a specific geopolitical transnational horizon. Such general issues, while being a way to consider humanity in general, are able to reveal, through the greatest sensitivity to the smallest details, some particularities in Iranian and German societies. Definitely, Shahid Saless is not only a transnational filmmaker, but also a key filmmaker for film history, and such a firm conviction is the precondition to the remarks that will be developed here.

The renewal of interest in screening the work of a filmmaker who has been rather forgotten for a long time has to be questioned. To start with, let us consider some reasons for this oblivion. Firstly, there is the biographical one: that of an Iranian filmmaker leaving his country to find a better environment for his art, in Europe and then in the USA. As we know, exile is not a simple matter to deal with in film history (with some noticeable exceptions, like the German–Jewish filmmakers fleeing from Nazism). Moreover, such a biography is not easy to understand in a Cold War context because it does not match with a polarised geopolitics. A second reason is the œuvre itself. Shahid Saless's very first works – around twenty-two shorts on different aspects of Iranian culture and folklore – happen to be part of the Iranian documentary tradition and had no transnational reach (to date, only one of these films has been screened: *Black and White*, 1972). After that, there are two Iranian films that achieved international circulation, mainly in the Federal Republic of Germany, thanks to the Berlinale, but were more generally appreciated because of the New Iranian Film wave from the 1960s and 1970s: these were *A Simple Event* (1974) and *Still Life* (1974). Both films are more likely to attract the interest of an Iranian transnational audience, while German films usually seem to have less appeal for migrated communities because of the language and setting.[3] In fact, the German part – the main part – of Shahid Saless's œuvre is divided into those movies aimed at a national and international public (mainly in the early years) and others made for a local or national circuit, mainly produced by and broadcast on TV channels in West Germany. To make a 'retrospective' out of such a complex and heterogeneous situation as this is, to some extent, to do violence to history, and even to film history, but also to do justice to Shahid Saless's own dream of being an acclaimed international auteur. That is a third difficulty to deal with: how to make sense out of it.

To sum up, film history has difficulties to negotiate with such auteurs, which defy traditional divides like Oriental/Occidental cultures, national film styles, production centres in contrast to more peripheral sites, and the geopolitical background during the Cold War. Shahid Saless's œuvre is disseminated in different countries (Iran and the Federal Republic of Germany) and in different places (he had various producers in West Germany), and by different institutions (film and/or TV).[4] Such a complex filmography also generates huge issues in curatorship because of archival difficulties and the negotiation of rights. In fact, there are film copies in Iran and in the German national archives, but also ones that are buried somewhere in the German TV archives, presenting complexities with rights and being rented only as Beta SP videos, while existing in 16 mm. This corresponds to a more general policy followed by European TV archives, distributing only video copies for TV broadcasting but also for film screenings: that implies that the quality of the copies may be quite poor, but it is sometimes better (or, rather, is poor in a different way) than old 16 mm copies. Moreover, the conditions of rental for TV broadcast may sometimes be quite complex and expensive. In the last few years, some institutions, like the Filmmuseum München, have tried to centralise more copies of Shahid Saless's films, but the question of rights still remains quite complicated and needs to be cleared for each film.

Last but not least, there is the question of subtitling, even if there is little dialogue in Shahid Saless's work. This is another quite important difficulty for curatorship because the price of translation, the making of subtitles (one or two lines of text with a limited number of characters) and their projection under the film copy in a cinema are quite expensive operations, and such costs have to be added to the rental fee and the clearing of film rights. Most of his films, being in German, do not present particular difficulties for a German audience, but there are few subtitled copies, and these are mainly in English.

During the last few years, Internet communities and passionate *cinéphiles* (for instance, the Karagarga community) created English subtitles for quite a few of Shahid Saless's films, making it possible to share the director's work more widely. This voluntary work has to be praised because it is a deciding factor in sharing films with a larger non-German audience. In any case, some screenings were also held without subtitles: for example, *Hans – A Young Man in Germany* (1985) in the Brussels Cinematek, such an international city allowing the freedom to show not only French or English (or Dutch) subtitled copies, but in this case a German film without subtitles. The same occurred in Paris for *The Willow Tree* (*Der Weidenbaum*, 1984), but with the inclusion of an introduction and a debate explaining what needs to be understood during the few dialogues in that particular film; on the same occasion, photocopies of the short tale by Chekhov that inspired Shahid Saless were given to the audience for reading before the screening. Once again, the specific work of the Iranian author, with his modern rarefied dialogue and the great importance given to bodies, movements, rhythm and gestures, made it a little simpler to screen some of his films without subtitles or with reduced costs, thanks to the assistance of volunteers and enthusiasts. This aspect is quite paradoxical because the singularity and modernity of his work make it a little simpler to show in particular cinemas or *cinémathèques*, as it allows a certain screening context to be created when it is accompanied by enthusiasts giving clues, discussing the work and making it acceptable to the audience.[5]

All these difficulties are well known to the film curator, in particular when he/she is trying to make audiences rediscover an author's work. In some ways, it was the Internet that allowed a remediation in both senses: a new chance to circulate Shahid Saless's work, and a new medium to experience it, mainly for domestic use. There has been a Shahid Saless revival among new generations of cinephiles, who are using the Internet as a way to discover new films and to make new constellations of auteurs. Such a way of circulating films goes far beyond commercial distribution (VHS, DVD, blu-ray or video on demand) and challenges traditional views on film history, classically mixing economic, geopolitical and socio-cultural hierarchies with personal attempts to valorise and canonise films responding to other criteria. The digital era condition may be a premise to new conditions for curating film programmes, but it weakens the conditions necessary for creating an audience because the movies seem to be available on the Internet, within a different apparatus to that in the cinema. The 'post-medium condition' generates, more exactly, 'remediations' through new media, and scattered screening conditions. The main political issue of new forms of cinephilia is divided between private reception (for individuals, couples or families) and new, quite ephemeral links, through Internet 'communities' (blogs, forums and so on). A screening is always in the present tense, be it the socio-political or the actual screening experience in a cinema. In fact, this is a peculiarity of film as a medium, which we perceive as a present experience (Roland Barthes or Christian Metz already stated this with respect to that question). The film screening, then, seems to be the best way to give a collective and philological actuality to the film history. On the other hand, the cultural policy of film programming needs to be as independent from commercial pressure as possible, defending a cultural policy that may offer a possibility of representing new interpretations of film history, new authors (and the rediscovery and re-interpretation of 'old' ones) and new constellations of films. Such a commitment may make it possible to establish a real link between the critical work of film scholars and the cultural policy of film curatorship, be it made by scholars or not.

Coming to transnational film works, the contemporary context is quite propitious for considering auteurs who have an internationally complex career. Since the 2000s, post-colonial and transnational studies have explored this new perspective, with many important results and discoveries, including some internal paradoxes or contradictions in post-colonial (many now prefer 'decolonial') and transnational perspective themselves. This may explain the reawakening of interest in Shahid Saless, but it brings together two main risks: firstly, such studies could not last (as the recent notion of 'decolonial' demonstrates, contesting the 'post-colonial'); secondly, Shahid Saless may just be used as another example for testing a general theoretical approach, and nothing more than that. Both risks join a more general issue, deeply linked to contemporary capitalist consumerism, which is the need for new products that are both original and obsolescent. In such a context, both the experience of collectively watching a movie that is already available on YouTube as a digital shared file, and the initiative to prepare a book on his œuvre that will last are very important, 'untimely' and concrete actions, in so far as they modify the perception of what cinema may be, and of general film history.[6]

The main issue for film history seems to be to consider the stylistic originality of a work, and to understand it through its cultural, geopolitical and economic context, but without historicist determinism. In other words, when defending an aesthetic understanding of film history, the main point is to consider the aesthetic qualities of the films to be screened. Aesthetics is not only the evaluative theory of canonical beauty; from a contemporary perspective, it is also the study of perceptions and judgements we can make relating to an artwork. For sure, that leads us to reconsider aesthetic value itself, including oppositional aesthetics like the 'imperfect cinema' of Julio García Espinosa or the 'aesthetics of hunger' of Glauber Rocha. Shahid Saless is a specific case because of his radical synthesis of classicism and modernity, of formal obsessions and singular narratives, of minimalist and radical mise-en-scène. His work is not specific because of the filmmaker's diaspora (on the contrary, we may be surprised that he kept such constant devices in plot and style), but it is so because he is an original author – while in contact and in dialogue with other original authors. Such a shift in accent is crucial and allows to reconsider Shahid Saless with regard to film history in general.

This is also the main way really to consider marginalised films and to be respectful to them. In other words, we ought to rely on their inner qualities and to understand them according to their specific context. Be it an Iranian diaspora or a Black American filmmaker, the main thing is to consider him/her as a filmmaker and for his/her work, not only because of his/her community and identity. This means that books on specific filmographies – such as one we may imagine on women filmmakers in South America – are, beyond their undoubted interest, not so effective from the point of view of general film history. We know such periods of infatuation, as was the case for non-aligned Eastern European cinema in the 1960s, or following a more general post-Soviet narrative during the 1990s. After following a long-term path to 'unthinking Eurocentrism' (Shohat and Stam 1994, 63), many studies on different authors, communities, nations and transnational constellations are left, but there have been few attempts really to modify general film history and to challenge its perception in the public sphere. Screenings and public debates, or meetings, then, seem to be the most important point of convergence between the public sphere and the experience represented by specialised curator/scholar/cinephile communities.

To conclude, as delighted as we may be about such a renewal of interest in Shahid Saless, it is still important to be clear about its context and implications. Trying to give a more general theoretical apprehension of it involves considering more general issues for cinema and for film studies, from the curatorial and the academic points of view. As an auteur trying to transcend cultural divides and creating his style out of that situation, Shahid Saless reminds us of the importance of art and culture as international (rather than 'transnational') practices in which mainstream geopolitical, economic and cultural differences are displaced and articulated in specific ways. When another Iranian migrant, Hamid Naficy, argued for the notion of 'accented cinema' (Naficy 2001), he aimed for a more general notion valorising stylistic and narrative tendencies that were common to many creative filmmakers of various origins. If Naficy, among others, left behind the idea of creating a link between these filmmakers (since then, he has worked mainly on Iranian cinema and television, and on its cultural issues for exiles), the path he showed us seems to be a decisive one for a better understanding of Shahid Saless and for making him dialogue with other great filmmakers. Films do exist on their own, and their singularities are the condition according to which they may exist for different peoples and make them feel, think and imagine. Just like history in general, film history has been written by the victors, and it is not enough just to reverse it. The strength of singularities within a plural film history needs to face up and object to the actual distribution (Rancière 2000) of economic, geopolitical and cultural divides. Film history and film as a medium need Sohrab Shahid Saless's films for a better understanding of how their potentialities may unfold in our times.

NOTES

1. As a lecturer at Lyon 2 University, my income is institutionally due to the activity of teaching and scholarly research.
2. Together with Stefanie Bodien (a freelance programmer), I screened a movie by Shahid Saless within a retrospective about lesser-known New German Cinema from the 1960s to the 1980s ('L'"autre' nouveau cinéma allemand' at the Brussels Cinematek, June 2015). We then organised a retrospective on Shahid Saless that featured eight films (Cinematek and Goethe Institut Brussels, June 2017). I also organised a three-film homage to Shahid Saless in Paris, with the assistance of the Goethe Institut there (January to March 2018).
3. As I was able to experience while showing Shahid Saless's films in Paris, for instance.
4. Exceptionally, a 16 mm copy of *Ordnung* received international distribution through the Goethe Institut network.
5. I am thinking about Stefanie Bodien supporting each screening (even the reruns) in the Brussels Cinematek, or Azadeh Fatehrad and Nikolaus Perneczky introducing screenings and leading debates in London.
6. A third and crucial aspect may be added: that is, the subjective experience of the single spectator, which I consider of equal importance to the other two points but of which I cannot speak, other than attesting to the success among the audience of screenings that I attended, and the enthusiasm of some spectators.

BIBLIOGRAPHY

Naficy, Hamid (2001), *An Accented Cinema: Exilic and Diasporic Filmmaking*. Princeton: Princeton University Press.
Rancière, Jacques (2000), *The Politics of Aesthetics: The Distribution of the Sensible*. London: Continuum.
Shohat, Ella, and Robert Stam (1994), *Unthinking Eurocentrism: Multiculturalism and the Media*. New York: Routledge.

Interview by Behrang Samsami (Journalist) with Bert Schmidt (Shahid Saless's Cinematographer)

'IT WAS AS IF IT WAS AN OPEN AIR STUDIO'

Sohrab Shahid Saless: he is one of the most important figures in modern Iranian film, and nowadays a real unknown quantity in New German Cinema. Saless was born in Tehran in 1944 and died in 1998 in Chicago; he spent his whole life working as a transnational screenplay author and director. During the 1960s, he studied film production and drama in Austria and France, and shot numerous films for cinema and television, as well as documentaries in Iran, the Federal Republic of Germany and the former Czechoslovakia. He then moved to the USA in the 1990s but was not able to produce films there. Since 2016, retrospectives in cities including Berlin (2016) and Munich (2017) have meant that the work of this award-winning Iranian filmmaker, who had been unjustly forgotten in Germany, is now being rediscovered, as well as discovered for the first time.

Two films, which Saless produced and which the following interview is about, were either predominantly or completely filmed in the former Czechoslovakia: *Hans – A Young Man in Germany* (*Hans – Ein Junge in Deutschland*, 1985) was produced in the spring and autumn of 1983. Saless based this black-and-white film on the 1977 novel, *The Blue Hour* (*Die blaue Stunde*), an autobiographical work by the author Hans Frick (1930–2003). Hans, the protagonist, lives in Nazi Germany with his mother, a factory worker, and his seriously ill grandmother in Frankfurt am Main. The family experiences the war years here: bombs fall, forced labourers are dragged through the streets and neighbours harass the boy. And the reason for this? Hans's father, who he does not know, is a Jew – so both mother and son live in fear of denunciation. When Hans sees Gestapo in front of the apartment, he flees the city and manages to survive until he is intercepted by incoming American soldiers.

INTERVIEW

Figure In.1 A break in filming: actor Josef Stehlik and director Saless. Saless is partially covering the written slogan on the Slovakian production company's car: 'Slovenská filmová tvorba Koliba Bratislava'. (Source: photograph by Bert Schmidt 1984.)

The Willow Tree (*Der Weidenbaum*) was shot in the spring and summer of 1984 and is a film version of the short story of the same name written by the Russian writer Anton Chekhov, which was first published in 1883. Archip, an old man, sits by the water fishing and observes a stagecoach driver, who passes him every day, killing a postman who was transporting money and hiding the bag containing the money in a hollow willow tree. The old man takes the bag and goes into the city with it to denounce the crime. Here, he is sent from one office to another.

Bert Schmidt, an author, filmmaker and producer, was involved in the production of both *Hans* and *The Willow Tree* as Sohrab Shahid Saless's assistant director. In a conversation with Behrang Samsami, with whom he is currently working on a book about the life and work of the Iranian director, Bert Schmidt reflects on the time he shared with Saless and the conditions under which both films were shot in communist Czechoslovakia in the mid-1980s.[1]

Behrang Samsami: Bert, you got to know Sohrab Shahid Saless in 1979. How did that happen?
Bert Schmidt: In mid-March 1979, my colleague Dieter Reifarth was making a retrospective about Saless's work – which at the time was less extensive – at the Communal Cinema in Frankfurt where he was the programmer and which is now the Deutsche Filmmuseum.

Figure In.2 The exterior shots for *The Willow Tree* on a tributary of the Danube on the Slovakian–Hungarian border. (Source: photograph by Bert Schmidt 1984.)

At that point, Saless had not been in a position to produce any projects at all for two years. Then he came to Frankfurt. I already knew his films. We got talking and discovered that we had studied at the same private film college in Paris, although I had been there a few years later. I asked him whether I could work for him as a director's assistant. He agreed immediately. In the autumn of 1979, when he was living with me, he wrote the screenplay for his film *Order (Ordnung)*. During the day he worked on this, and in the evening Dieter Reifarth and I kept him company. But Saless was so independent in his ideas when it came to aesthetics and dramaturgy that we were only able to discuss it to a limited extent. It was of course always his own story that he was telling. He was a film author.

In January 1979, the Shah left Iran. Ayatollah Khomeini returned to the country. Soon afterwards, an Islamic Republic was declared.

The events in Iran preoccupied Saless, but he did not want to return under any circumstances. At least, not initially. Many of his acquaintances, who, like him, were left-wing, went back at that point, only to come back to Germany disappointed, as they had come to the realisation that the clergy held the upper hand.

In 1983 and 1984, Saless shot two films in what was at the time the part of Czechoslovakia that belonged to the Eastern Bloc: *Hans – A Young Man in Germany* and *The Willow Tree*.

Figure In.3 Behind the scenes of *Hans – A Young Man in Germany*. At the table: actor Hans Zander (who played the SS man, Martin Weiss) and director Sohrab Shahid Saless. Behind Saless: the Iranian cameraman Ramin Reza Molai. (Source: photograph by Bert Schmidt 1985.)

Schmidt: Many intellectuals from the Third World – and I am including Iran as it was at that time – harboured sympathies with the Soviet Union back then and saw Moscow as a protective power. Of course, they were not confronted with the GDR and the Stasi, but saw a glimmer of hope for their own country in the East.

Samsami: Where did filming take place in the Czechoslovak Socialist Republic?

Schmidt: *Hans – A Young Man in Germany* was originally meant to be filmed in Frankfurt, in the original quarter of Gallus, a former industrial and working-class area. However, residents were resistant to the filming taking place. It was also difficult for the production designers to portray war scenes, as this area of the city had become too modern in the mean time. The Hessische Rundfunk, the regional public service broadcaster of Hesse, which was producing the film, searched for alternative locations and finally found one in Czechoslovakia – at Studio Koliba in Bratislava. It was much cheaper to shoot the film there, and we also found Ostrava to be a city with very German characteristics; its architecture would not have been out of place in Frankfurt. I went along on the location recce to Ostrava in late autumn 1982. It was ideal – it was as if it was an open air studio. We filmed in a redevelopment area in the middle of the city, which was quite run down – just like it would have been during wartime. We were able to use several streets and didn't have to dismantle or conceal anything.

Samsami: In *Hans*, the cast includes local actors and *The Willow Tree's* cast is exclusively local.

Schmidt: We cast over one hundred extras in Ostrava and filled minor roles. Again and again I witnessed how Saless had a really keen sense for finding exactly the right person for a particular role. That was also the case for the actor who played Hans. The young actor, Martin Paško, was naturally talented. His acting was one-for-one – meaning that we shot the scene once and it was a wrap. As the actor was Czechoslovakian and could speak no German, we had a colleague specifically in charge of guiding the actor. He translated the director's instructions. We also cast students in the film from African countries who were studying at a mining university. They played US soldiers in *Hans*.

Samsami: What were the production conditions like? Was any censorship involved?

Schmidt: No. Our Czech colleagues were simply co-producers. The Hessische Rundfunk was in charge of the project. There was also no plan to show *Hans* in the Czechoslovak Socialist Republic. Studio Koliba was simply providing a service.

Figure In.4 On the film set: Sohrab Shahid Saless and Bert Schmidt, his assistant director. (Source: photograph by Bert Schmidt 1985.)

During the same period, Miloš Forman's *Amadeus* was also being filmed in Prague. A couple of scenes from *Hans* were also shot in Germany. A delegation of actors and technical staff therefore came from Czechoslovakia for this. Collaboration with them was very professional. They were very loyal colleagues.

Samsami: Let's talk about *The Willow Tree*, which was produced by Radio Bremen and a Slovakian film company.

Schmidt: Chekhov was Saless's favourite poet. He made a film about his life in 1981. Saless had various projects. He wanted to make a film of the novella *Der schwarze Mönch* (*The Black Monk*). However, this never came to fruition. *The Willow Tree* is a very brief story, which Saless recounts in 90 minutes. Saless communicates the slowness and the torment of existence perfectly. Jürgen Breest, who was head of television plays at Radio Bremen, was very impressed. But right from the beginning it was absolutely clear that the film wouldn't be shot in Germany. Saless therefore used his contacts in Slovakia. We filmed the exterior shots for the film around 80 kilometres east of Bratislava on a tributary of the Danube on the Hungarian border; the scenes which are shot in the city were filmed near Poprad, at the base of the High Tatra mountain range. I would also like to mention the actors: both Josef Stehlík, who played the old man, Archip, and Peter Stanik, who played the coach driver, were excellent.

Samsami: *List z Kábulu, A Letter from Kabul* in English, is a film which Saless filmed for Slovakian television and which is barely known.

Schmidt: In 1984, Saless remained in Slovakia after *The Willow Tree* had been edited. He had also met a young woman at the time. He was a well-regarded guest in the ČSSR, because his world view was 'right'. In 1985, he came to West Germany to film *Changeling* (*Wechselbalg*), which was based on a story by Jürgen Breest, and then returned to Czechoslovakia. It must have been 1986 or 1987 when *A Letter from Kabul* was made. Back then, Saless flew to Soviet-occupied Afghanistan with a Slovakian film team.

Samsami: What is it about?

Schmidt: A boy called Mahmud writes a letter to his friends out there in the world, telling them about life in the Afghan capital city. The film is a poetic documentation of life there. However, once it had been completed, Saless experienced some aggravation. The film was censored. I think the issue was that there were scenes which placed too much emphasis on daily life during wartime and which showed that there were problems there. This did not fit with the propaganda at the time, according to which the Soviets had the situation under control. Saless told me that rockets were constantly exploding when they were filming in Kabul. The scenes, in which Saless showed the destructions and victims of those attacks, were cut from the film, shortening it by 15 minutes. Because he protested, *A Letter from Kabul* was never shown on Slovakian television.

Samsami: What brought Saless's time in Czechoslovakia to a close?

Schmidt: I was visiting him in winter 1987. At the time he was living in Poprad, and had married a different woman. We talked about Gorbachev and his perestroika politics, which Saless was critical of. At that time he had to put preparations for a film version of Ludwig Fels's novel, *An Absurdity of Love* (*Ein Unding der Liebe*), on hold, for which he had written the screenplay. He had fallen ill with bowel cancer, and underwent a successful operation. However, he was then no longer able to film in the ČSSR – the year 1989 was approaching. He returned to Germany to shoot his final film, *Roses for Africa* (*Rosen für Afrika*) of 1992, based on the novel of the same name by Ludwig Fels.

NOTE

1. *It Was as if it Was an Open Air Studio* (*Es war wie im Freilichtstudio*), the interview by Behrang Samsami with Bert Schmidt, including an introduction by Behrang Samsami entitled *The Quiet Life* (*Das stille Leben*), was first published in June 2017 in German and Czech in jadumagazin.eu, the German and Czech online magazine published by the Prague Goethe Institute: <http://www.goethe.de/ins/cz/prj/jug/kul/de16380481.htm> (last accessed 17 December 2018). The introduction has been abridged and updated for the English language edition. Copyright: jádu | Goethe-Institut Prague.

Sohrab Shahid Saless's Filmography

Bojnurd Folkdances (*Raqs ha-ye Mahhali-ye Bojnurdi*), **Iran, 1970, 15 min, 35 mm, Farsi.**
Written and directed by Sohrab Shahid Saless. Cinematography by Naghi Ma'soomi. With Fereydun Reypoor with Zai Khalaj, Mohammad Sadeq Alami, Mohammad Kazem Kazemi and Azzatollah Ramazanifar.

Dance of Daravish (*Bazm-e Daravishan*), **Iran, 1969, 15 min, 35 mm, Farsi.**
Written and directed by Sohrab Shahid Saless. Cinematography by Naghi Ma'soomi. With Fereydun Reypoor with Zai Khalaj, Mohammad Sadeq Alami, Mohammad Kazem Kazemi and Azzatollah Ramazanifar, Esmail Vasseghi, Jahansooz Fooladi, Farzaneh Kanoli.

Torbat-e Jam Folkdances (*Raqs ha-ye Mahhali-ye Torbat-e Jam*), **Iran, 1970, 35 mm, 15 min, Farsi.**
Written and directed by Sohrab Shahid Saless. Cinematography by Naghi Ma'soomi. With Fereydun Reypoor with Zai Khalaj, Mohammad Sadeq Alami, Mohammad Kazem Kazemi and Azzatollah Ramazanifar, Esmail Vasseghi, Jahansooz Fooladi. Farzaneh Kanoli.

Turkman Folkdances (*Raqs ha-ye Mahhali-ye Turkaman*), **Iran, 1970, 16 min, 35 mm, Farsi.**
Written and directed by Sohrab Shahid Saless. Cinematography by Naghi Ma'soomi. With Fereydun Reypoor with Zai Khalaj, Mohammad Sadeq Alami, Mohammad Kazem Kazemi and Azzatollah Ramazanifar, Esmail Vasseghi, Jahansooz Fooladi. Farzaneh Kanoli.

Black and White (*Siah-o sefid*), **Iran, 1972, 4 min, 35 mm, no dialogue.**
Directed by Sohrab Shahid Saless. Commissioned by Kanoon: The Center for the Intellectual Development of Children and Young Adults.

A Simple Event (*Yek ettefāq-e sāda*), **Iran, 1974, 81 min, 35 mm, Farsi.**
Written and directed by Sohrab Shahid Saless. Cinematography by Naghi Massumi. With Mohammad Zamani, Ane Mohammad Tarikhi, Habibollah Safarian, Hedayatollah Nawid.

Still Life (*Tabi'at-e bijān*), **Iran, 1974, 93 min, 35 mm, Farsi.**
Written and directed by Sohrab Shahid Saless. Cinematography by Hushang Bahariu. With Zadour Bonyadi, Zahra Yazdani, Habibollah Safarian.

Far From Home (*Dar Ghorbat a.k.a. In der Fremde*), **Iran/West Germany, 1975, 91 min, 16 mm, Turkish and German.**
Directed by Sohrab Shahid Saless. Written by Sohrab Shahid Saless and Helga Houzer. Cinematography by Ramin Reza Molai. With Parviz Sayyad, Anasal Cihan, Muhammet Temizkan, Hüsamettin Kaya, Ursula Kessler, Ute Bokelmann.

Time of Maturity aka Coming of Age (*Reifezeit*), **West Germany, 1976, 111 min, 35 mm, German.**
Directed by Sohrab Shahid Saless. Written by Sohrab Shahid Saless and Helga Houzer. Cinematography by Ramin Reza Molai. With Mike Hennig, Eva Mannhardt, Eva Lissa, Charles H. Vogt, Heinz Lieven.

Diary of a Lover (*Tagebuch eines Liebenden*), **West Germany, 1977, 91 min, 35 mm, German.**
Written and directed by Sohrab Shahid Saless. Cinematography by Mansur Yazdi. With Klaus Salge, Eva Manhardt, Edith Hildebrandt, Ingeborg Ziemendorff, Robert Dietl, Ursula Alexa, Dorothea Moritz.

The Long Vacation of Lotte H. Eisner (*Die langen Ferien der Lotte H. Eisner*), **West Germany, 1979, 60 min, 35 mm, German.**
Directed by Sohrab Shahid Saless. Cinematography by Ramin Reza Molai.

The Last Summer of Grabbe (*Grabbes Letzter Sommer*), **West Germany, 1980, 204 min, 35 mm, German.**
Written by Thomas Valentin. Directed by Sohrab Shahid Saless. Cinematography by Rolf Romberg. With Günther Naumann, Ute Burgmann, Tberhard Fechner, Gabriele Fischer.

Order (*Ordnung*), West Germany, 1980, 96 min, 35 mm, German.
Written by Sohrab Shahid Saless, Dieter Reifarth and Bert Schmidt. Directed by Sohrab Shahid Saless. Cinematography by Ramin Reza Molai. With Heinz Lieven, Dorothea Moritz, Ingrid Domann, Peter Schütze, Dagmar Hessenland, Dieter Schaad.

Utopia, West Germany, 1982, 198 min, 35 mm, German.
Written by Sohrab Shahid Saless and Manfred Grunert. Directed by Sohrab Shahid Saless. Cinematography by Ramin Reza Molai. With Manfred Zapatka, Imke Barnstedt, Gundula Petrovska, Gabriele Fischer, Johanna Sophia, Birgit Anders.

Empfänger Unbekannt (*Addressee Unknown*), Germany, 1983, 86 min, 35 mm, German.
Written by Imke Beilfuss and and Sohrab Shahid Saless. Directed by Sohrab Shahid Saless. Cinematography byRamin Reza Molai. With Klaus Crütz, Eckart Stein, Cornelia Palme, Claus-Jürgen Pfeiffer, Monika Grube, Serge Eymann, Max Galinsky.

The Willow Tree (*Der Weidenbaum*), West Germany/Czechoslovak Socialist Republic, 1984, 97 min, 35 mm, German.
Written and directed by Sohrab Shahid Saless, based on a story by Anton Chekhov. Cinematography by Ramin Reza Molai, Stanislav Dorsic. With Josef Stehlik, Peter Stanik, Milan Drotar, Marian Sotnik, Michal Suchanek, Stefan Adamec.

Hans – A Young Man in Germany (*Hans – Ein Junge in Deutschland*), West Germany/France/ Czechoslovak Socialist Republic, 1985, 148 min, 35 mm, German.
Directed by Sohrab Shahid Saless. Written by Sohrab Shahid Saless and Hans Frick. Cinematography by Ramin Reza Molai. With Martin Pasko, Imke Barnstedt, Yane Bittlová, Ulrich von Bock, Jirina Barásova, Hans Zander.

Changeling (*Wechselbalg*), West Germany, 1987, 135 min, 35 mm, German.
Directed by Sohrab Shahid Saless. Written by Jürgen Breest, adapted from his novel. Cinematography by Michael Faust. With Friederike Brüheim, Henning Gissel, Katharina Baccarelli, Erika Wackernagel, Helga Jeske.

Roses for Africa (*Rosen für Afrika*), Germany, 1992, 183 min, 35 mm, German.

Written by Ludwig Fels and Sohrab Shahid Saless. Directed by Sohrab Shahid Saless. Cinematography by Eberhard Scheu. With Barbara Siebner, Barbara Ehret, Monika Gold, Dietmar Hochberger, Manfred Korytowski, Heinz Beck, Josef Hecker and Egon Paschke.

A Film about Shahid Saless

Safar-e Sohrab (*Sohrab, A Journey*), Iran 2016, 77 min, 35 mm, Farsi with English subtitles

Written and produced by Omid Abdollahi. Cinematographer Reza Teimoori with Mehdi Ahmadi, Hassan Shabankareh, Amir Bayat, Meysam Abbas, Elham Abdollahi Rad, Saman Byat, Leila Qodratollahifard, Mehdi Fatehi, Mohsen Kheyrabadi.

Synopsis: A portrait documentary about one of the most prominent pioneers of the Iranian modern cinema, Sohrab Shahid Saless. In 1969, a young man of twenty-six years of age returns to his home country, Iran, after years of studying cinema and going through the hardships of living abroad as a university student. He does not want to become a filmmaker in the commercial and valueless cinema of that time, so he chooses a different and – of course – a very hard path for the making of his films. The results of this daring choice are the two features *A Simple Event* and *Still Life*, which are remembered today as the most important and most influential first examples of the formation of Iranian modern cinema. The pioneer filmmaker is nobody but Sohrab Shahid Saless. But how did he succeed in the making of these unconventional films? And how are his films related to the vicissitudes in his own life?

A picture from Sohrab's youth. I'd read and heard a lot about his perplexities and dysphoria, but there was no picture to complement what I knew. That was until, thanks to Homayoon Emami's kind contribution, I came across a collection of photos that quenched my thirst at once during the last days of my archival research for the documentary *Sohrab: A Journey* (2017).

Figure OA.1 Sohrab Shahid Saless in his studio. (Source: unknown photographer, Tehran, 1958.)

These black-and-white photos depict young Sohrab in his private room at his paternal home. These are the days in which he must have been dreaming up big ideas and, according to a close friend of his, was fully immersing himself in Chekhov's work. Ultimately, only two of those photos were left out of the documentary.

One photo depicts Sohrab and his only child from his German wife, his daughter Masha. There are not a lot of pictures of him and his daughter and this one is amongst the handful of photos that show father and daughter together. Sohrab abandoned the mother and child before his daughter had a chance to come to a proper understanding of the word 'father'. He later elaborated on the subject somewhere: 'Filmmaking has always been and is the most important priority for me. It does not matter if my films are good or bad. Filmmaking has been everything to me. It has been my father, mother, wife, child and love.'

One depicts Sohrab alongside Manouchehr Tayyab and probably one of the locals from the Turkman Sahra region. Sohrab has never mentioned working as an assistant director or being part of the directing team of any films.

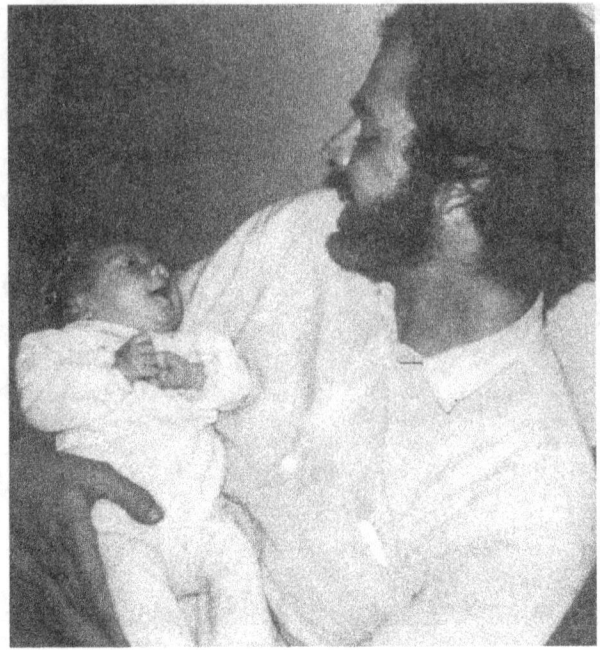

Figure OA.2 Sohrab Shahid Saless in Germany. (Source: unknown archival photo, documented by Omid Abdollahi, Tehran, 2013.)

However, there are images of him on the set and behind the scenes of two films. One is from Khosro Sinaie's *Beyond the Noise* (1968), in which Sohrab appears in front of the camera for a few brief seconds, and the other one is this photo in which he appears to be behind the scenes on one of Manouchehr Tayyab's films.

It had been a few months since I started researching for the documentary *Sohrab: A Journey* (2017). I had left no stone unturned, trying to get the consent of the people whose presence and opinions were crucial for the film, or so I thought. However, the more I tried, the less I achieved. Apart from one or two people, the others were reluctant to take part in the project and kept coming up with different excuses. As my meetings kept getting cancelled, I was losing my spirits and my motivation to continue with the film. That is until one morning when I decided to put an end to the whole cat and mouse game once and for all. I went into a photo studio, printed one of Sohrab's portraits and pinned it to a clipboard. I hung the photo frame on the white wall facing my bed as a constant reminder, each morning I woke up and each night before I fell asleep, that the only person I can truly count on and who can help me in the process of making this film, is Sohrab himself.

A FILM ABOUT SHAHID SALESS 173

Figure OA.3 Sohrab Shahid Saless in Bandar Torkaman, Iran. (Source: unknown archival photo, documented by Omid Abdollahi, Tehran, 2013.)

Figure OA.4 Sohrab Shahid Saless: portrait (Source: unknown archival photo, documented by Omid Abdollahi, Tehran, 2013.)

Figure OA.5 Bandar Torkaman site visit. (Source: Omid Abdollahi, 2012.)

Figure OA.6 Bandar Torkaman site visit. (Source: Omid Abdollahi, 2012.)

Figure OA.7 Bandar Torkaman site visit. (Source: Omid Abdollahi, 2012.)

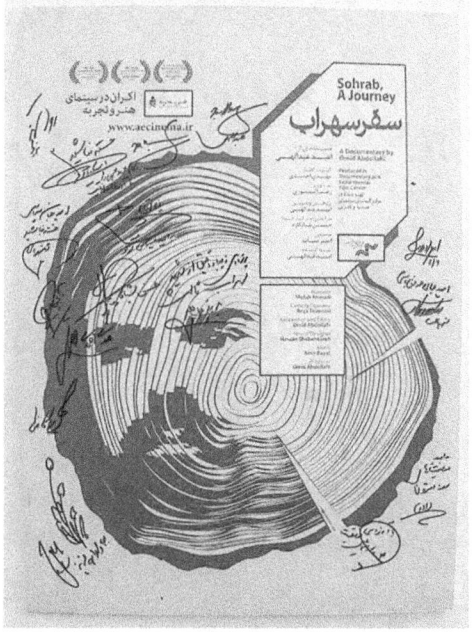

Figure OA.8 Poster for the film. (Source: Photograph by Omid Abdollahi, design by Mehdi Fatehi, Tehran, 2018.).

I travelled to Turkman Port, where both *A Simple Event* (1974) and *Still Life* (1974) were shot, three times during the days when the script for *Sohrab: A Journey* (2017) was still incomplete and shaping up. Oddly, roaming around in the shooting locations of these films invigorated me and I knew that they would compromise a part of my film, I just had no idea where and how. Things had changed there on the surface, but the overall mood and spirit of that place made me feel the same way I'd felt when I watched Sohrab's films. Eventually, the outcome of those days and those trips formed and accentuated the opening and closing chapters of my film.

NOTE

1. *Sohrab: A Journey: Scripts, Critics and Documentations* was first published in September 2018 in Farsi in an online magazine titled *Eestar*: <http://www.eestar.ir/نامه،-اسناد%E2%80%8Cسفر-سهراب؛-نقد،-فیلم/> (last accessed 17 October 2019). The introduction has been abridged and updated for the English language edition. Copyright: Eestar, Tehran, Iran.

Index

abstraction, 44, 56, 145
accented, 7, 10, 12, 13, 14, 15, 18, 22, 23, 24, 26, 42, 63, 100, 157, 158
adaptation, 17, 23, 58, 59
aesthetically, 34, 147
agency, 2, 17, 33, 34, 101
alienating, 41, 54
allegorical, 50, 69, 70
ambika P3, 123, 124, 125, 126, 127, 129
anger, 116
anti-formalist, 153
Arab Spring, 143
archive, 59, 85, 100, 129, 141, 154
art-house, 7, 10, 20, 24, 74, 92, 93, 95
audience, 7, 15, 37, 42, 45, 65, 74, 91, 92, 94, 126, 127, 128, 129, 131, 141, 143, 144, 145, 146, 149, 150, 151, 154, 155, 158
audition, 33
Ausländer, 81, 86, 142, 150
authors, 14, 24, 152, 156, 157

autobiographically, 22, 39
autobiography, 37, 104
automatisation, 51
Autoren, 79, 83, 95
avant-garde documentary, 19, 144

belong, 15, 16, 20, 22, 23, 25, 44, 61, 103, 109, 110, 112, 113, 116, 118, 121, 161
Berlin, 9, 28, 32, 34, 62, 79, 84, 85, 86, 88, 89, 95, 96, 97, 98, 99, 100, 101, 102, 104, 108, 109, 110, 113, 114, 115, 116, 119, 120, 132, 140, 143, 145, 148, 149, 154, 159
borders 104, 109, 131, 146
boundaries, 123, 124, 143, 144, 148, 150, 153
broadcast, 12, 23, 87, 90, 91, 92, 126, 131, 154, 162
brothel, 28, 29, 31, 32, 33, 34, 35, 37, 38, 40, 85, 114
brutal, 31, 33, 55, 60, 111, 112, 118

censorship, 5, 52, 163
characters 9, 10, 13, 20, 28, 30, 31, 32, 34, 35, 37, 38, 39, 41, 45, 46, 47, 48, 49, 53, 54, 58, 59, 60, 65, 67, 69, 91, 106, 111, 114, 116, 150, 154
Chekhov, 2, 8, 28, 30, 45, 47, 49, 50, 62, 64, 68, 69, 70, 114, 155, 160, 164, 168, 171
cinémathèques, 151, 155
cinematic gaze, 41, 59
cinephilia, 153, 155
claustrophobia, 51
climate change, 149
close-up, 30, 31, 38, 43, 44, 47, 50, 65, 107, 116
coexistence, 105
Cold War, 65, 100, 102, 119, 142, 153, 154
commercial, 7, 10, 52, 67, 74, 82, 83, 84, 87, 91, 93, 94, 124, 128, 142, 144, 145, 149, 150, 155, 170
commodification, 51
conflicts, 116, 142, 148
contemporary, 8, 49, 75, 151, 123, 124, 127, 128, 129, 141, 142, 143, 144, 149, 151, 153, 155, 156, 157
corridor, 38, 53
creative exile, 77, 105, 109, 113
crisis, 19, 37, 83, 86, 99, 102, 109, 111, 143, 148
curatorial, 124, 126, 128, 129, 130, 132, 141, 151, 152, 157
curatorial practice, 124, 128, 141, 157
curatorship, 151, 152, 154, 156

dash mashti, 7
de-fetishising, 47
diasporic space 104, 109, 115

dictation, 55, 56
dislocation, 77
displacement, 5, 10, 14, 15, 17, 22, 30, 39, 41, 77, 104, 113, 115, 118, 126, 132, 141, 142, 143, 149
distance, 8, 28, 43, 44, 45, 49, 112, 115, 144, 145
distributor, 12, 84, 86, 88, 94
documentaries, 8, 16, 17, 28, 64, 83, 113, 159
domestic, 95, 105, 109, 110, 112, 142, 155
domestic chores, 109
double agency, 101
dysphoric films, 8, 22
dystopian, 50

economic, 10, 14, 24, 35, 60, 61, 69, 77, 80, 81, 83, 87, 98, 104, 112, 119, 151, 152, 155, 156, 157, 158
émigré, 2, 7, 14, 17, 18, 19, 23, 24, 39, 41
empowerment, 40, 60
encounter, 33, 34, 37, 41, 44, 57, 67, 80, 112, 114, 123, 131
Eurocentrism, 8, 157, 158
everyday, 3, 9, 28, 41, 44, 53, 58, 103, 114, 116, 118, 153
excluded, 44, 109
exile, 8, 9, 12, 14, 15, 16, 19, 20, 21, 22, 23, 24, 25, 26, 27, 39, 44, 50, 64, 77, 80, 87, 101, 103, 105, 109, 112, 113, 118, 131, 132, 141, 142, 143, 144, 145, 147, 148, 149, 150, 153, 157
exilic, 2, 7, 10, 11, 12, 14, 17, 18, 21, 22, 24, 25, 26, 42, 63, 84, 100, 158
exilism, 21, 22
experimental, 17, 20, 66, 92, 123, 124, 126, 128, 144, 145, 150

exploitative, 35, 145
exterior, 60, 61, 105, 110, 161 164

festival, 9, 10, 20, 65, 79, 80, 81, 82, 84, 85, 87, 89, 90, 92, 93, 94, 95, 97, 116, 131, 144, 147, 149
Filmfarsi, 7, 67, 74, 75
filmically, 87
finance, 25, 81, 83, 88, 100, 131
forced, 36, 38, 44, 49, 51, 54, 55, 56, 60, 88, 102, 108, 115, 132, 143, 149, 159
foreign, 3, 8, 10, 15, 20, 24, 81, 86, 89, 99, 100, 102, 116, 142, 148

Gastarbeiter, 102, 132, 133
geopolitical, 148, 151, 153, 155, 156, 157, 158
Germanness, 114
ghorbatzadeh, 15
global cinema, 12, 14
greet, 68, 69, 70
guest worker, 5, 10, 45, 50, 54, 56, 60, 79, 102, 103, 114, 119

hashti, 43, 44
high art, 37
historical, 43, 44, 60, 64, 65, 66, 69, 71, 73, 75, 81, 101, 128, 131, 153
home, 9, 10, 11, 13, 15, 16, 17, 18, 20, 21, 22, 23, 24, 25, 26, 28, 30, 31, 34, 36, 39, 40, 44, 48, 50, 52, 53, 54, 55, 56, 58, 59, 60, 61, 68, 69, 71, 79, 80, 81, 83, 84, 86, 90, 92, 95, 97, 99, 102, 103, 104, 105, 107, 109, 110, 111, 112, 113, 114, 115, 118, 119, 131, 144, 148, 150, 161, 167, 170
homeland, 10, 15, 16, 17, 18, 22, 23, 25, 39, 52, 79, 104, 105, 115

horror, 33
host societies, 77

identity 15, 16, 17, 19, 21, 26, 27, 37, 44, 61, 74, 103, 104, 113, 115, 124, 127, 129, 143, 148, 157
immersive space, 126, 129
in-betweenness, 2, 101, 103, 105
inaccessible, 41
independent, 35, 62, 84, 86, 145, 156, 161
individual purchase, 123
inhospitable foreign land, 10
inspector, 67, 68, 70
installation, 123, 124, 125, 126, 127, 128, 129, 145
institutional, 50, 53, 131, 144, 147, 151, 152, 153, 158
intellectual, 2, 16, 51, 62, 69, 70, 74, 83, 142, 143, 144, 145, 148, 162, 167
interior, 32, 49, 105, 106, 110, 112
interpreters, 152
intersectional, 12, 19, 20, 104
intimate, 109, 112, 116, 144, 145
Iranian, 7–28, 39, 42, 44, 51, 52, 60, 61, 62, 64, 65, 66, 68, 69, 72, 74, 75, 79, 84, 86, 87, 99, 100, 101, 113, 115, 132, 141, 142, 148, 150, 153, 154, 155, 157, 159, 160, 162, 170

jaheli, 7

Kreuzberg, 101, 102, 103
Kuratorium, 83, 89

Liberty Bell, 102
lobbying, 82, 83, 90
loneliness, 10, 22, 38, 69, 103, 108, 111

long shots, 8, 28, 44, 65, 66, 109, 111, 116, 161
long takes, 8, 28, 44, 66, 71, 85, 109, 111, 116

mainstream, 13, 15, 17, 74, 142, 149, 157
margins, 105, 112
melancholic, 67
micro history, 43, 44
'Middle Easternness', 103
migration, 3, 5, 11, 12, 13, 14, 15, 26, 52, 100, 102, 103, 109, 114, 118, 119, 120, 143, 144, 146, 148, 149
minimalism, 64, 66, 70, 75
mirror, 9, 31, 37, 43, 45, 47, 49, 51, 53, 55, 57, 58, 60, 61, 63, 127, 129, 137, 148
mise-en-scène, 2, 156
misogyny, 34, 41
modernity, 19, 43, 51, 52, 53, 59, 60, 61, 62, 112, 155, 156
Moving Image, 55, 59, 77, 101, 104, 109, 118, 121, 127, 141, 142, 144, 149
museology, 124
mythology, 142

national affiliation, 21, 114, 128
national identities, 17
New Film Group, 5
no-man's land, 44
non-actors, 9, 65, 66
non-institutional, 153

Occidental cultures, 154
one-for-one, 163
optimistic, 8, 36
ordinary people, 7, 8, 9, 23, 28, 68, 114, 129

Oriental, 154
outsider, 23, 24, 28, 39, 41, 103, 110, 114, 115, 118, 141

Persian Motown, 12
perspective, 30, 31, 42, 43, 44, 50, 64, 65, 67, 69, 71, 73, 75, 90, 93, 103, 118, 126, 141, 151, 153, 155, 156, 157
pimp, 28, 29, 53, 59, 85, 87, 114
plots, 67, 74
poetic, 37, 62, 110, 114, 126, 129, 153, 164
poetry, 132
polemics, 148
political, 12, 14, 15, 16, 51, 52, 60, 61, 62, 77, 79, 81, 104, 115, 116, 119, 127, 128, 132, 143, 145, 146, 147, 148, 151, 153, 155, 156, 157, 158
positive unconscious, 54
post-colonial theory, 26, 143, 156
post-medium condition, 155
post-war German film industry, 82, 83
premiere, 85, 90, 92, 94, 95, 96, 97
principal, 15, 20, 67, 70, 72, 73
prisoner, 35, 41, 53
promotional, 131
prostitutes, 23, 35, 53, 56, 103, 114
protagonist, 23, 30, 32, 36, 65, 66, 69, 109, 159
protocol style, 47, 49, 50, 51, 54, 58
public acceptance, 149

rationalisation, 51, 60
readjustment, 113

realism, 7, 64, 66, 67, 69, 71, 72, 74
refugee communities, 147
reification 51, 60
remediations 155
repetition, 41, 111
retrospective, 97, 127, 131, 151, 152, 154, 158, 159, 160
reverse shot, 45, 46, 47, 49
roughness, 153

sadness, 22, 52, 109, 111, 112, 116
sadomodernism, 50, 63
scale, 129, 131
schizophrenia, 60
schizophrenic, 106
screening, 9, 62, 91, 96, 100, 108, 131, 141, 151, 152, 153, 154, 155, 156, 157, 158
script, 85, 112, 176
self-effacing, 152
selfhood, 37
separation, 116, 118
sex worker, 28, 29, 30, 31, 33, 35, 56, 119
silence, 61, 67, 68, 71, 72, 74, 109, 115, 116, 118
site-specific, 124, 126, 128
slow pans, 8, 29, 105
social, 2, 11, 13, 14, 19, 22, 26, 37, 42, 54, 55, 56, 57, 59, 60, 62, 69, 74, 82, 89, 90, 101, 103, 114, 115, 126, 128, 129, 144, 149
social revolution, 14
socio-political, 2, 77, 119, 155
spatial manifestation, 127
spectacle, 7, 105, 110, 145
staged, 8, 107, 146
staircase, 36, 38, 105, 106, 107, 108, 110, 116

state subsidies, 80, 83
state-subsidised funding, 23
statelessness, 132, 141, 142, 143, 144, 146, 148
stipulation, 89
storyline, 65, 67, 74, 109
struggle, 25, 77, 79, 84, 85, 94, 95, 96, 103, 110, 111, 114, 132, 144, 150
suffering, 22, 29, 104, 108, 111, 116, 150
surveillance, 49, 51, 53, 62, 105
symbolism, 28, 29, 31, 33, 35, 36, 37, 39, 41

television, 11, 12, 15, 17, 22, 27, 80, 81, 83, 84, 85, 86, 87, 88, 89, 90, 91, 92, 93, 98, 100, 126, 131, 157, 159, 164, 165
tenderness, 131, 133, 135, 137, 139, 153
theatre, 55, 83, 94, 96, 110, 145
topographically, 132
transmission, 121
transnational, 7, 20, 115, 119, 121, 142, 151, 153, 154, 156, 157, 159
trapped, 35, 37, 40, 41, 110
traumatised, 38
tributaries, 132
Turkish guest-workers, 10, 54, 103, 114

unbeknownst, 31
uncharacteristic, 30, 36
uncompromising, 23, 41, 92

viewer, 32, 36, 41, 42, 74, 91, 92, 101, 106, 107, 108, 109, 111, 114, 116, 118, 126, 144, 145, 150, 153
violence, 29, 32, 41, 45, 50, 56, 59, 115, 154

voiceover, 50, 70, 112
voluntary exile, 9, 103

West Berlin, 28, 34, 85, 88, 101, 102, 103, 104, 108, 113
West Germany, 5, 23, 28, 30, 39, 80, 84, 89, 101, 102, 154, 164, 167, 168
Western culture, 142, 143
witness, 9, 29, 33, 42, 44, 45, 47, 49, 55, 60, 106, 109, 113, 114, 115, 118, 163
World War Two, 10, 32, 82, 101, 150
worn-out, 68
Wunderkinder (prodigies), 80

EU representative:
Easy Access System Europe
Mustamäe tee 50, 10621 Tallinn, Estonia
Gpsr.requests@easproject.com